Images, Issues, and Attacks

LEXINGTON STUDIES IN POLITICAL COMMUNICATION

Series Editor: Robert E. Denton Jr., Virginia Tech

This series encourages focused work examining the role and function of communication in the realm of politics including campaigns and elections, media, and political institutions.

TITLES IN SERIES:

Governing Codes: Gender, Metaphor, and Political Identity, By Karrin Vasby Anderson and Kristina Horn Sheeler

Paving the Way for Madam President, By Nichola D. Gutgold

Maryland Politics and Political Communication, 1950-2005, By Theodore F. Sheckels

Images, Issues, and Attacks: Television Advertising by Incumbents and Challengers in Presidential Elections, By E. D. Dover

Images, Issues, and Attacks

*Television Advertising by Incumbents
and Challengers in Presidential
Elections*

E. D. Dover

LEXINGTON BOOKS

A division of
ROWMAN & LITTLEFIELD PUBLISHERS, INC.
Lanham • Boulder • New York • Toronto • Plymouth, UK

LEXINGTON BOOKS

A division of Rowman & Littlefield Publishers, Inc.
A wholly owned subsidary of The Rowman & Littlefield Publishing Group, Inc.
4501 Forbes Boulevard, Suite 200
Lanham, MD 20706

Estover Road
Plymouth PL6 7PY
United Kingdom

British Library Cataloguing in Publication Information Available

Library of Congress Cataloging-in-Publication Data

Library of Congress Control Number: 2006933220

ISBN-13: 978-0-7391-1545-9 (cloth : alk. paper)
ISBN-13: 978-0-7391-1546-6 (pbk. : alk. paper)
ISBN-10: 0-7391-1545-6 (cloth : alk. paper)
ISBN-10: 0-7391-1546-4 (pbk. : alk. paper)

Printed in the United States of America

™ The paper used in this publication meets the minimum requirements of American
National Standard for Information Sciences—Permanence of Paper for Printed Library
Materials, ANSI/NISO Z39.48–1992.

To Molly

Contents

1 Introduction and General Overview   1

2 Elections with Strong Incumbents: 1984 and 1996   21

3 Elections with Weak Incumbents: 1980 and 1992   51

4 Elections with Surrogate Incumbents: 1988 and 2000   79

5 The 2004 Election: Nomination Campaigns   109

6 The 2004 Election: The Bush Campaign   123

7 The 2004 Election: The Kerry Campaign   139

8 Summary and Interpretations   153

References   159

Index   177

About the Author   181

CHAPTER 1

INTRODUCTION AND GENERAL OVERVIEW

Several months after the conclusion of the 2000 presidential election, the journal Great Plains Quarterly asked me to review *Videostyle in Presidential Campaigns: Style and Content of Televised Political Advertising*, by Lynda Lee Kaid and Anne Johnston. These two scholars described and defined videostyle by saying that it is composed of "the verbal content, the nonverbal content, and the film/video production techniques used in political ads." They also wrote that "the style of a candidate initially is revealed through a general communication style, a pattern of behavior that is apparent, consistent, and recurring (Kaid and Johnston 2001, pp. 25-26)." The book focused on how presidential candidates had used television advertising to advance their own efforts and attack those of their rivals in the elections from 1952 thru 1996. I was very impressed with the work and found some of its findings complementary to several themes I had employed in my own work relating to political communication in recent presidential elections. Perhaps even more important, it also gave me an idea for undertaking a new research project that has now resulted in this book. In three previous works related to mediated communication in presidential elections, I have argued that mediated incumbency is the most important explanatory factor in the outcomes of modern American presidential elections. The performances by specific incumbents during their tenure in office and the effectiveness by which those performances are defined and then communicated to voters plays a much greater role in determining election outcomes than other factors such as partisanship. Unlike Kaid and Johnston, however, I directed my attention to the mediated messages that derive from television news rather than to those from advertising (Dover, 1994, 1998, 2002).

Videostyle provides a thorough analysis of the vast range of televised messages that presidential candidates have employed, and even includes one chapter that compares and contrasts the approaches of incumbents and challengers. Individual candidates from these two incumbency related categories always enter their respective campaigns from different vantage points. The characteristics of these vantage points derive from the specific roles played by incumbents and challengers, are recurring through a series of elections, and provide both types of candidates with a variety of communicative needs and opportunities that are not always available to their rivals. In order to win, incumbents and challengers must implement strategies that exploit or mitigate the opportunities and constraints that derive from their different vantage points. While not focusing specifically on televised advertising, I raised a similar set of arguments in my previous works. Incumbents and challengers vary in both their communicative needs and in their responses to those needs. I directed my attention to how the two different types of candidates addressed their unique needs and of how television news interpreted those efforts and reported them to their viewing audiences.

My work differs from Kaid and Johnston, however, and from other writers who have compared and contrasted the strategies of incumbents and challengers, in one important way. I have subdivided incumbency into three categories based upon the political strength of the incumbent and have shown how the campaign strategies of incumbents differ not only from those of their challengers, but also from those of the incumbents who comprise the other two categories of political strength. The categories are 1) elections with strong incumbents, 2) elections with weak incumbents, and 3) elections with surrogate incumbents. Elections with strong incumbents occur when the president wins another term while elections with weak incumbents take place when the president fails in his bid to remain in office. While the placement of a specific election into one of these categories is ultimately determined by the final choice of voters, presidential elections tend to be retrospective evaluations of incumbents where the political strength of individual candidates results from actions and evaluations that have occurred over many months and sometimes years before an actual election takes place (Fiorina, 1981). This feature makes the placement of an incumbent into a strong or weak category quite predictable many months in advance of the actual election. I support these conclusions with survey results from the Gallup Poll, discussed below. The final category, those with surrogate incumbents, contains elections where the incumbent retires and thereby forces his party to nominate some other candidate as its standard bearer.

Six presidential elections during the past half-century have resulted in the reelection of the incumbent. These were in 1956 (Dwight D. Eisenhower), 1964 (Lyndon B. Johnson), 1972 (Richard M. Nixon), 1984 (Ronald Reagan), 1996

(Bill Clinton), and most recently, 2004 (George W. Bush). During this same time, three elections saw the failure of the incumbent to secure another term; 1976 (Gerald Ford), 1980 (Jimmy Carter), and 1992 (George Bush). Finally, in all four elections over the past half century in which the incumbent did not seek another term, the presidential party nominated the vice president as a potential successor. These were in 1960 (Richard M. Nixon), 1968 (Hubert H. Humphrey), 1988 (George Bush), and 2000 (Albert Gore Jr.).

Since it began in 1935, The Gallup Poll has frequently asked respondents to express their approval or disapproval of a president's performance in office. In determining the relevance of the abovementioned election categories, I have calculated the average approval rating of presidents during these various elections. A rating score was obtained by averaging the approval rating from each Gallup Poll taken during the six month period that began on November 1 of the year before the presidential election and ended on April 30 of the election year. The choice of the six month period was designed to determine long-term trends in presidential approval and avoid temporary fluctuations that can derive from the influence of short-term events. The November to April dates were chosen to show that presidential approval tends to be consistent throughout a campaign and that its effects are not merely limited to the final days before an election. This is important because the political strength of an incumbent can influence the behavior of other actors, such as rival candidates and news reporters, throughout the duration of a campaign. The six strong incumbents had average ratings that ranged from a low of 51 percent for Clinton to 75 percent for Johnson. Moreover, Clinton's approval rating was growing and was stronger in April than it had been the previous November. In contrast, the weak incumbents, and this includes Lyndon Johnson during the early weeks of 1968 before he withdrew from the campaign in late March, ranged from a low of 39 for Johnson to 48 for Carter. Carter's ratings were falling and were less than forty percent by April. His favorable ratings had been low throughout most of 1979 but increased temporarily during the first weeks after the beginning of the Iranian hostage crisis in November, 1979 (Gallup Poll, 2006).

My purpose in writing this book is to determine how incumbents from the three different categories of modern presidential elections differ from one another and from their challengers in their uses of televised advertising. I seek to learn how political vantage points and variations in popular support can influence videostyles of individual candidates. In doing so, I focus attention exclusively on the candidates themselves rather than on all advertising. I advance several research questions later in this chapter.

Incumbency

A first question that needs to be addressed is to determine why incumbency is a topic worthy of consideration in any analysis of modern election campaigns. Numerous differences always exist between the various candidates in any given election but ultimately many of them prove to be inconsequential as determinants of final outcomes. Perhaps incumbency is one of these. In *The Presidential Election of 1996: Clinton's Incumbency and Television,* I discussed the importance of incumbency as a determining factor in the outcomes of presidential elections during the television age. I summarize my arguments here. Incumbency has taken on particular importance in recent decades because of a variety of distinct but highly interrelated changes that have occurred in the organizational structure and political behavior of American government and election campaigns.

One of these, and which often receives only limited attention in the field of communication studies, is the substantial growth of the presidency as a bureaucratic institution of government. Prior to the administration of Franklin D. Roosevelt in 1933, the institution of the presidency consisted only of the president himself and his relatively small office staff of less than forty persons (Hart, 1995). As an indication of the limited extent of the presidency, the vice president was considered to be a member of the legislative branch and his office was located in the Capitol Building (Light, 1984). The small nature of the institutional presidency changed forever in 1939 when Congress, responding to a request advanced by a committee on governmental reorganization that Roosevelt had started, created the Executive Office of the President (EOP) (Polsby, 1983). While initially limited in both its size and scope, the EOP of today is a complex, and essentially private, bureaucracy under the direct control of the president. Its current staff may be as large as 3,000 persons (Barilleaux, 1988). The various component parts of the EOP are located either in the White House itself or in the adjacent Executive Office Building which is part of the White House office complex. The major components of the EOP include the White House Office, the Office of Management and Budget, the National Security Council, and the Council of Economic Advisors. There are additional components that sometimes differ from one administration to the next (Hart, 1995). While each of the component parts is powerful in its own right, together, they enable the president to dominate much of the decision making processes of the national government while having little, if any, accountability to Congress (Cronin and Genovese, 1998).

The White House Office of today is often referred to as the "West Wing." It consists of the president's closest political advisors, many of whom have held major positions in the incumbent's previous election campaign or who will lead in his next one (Cronin, 1980). It also includes the vice president who has been a member of the executive branch since the 1950's (Light, 1984; Nelson, 1988). The Office of Management and Budget of today is one of the most significant tools the president has available to help him control the actions of government. All governmental agencies must submit their requests for funding or new laws to the budget office which then determines if those requests conform to the president's program (Cronin and Genovese, 1998; Wildavsky and Caiden, 2004). If not, the requests cannot be sent forward to Congress for enactment. This practice of "central clearance" enables the president to control many features of agency behavior (Barilleaux, 1988). The National Security Council and the Council of

Economic Advisors serve the president in ways similar to that of the budget office with respect to the policy areas of national security, war, diplomacy, economic planning, fiscal policy, and economic stabilization. Concentration of bureaucratic power in the presidential office has helped make incumbent presidents exceptionally formidable in their quests for reelection in ways that their challengers cannot even hope to emulate (Lowi, 1985; see also Fisher, 1993; Hess, 2002; Light, 1995; Mayer, 2001; Milkis and Nelson, 1994; Nathan, 1983; Neustadt, 1990; Pfiffner, 1999).

A second reason for the added importance of incumbency is the phenomenal growth of primary elections as the major method for nominating candidates for the presidency. The use of primary elections to choose the national convention delegates who eventually nominate each party's candidate for president and vice president is a phenomenon of the twentieth century and expanded in use extensively during the final three decades of that century, particularly after the election of 1968. Previously, convention delegates from each state were chosen by party committees or in some instances, were appointed by party officials. In current elections, the various aspirants for a party nomination must devote many months and considerable finances as well, to competing against one another in about forty primaries that are held between late January and early June of each campaign year. Primaries encourage a phenomenon called "candidate centered campaigns (Nie, Verba, and Petrocik, 1979)." In such campaigns, individual candidates bypass party leaders and make direct appeals to voters whose support will enable them to win the various primaries and enough convention delegates to secure the nomination. Through such a process, a successful candidate will develop a direct relationship with a core of partisan voters that is so strong party leaders will eventually rally around the winner rather than actually select him. If elected, the new incumbent president is no longer accountable to the leaders of his own party. In a result paralleling the relations between the presidential bureaucracy and Congress, primary elections also serve to prevent other officials, in this instance, the leaders of political parties, from exercising effective institutional restraints on modern presidents. This development, in turn, serves to further enhance the powers of incumbency (see Bartels, 1988; Ceaser and Bush, 2005; CQ Press, 2005; Mayer, 1999, Nelson, 2005, Polsby and Wildavsky, 2004; Wayne, 2003).

The third reason is the growth of television as the most important medium of presidential communication with the electorate. Television enables the president to speak directly to the electorate while bypassing the filtering processes that are inherent with print media. He can address voters from his desk in the Oval Office where he appears to be speaking to each of them individually or he can reach people through ceremonial occasions such as the annual State of the Union Address. In either instance, the president can appeal to voters in a manner that can seem very personal (Tulis, 1987). Moreover, television news reporting enhances the president's connections with the electorate. Television new media devote a considerable amount of their airtime to the general topics of politics and government but focus a predominate amount of their attention within these topics on the president. The president's remarks, actions, goals, strategies, travels, problems, and much more are constant themes of televised news reporting (Ceaser et al., 1981). Moreover, television news media often depict the behavior of other governmental institutions from the perspective of how that behavior relates to the president (Lowi, 1985). This extensive emphasis on presidential behavior, and particularly because it often comes at the expense of other institutions, has provided incumbents with the ability to run for reelection simply by performing their jobs. The "Rose Garden Strategy," where an incumbent president runs for reelection from the White House while television news media tell the nation about what he does each day has been a major feature in recent campaigns (Popkin, 1991). Presidents have opportunities for action that are simply not available to their challengers and many of these actions are televised. They can order military attacks, engage in diplomacy, sign bills into law, issue executive orders, make proclamations, visit the scenes of major national disasters, such as George W. Bush touring Florida after four hurricanes had devastated substantial portions of that battleground state during the election campaign. Presidents are newsworthy even when they leave or return to the White House after a weekend at Camp David. In contrast, television news media frequently limit their reporting about challengers only to those instances when the challengers perform in their roles as aspirants for office (see Hinckley, 1990; Farnsworth and Lichter, 2003; Graber, 2002; Kernell, 1997; Maltese, 1994; Ornstein and Mann, 2000).

The combination of these three factors; a powerful presidential bureaucracy under the incumbent's personal direction, nomination through a series of primaries where successful candidates develop direct personal relations with voters, and the emergence of television as the most influential medium of political communication have helped create the conditions where incumbent presidents occupy the most strategically important vantage point of all aspirants in candidate centered campaigns.

Television Advertising

There is considerable scholarly work relating to the value and uniqueness of televised political advertising. Kaid said there are two defining characteristics of such advertising, 1) the ability of the source to control the massage, which she considers to be its greatest advantage, and 2) the delivery of the message through the channels of mass communication (Kaid, 1999. p. 423). Kathleen Hall Jamieson distinguished the superior persuasive capacity of broadcast messages from those of print media when she wrote that "some arguments could be visualized through the magic of television editing that could not be plausibly verbalized." She defined this difference as "argument by association" and divided it into two categories, "positive images of favored candidates and negative images of the opponent (Jamieson 1986, p. 15)."

Televised advertising differs from print advertising in two fundamental ways; the relatively large size of the viewing audience and the passive nature of that audience. Television advertising reaches a "larger number of voters simultaneously than any other communication channel (Kaid and Johnston 2001, p. 1)." Moreover, and unlike printed material where persons must actively choose topics and then engage extensively in them while reading, television viewing requires little effort on the part of an individual except to watch and listen (Kaid and Davidson 1986, p. 207). The combination of these features is particularly valuable to candidates for office in the sense that they have control of both the content and presentation of their messages. Candidates can use televised advertising to "link with the voter directly and in an unfiltered way" and "to make every voter feel that he or she has personal knowledge of the candidate (Kaid and Johnston 2001, pp. 13-14).

This optimistic view of the usefulness of mass media is of fairly recent origin. Scholars from earlier decades, essentially pre-television, wrote of the "limited effects" of media influences on political attitudes and voting behavior. Mediated messages often ran into the problem of selective exposure in that voters tended to read only those news stories or ads that reinforced their own preferences (Lazarsfeld, et al., 1948). Television ads are different, however, in that passive viewers essentially have an ad thrust in front of them and frequently respond by watching it. Such exposure helps voters become more aware of the issues a candidate may advocate, even if those issue stands differ from their own (Atkin and Heald, 1976). A variety of more recent scholars have found that televised ads are effective at informing voters. Based upon their study of media effects in the election of 1972, Patterson and McClure concluded that voters, by a margin of about four to one, learned more about issues from political advertising than from network news programming (Patterson and McClure, 1976; see also, Just, Crigler and Wallach, 1990; Brians and Wattenberg, 1996). William L. Benoit attributes these findings to the fact that campaign news is only one story out of many on a typical broadcast, that reporters usually focus more of their attention on the "horserace" feature of a campaign, that is, which candidate is ahead and which one is not, and to the growing practice of news programming devoting less and less time to the remarks of individual candidates, thus creating difficulties for voters in attributing specific issue positions to those candidates (Benoit, 1999).

Academic studies of televised political advertising focus attention on three leading themes; 1) messages that advocate specific points of view on questions of public policy (issues) versus messages that emphasize the personal characteristics of candidates (images); 2) messages which speak of the more desirable characteristics of candidates or causes (positive) versus ones that raise questions and seek to generate doubt about the characteristics of rival candidates or causes (negative); and advertisements that direct attention to various other personal or political matters such as emotion, fear, or partisanship (Kaid, 2004, p. 160). Several scholars who have directed their attention to candidate strategies relating to televised advertising have tended to focus on their first two of those themes, the issue/image and the positive/negative.

Several scholars have written about the functions of political advertising. Benoit says that it serves three functions for political candidates. The candidates seek to "enhance their own credentials as a desirable office holder (acclaims); or downgrade their opponent's credentials as an undesirable office-holder (attacks); or respond to those attacks (defenses) (Benoit, 1999)." Karen Johnson-Cartee and Gary Copeland offer similar categories, albeit with different names, calling them supportive and negative. Candidates use supportive strategies in order to increase their name recognition, or link themselves with popular issues, or develop personal imagery emphasizing their character or leadership abilities. They employ negative strategies to attack the images or issues of their rivals (Johnson-Cartee and Copeland, 1997). L. Patrick Devlin also has found that televised advertising performs a number of vital functions. Perhaps the most important, in his view, is the opportunity it provides candidates for introducing themselves to voters. "Ads can make an unknown candidate a better known candidate," he writes (Devlin, 1986, pp. 22-24)."

Senator John F. Kennedy (Massachusetts) used one of the most famous ads designed for introducing a candidate to the voters during the presidential election of 1960. The strength of the ad, named *Kennedy-Kennedy*, rested with its repeated use of the candidate's name. It contained a number of pictures of Kennedy shown alone and additional pictures where he appeared in the company of such famous Democrats as former president Harry Truman and former first lady Eleanor Roosevelt. There were also images of campaign posters and banners with the name "Kennedy" written on them in large letters. These images were accompanied by a song in which the candidate's name was repeated numerous times. The chorus, used twice, went "Kennedy, Kennedy, Kennedy, Kennedy, Kennedy, Kennedy, Kennedy, Ken-Ken, Kennedy for me, Kennedy, Kennedy, Kennedy, Kennedy."

Devlin also found that televised advertising can help candidates raise money, reinforce the views of supporters and partisans, attack opponents, develop personal images, and explain the issues that they hope will ultimately define their campaigns. While one might intuitively think that images related to the personal characteristics of individual candidates and issues that essentially deal with possible answers to public problems are analytically distinct from one another, Devlin and others have found that the two are often linked in televised advertising. He says that the best way for a candidate to make a positive image impression with voters is to emphasize issues. In doing so, candidates can convey image impressions that they can handle issues, and ultimately, can also handle the job of president (Devlin, 1986). Johnston and Kaid find that a distinction between issues and images is false because political ads that focus on either of these themes generally blend the two in ways that make distinctions difficult (Johnston and Kaid, 2002). Benoit, drawing from his analysis of the televised debates from the presidential election of 1992, explains that a candidate's stance on issues often helps shape his image with voters and conversely, such images also tend to influence voters' perceptions of issues. Sometimes, images can even become issues (Benoit, 1999). Other scholars support this view. Popkin writes that issues can be effective in campaigns only if voters see connections between certain issues and the office, their personal concerns, and the candidate who advocates them (Popkin, 1991). Ridout finds that issues and images are particularly interrelated during the nomination campaign. It is during this phase of the election year that candidates must decide which issues to advance and which themes will prove most effective in their efforts at presentation of self to voters (Ridout, 2004).

One can see examples of the interrelation between issues and images in two ads used in the elections of 1968 and 1976. In *Ahead of his Time*, Hubert Humphrey tried to connect himself with several important accomplishments of the national government during his campaign for president in 1968. Humphrey was Lyndon Johnson's vice president at the time. The image portion of the ad included a picture of Humphrey that constantly enlarged in size as a narrator spoke of Humphrey's past accomplishments. The narrator would mention a policy that had been enacted during the Kennedy or Johnson administrations and then refer to Humphrey's long time association with it. The purpose was to develop the theme of Humphrey as an advanced political thinker who was the kind of leader the nation needed. The narrator started the ad by talking about Humphrey and civil rights. "When he voted for civil rights twenty years ago, a lot of people said he was ahead of his time. He was." Similar wording followed about such laws and programs as the Nuclear Test Ban Treaty, Medicare, the Job Corps, Food for Peace, and the Peace Corps. The narrator concluded by linking Humphrey with these issues by stating, "Hubert Humphrey has been ahead of his time for the past twenty years. That's why he is the man that you need for the future. Don't just vote for the right ideas. Vote for the man who thought of them."

Eight years later, in 1976, Gerald Ford was seeking a second term as president, although he had not been elected to his first one. After two and one-half years in office following Richard Nixon's resignation over the Watergate scandal, Ford was in significant political trouble. He fought for months to narrowly overcome a strong challenge for the Republican nomination from Ronald Reagan but then lost the general election to Jimmy Carter. He used an ad designed to emphasize the idea that he possessed the strong personal character that was needed for national leadership. In the ad *Accomplishment,* Ford relied upon visual imagery to illustrate how he acted in his role as president. He was shown working and talking in the Oval Office while seated at the president's desk and standing next to a window. Ford was also shown speaking from a podium which contained the presidential seal and the phrase "President Ford '76." Throughout the ad, the narrator referred to Ford's character and tried to link them with the needs of national leadership. "He came to the office of president in troubled times. He began an open administration . . . he is leading us out of the worst recession in years . . . he has made hard decisions . . . he has had the courage to say no. President Ford is your president. Keep Him."

Political candidates do not limit their advertising exclusively to positive themes about images and issues. Instead, they also rely upon negative advertising that questions the images and issues developed and articulated by their opponents. Many scholars have found that positive and negative advertising are related. Jamieson writes that negative ads, when used in combination with positive ones, help voters make distinctions between candidates (Jamieson, 1992).

Other scholars advance the argument that negative ads may be more informative and effective than positive ones. Garramone et al. say that "negative commercials may lead to greater candidate image discrimination and greater attitude polarization than their positive counterparts (Garramone, et al., 1990)." Dolan says "the majority of negative ads contain relatively more accurate information about the candidates than issue ads, which tend to gloss over the issues and present rosy scenarios (Dolan, 2004, p. 47)." Johnson-Cartee and Copeland support this contention when they state that positive ads are "simply not persuasive." They point out that positive ads are rarely argumentative because they "merely establish the political issues associated with a given candidate before the argumentation period of negative political advertising begins (Johnson-Cartee and Copeland, 1997, p. 15)." They express this view in their definition of negative advertising. It is "political advertising that implicitly or explicitly places the opposition in an inferior position . . . an argument that calls into question a given candidate's fitness for office-that is, his or her leadership ability (Johnson-Cartee and Copeland, 1997, p. 20)." In showing the linkage between positive and negative advertising strategies, Johnson-Cartee and Copeland demonstrate that the most effective ads are those which compare the records, issue positions, or personal experiences of candidates (Johnson-Cartee and Copeland, 1991).

While positive advertising is aimed at emphasizing a candidate's personal character and linking that character with certain specified issues, negative advertising seems to be linked more at preventing the rival's positive ads from weakening a candidate's partisan base of supporters. Iyengar and Petrocik state that holding on to one's partisan base is essential in a successful campaign and that "there is no better way to do this than to emphasize issues that represent the core programmatic commitments of the party (Iyengar and Petrocik, 2000)." These commitments include domestic social programs such as education, health care, social security, racial and gender equality, labor unions, jobs, poverty, and the environment for Democrats and lower taxes, reduced government spending, national defense, foreign policy, crime, and a variety of family values for Republicans (Iyengar and Petrocik, 2000; see also Benoit, 1999). Positive ads attempt to persuade a candidate's partisan base of his commitment to widely held views they have on certain issues; negative ads seek to convince that same base of the rival's lack of commitment to those issues. Ansolabehere and Iyengar write that the most important effect of negative advertising is to reinforce preexisting views of voters rather than change opinions. They state that "Campaign commercials work to the extent that they resonate with the viewers' concerns and political beliefs. Voters cull out of political advertisements information that squares with their predispositions (Ansolabehere and Iyengar 1995, p. 96)." They point out that exposure to advertising "makes it more likely voters will take their own preferences on the issues into account (Ansolabehere and Iyengar, 1995, pp. 9-10)." In essence, candidates use attacks to complement their image and issue advertising. They begin their campaigns by using positive image and issue advertising for the purpose of introducing themselves to and then and motivating their own partisans, and then they employ negative advertising in hopes of preventing those partisans from being seduced by their rivals. One can see examples of this strategy of prevention in two classic attack ads from the elections of 1964 and 1972.

One of the most famous attack ads in history was *Daisy Girl*, which was used by the incumbent president Lyndon Johnson against his Republican challenger Senator Barry Goldwater (Arizona) in 1964. Johnson used the ad to exploit a weakness in Goldwater's public image; the habit the senator had of making statements that all too often sounded rash. Goldwater had made one such remark relating to the use of nuclear weapons when he said we should fire one into the men's room at the Kremlin. The ad featured imagery of a young girl in a flower garden picking petals from a daisy. She was counting the petals when an adult male voice quite suddenly came forth and began counting numbers backwards in the style used when rockets were about to be launched. At zero, the girl looked frightened as the imagery changed to that of a nuclear explosion. Viewers could then hear Johnson's voice when he said "these are the stakes; to make a world in which all God's children can live, or go into the dark. We must either love each other or we must die." This ad was an attempt at illustrating that Goldwater was not committed to peace, an issue the Democrats tried to claim as their own that year.

Eight years later in 1972, Richard Nixon, this time acting in the role as the Republican incumbent, attacked his Democratic challenger Senator George McGovern (South Dakota) over national defense. McGovern had been a strong opponent of the Vietnam War and a constant critic of what he claimed were excessive levels of defense spending. In an ad entitled *McGovern Defense*, the Nixon campaign tried to claim the national defense issue as Republican and to portray McGovern as a threat. The ad contained a table with numerous toy soldiers and other military toys. While a narrator talked about how McGovern's defense plans would bring about widespread reductions in the size of existing armed forces, a hand would sweep some of the toys off the table. The narrator said that McGovern would cut the marines by one-third while a hand swept away about one-third of the toy marines. Different versions of this same act was repeated several times with references made to the numbers of soldiers, sailors, airmen, interception planes and ships that McGovern would eliminate. In addition, the narrator linked the power of the presidency with Nixon by saying "President Nixon doesn't believe we should play games with our national security. He believes in a strong America to negotiate for people from strength."

Incumbent and Challenger Advertising

Several scholars who have studied televised political advertising have focused attention on the different needs and strategies of incumbents and challengers. Popkin has looked at variations in the circumstances and opportunities of these two different kinds of candidates. He writes that, "Incumbents deal with acts of state and challengers deal with media events (Popkin 1991, p. 66)." Popkin says that incumbents prefer to use the "Rose Garden" strategy so that public evaluations of them can rest on their records as president rather than on their images as campaigners. He adds that incumbent presidents can also claim credit for many routine activities of government even though they may have contributed little to them because many voters do not directly observe much of what government does.

Judith Trent and Robert Friedenberg have studied the strategies that incumbents and challengers tend to employ in their election campaigns. While they have compared the two categories of candidates on a number of variables, they have not subdivided either category into subsets based on the political strength of the incumbent. They have found that incumbents rarely need to create personal and public identities during election campaigns because they have already accomplished this requisite need by virtue of serving in office. These scholars describe incumbency campaigning as "a blend of symbolic and pragmatic communication strategies designed to make candidates be perceived by voters as not only good enough for the office sought but appear as if they already possessed the office." In contrast, they view challenger campaigning as "a series of communication strategies designed to persuade voters that change is needed and that the candidate is the best person to bring about change (Trent and Friedenberg 2004, p. 111)."

The symbolic component of incumbent strategies relies on manipulating the imagery of the modern presidency. This includes the symbolic trappings, legitimacy, competency, and charisma that are now inherent in the institution of the presidential office. Symbolic trappings involve scenes of the White House and its accompanying grounds, the Oval Office, the presidential airplane among others. Legitimacy derives from widespread public beliefs that the occupant of the presidential office is worthy of public trust until he proves otherwise. The competency dimension reflects a point of view where people of different ideologies agree that American government cannot work effectively without strong presidential leadership. Finally, public actions by presidents tend to be exciting, patriotic, and/or glamorous and these contribute to the office's charismatic nature. An effective use of these strategies provides an incumbent with an unusual opportunity to link his own personal bid for another term with the symbolic dimensions of the institutional office. This opportunity is unavailable to any of his rivals, either for the nomination or in the general election.

Trent and Friedenberg have outlined eleven pragmatic strategies that are available to incumbents. Most of these involve different versions of using the various components of the presidential job to campaign for reelection. One is the creation of pseudoevents, activities such as ceremonies or announcements that attract media attention. Incumbents can use these to generate news coverage and later employ imagery of them in their televised advertising. Other pragmatic strategies include making appointments, creating special task forces, appropriating funds, consulting with foreign leaders, manipulating domestic issues, receiving endorsements, emphasizing accomplishments, appearing to stay "above" political trenches, and using surrogates to campaign.

In seeking to accomplish their requisite strategies of persuading voters that change is needed and that they are the best persons to bring it about, challengers must create dissatisfaction and doubts about that incumbent's policies and actions. Challengers must take the offense on issues and must probe, question and attack the incumbent's record, Trent and Friedenberg write. Calls for change often vary and might include the enactment of new programs, reliance upon a different governing philosophy, or even the use of altered styles of personal leadership. Challengers must convey a sense of optimism for the future while serving to reinforce what are often perceived to be majority values. One of the greatest problems that challengers must overcome is to offer voters better futures without frightening them into believing the challengers are too radical or distinct from the political mainstream. In a statement reflecting the daunting nature of presidential incumbency, Trent and Friedenberg emphasize that challengers, even when they have carried out their campaigns with great expertise, often run into the perennial problem that incumbents are quite simply almost impossible to defeat. They say that "challengers may be only as successful as incumbents are incompetent to employ the symbolic and pragmatic strategies their office provides (Trent and Friedenberg 2004, p. 107)."

Kaid and Johnston employed Trent and Friedenberg's strategic categories in *Videostyle* and in several of their other works about televised advertising. They found that incumbents and challengers differ significantly in most categories. With respect to symbolic strategies, the two types of candidates differed in use of symbolic trappings (27 percent of all ads versus 5 percent, with incumbents listed first), presidential legitimacy (26 to 12), and competency of the office (73 to 47). The candidates also differed on some of the incumbent's pragmatic strategies; consulting with world leaders (12 to 6), emphasizing accomplishments (50 to 16), employing an above the trenches political posture (28 to 17), and having surrogates speak on their behalf (42 to 35). In addition, they differed on three of the challenger's strategic categories; calling for changes (14 to 71), taking the offensive position (34 to 51), and attacking their opponent's record (37 to 47), Kaid and Johnston 2001, p. 86).

In addition to these strategic categories, Kaid and Johnston found that incumbents and challengers differ in their advertising strategies in several other important ways. Among these are such content related variables of general issue concerns (55 to 74), personal characteristics (69 to 53), and performance and success (33 to 5), and the presentation related variables of the candidate serving as the dominant speaker in an ad (26 to 46) and reliance upon anonymous announcers (49 to 32). In general, they found that incumbents were more likely to use anonymous announcers to speak of their personal characteristics and accomplishments, to focus on social and foreign policy issues, and to use visual imagery of the symbolic trappings of the presidential office. Challengers were more likely to speak for themselves with head on camera images, to attack the incumbent's record while calling for change, and to take the offensive on issues, particularly those of an economic nature (Kaid and Johnston 2001, p. 94).

Benoit's work is quite helpful in distinguishing the advertising strategies of the different types of incumbents and contrasting them with challengers. He compared the utterances of all candidate ads used by the major party nominees in the presidential elections from 1952 through 1996 on a number of variables, including incumbency. He found a number of important differences between incumbents and challengers, although he did not divide incumbents into categories based upon any particular variables, including their political strength. Nonetheless, his findings demonstrate that incumbents differ among themselves in their employment of televised advertising. His findings are centered on the application of his functional approach to the two major dimensions that have dominated research in recent decades; 1) positive messages (acclaims) versus negative ones (attacks) and 2) ads with themes of issues-images. He found that both incumbents and challengers tend to use more acclaims than attacks, but that incumbents use them far more frequently. Incumbents used acclaims in 66 percent of the utterances in their ads while challengers employed them in only 54 percent of theirs. In providing another test of his assertion that incumbents rely more on acclaims than challengers, Benoit looked at the specific strategies that five presidents who had ran as challengers during their initial victories and as incumbents in their reelection efforts had used during two consecutive elections. These candidates in question were Eisenhower, Nixon, Carter, Reagan, and Clinton. Benoit verified that all five had relied more on acclaims as incumbents than they had as challengers (Benoit, 1999, p. 177).

One can see examples of this pattern in two ads used by Richard Nixon in his consecutive election victories of 1968 and 1972. In 1968, when he was the challenger, Nixon questioned the practices of the incumbent Democratic administration of which his opponent, Hubert Humphrey, was an integral part. In the ad *Law and Order*, Nixon spoke to his audience about the public disorder that had marked the late 1960s. In accompaniment with imagery of anti-war demonstrators clashing with police, Nixon said, "It is time for an honest look at the problem of order in the United States. Dissent is a necessary ingredient of change. But is a system of government that provides for peaceful change, there is no cause that justifies a resort to violence. Let us recognize that the first civil right of every American is to be free from domestic violence. So I pledge to you, we shall have order in the United States." Four years later, when he was a strong incumbent seeking reelection against a challenger, George McGovern, who had made war and peace a central issue of his campaign, Nixon used an acclaims approach to emphasize his successes in national security. In the four minute film, *Russia*, Nixon spoke of his state visit to Moscow in May, 1972. The film began with imagery of Nixon meeting with the leaders of the Soviet Union when he was signing the Strategic Arms Limitation Treaty (SALT). The imagery included the many symbolic trappings that are associated with the presidency and international diplomacy. A narrator described Nixon's actions but his words were soon followed by remarks Nixon had made while addressing the Russian people in a televised address. Nixon spoke about the importance of the treaty in leading to peace between the two superpowers, and of the diary of a young Russian girl about the horrors that her family had encountered during the siege of Leningrad during World War II. The ad ended with the slogan, "President Nixon-Now More than Ever."

In addition to his discussion about acclaims and attacks, Benoit divided the issues-images dimension into two broad categories; public policy questions and matters related to candidate character. The policy category had references to past deeds, future plans, and general goals while the character category contained subcategories about personal qualities, leadership ability, and ideals. His findings, although not reported in the manner described here, allow for comparisons of the advertising strategies used by incumbents of the various categories of political strength discussed above. The five strong incumbents from 1956, 1964, 1972, 1984, and 1996 devoted about 65 percent of their advertising utterances to policy related questions and only 35 percent to personal character. In contrast, the three weak incumbents of 1976, 1980, and 1992 divided their utterances more evenly, 49.3 percent for policy and 50.7 percent for character. Surrogate incumbents and all challengers, whose collective utterances were very similar to one another, fell between these two with a division of about 58 percent policy and 42 percent character (Benoit, 1999, p. 174).

In relying upon the variety of research findings that I have discussed throughout this chapter, I have concluded that two important differences appear to exist between the advertising strategies of incumbent presidents when the political and popular strength of their incumbency is taken into account. Strong incumbents seem to differ from other candidates, including weak or surrogate incumbents and all challengers, in their reliance upon acclaims to emphasize their successful deeds, optimistic plans, and visionary goals. They often use the institutional power, symbolism, legitimacy, and charisma of the presidential office in their presentation of self through political advertising. In contrast, weak incumbents seem to differ from strong or surrogate incumbents and from all challengers in their extraordinary willingness to use those same institutional, symbolic, legitimating, and charismatic resources to draw attention to the personal qualities, leadership ability, and ideals that constitute character. These observations are consistent with the findings of Trent and Friedenberg, who have said that challengers may be only as successful as incumbents are incompetent in employing the symbolic and pragmatic strategies of the presidential office; of Benoit, who has explained and tested the various components that comprise issues-images and acclaims-attacks messages; and Kaid and Johnston who have developed the concept of videostyle as a requisite feature of political candidates in an age when televised advertising is the most effect means of communicating with voters in national campaigns.

While incumbents have many important advantages over their challengers that derive from their unique vantage point as the sole occupant of the presidential office, they must still address three interrelated matters that are essential in modern political advertising. All candidates must develop public images that convince voters they have the personal qualifications to lead the nation. A second is to develop of a set of issue stands that distinguishes them from their rivals and which provide a rationale for their pursuit of office. Finally, they need to attack their rivals in order to convince their own partisans that those rivals constitute a serious threat to the enactment or preservation of policies those partisans support. All presidential candidates must develop advertising strategies that unite the key concepts of images, issues, and attacks into a coherent set of themes.

Campaign Time Periods

Observers of modern presidential elections tend to divide the campaigns of individual years into two distinct components or time periods; the quests for the nominations of the two major political parties and the battle in the general election between the winners of those nominations. The political demands placed upon candidates by the events of these two periods are not always compatible. The quests for the nominations frequently involve battles among a relatively large number of candidates who aim their appeals at a partisan constituency whose members share many of the same political values. Candidates must convince their own partisans of their personal commitment to the party's core values in order to win the nomination. In addition, the existence of numerous candidates for the nomination often prevents any particular candidate from concluding that he has only one significant rival. To win, a candidate needs to convince enough of his own partisans that he offers a better combination of ideological consistency and prospects for a general election victory than any of his rivals. He must do this in a manner that minimizes the divisions that might develop among his own partisans so that unity for the general election is likely. The general election campaigns differ in the sense that they involve fewer candidates competing for the votes of a much more diverse electorate. A candidate does not need to attain national unity; he simply needs to acquire enough support to win a majority of the nation's electoral votes. In order to garner enough of these votes, the candidates frequently strive to sound less partisan and more conciliatory than they did while seeking the nomination. The different demands of these two time periods encourage candidates to vary the themes of their televised advertising. I refer the reader to the various scholars cited above in the section *Incumbency,* and more specifically to the ones mentioned in the discussion about modern election campaigns, for a more thorough and detailed explanation of the points summarized here.

This practice of dividing presidential campaigns into these two periods may be limiting, however. My previous research suggests that a division into five periods rather than two may offer a more realistic view of the development of modern media oriented campaigns (Dover, 2002). These periods consist of the nomination, which is clearly the first one to occur in any election year, and four different components of the general election. The second time period comprises the interim between the nomination battle and the national conventions. The existence of this time period is a recent development, a result of the front-loading of primaries and the reporting practices of television and other news media. Many states are scheduling their primary elections at dates far earlier than in past years. This practice encourages nomination campaigns to conclude many weeks and even sometimes many months, before the national conventions take place. The conventions tend to occur in July and August. Television news media focus extensive attention on the candidates during the primaries but reduce their coverage when they conclude. For example, during the most intense part of the 2004 primaries, from the first week in January through the first week in March, the three major television networks of ABC, CBS, and NBC devoted an average of 320 minutes of air time monthly on their evening newscasts to reporting about the Democratic candidates. They reduced their election related coverage to only 77 minutes per month between early March, when the nomination of John Kerry became obvious, and July 4. While coverage of every candidate diminished during this time, George W. Bush continued to attract substantial daily and ongoing news attention while acting in the role of president. Such coverage was not available to the challenger John Kerry (Vanderbilt Television News Archive, 2006).

The third period involves the national conventions. Here, the two major party candidates individually attain some extensive news coverage for about three weeks that is not available for their rival. This coverage involves the events that lead into the convention, such as the possible announcement of a running mate, potential themes that might be used in the convention and in the nominee's acceptance speech, the actual events of the convention, and a major campaign trip by the two members of the party ticket that begins immediately after the convention ends. The fourth period consists of the events during the time between the end of the conventions and the onset of the nationally televised debates. The candidates tend to direct their efforts during this time to the vital political task of attaining the support of undecided voters in specific states where the election appears to be relatively close. Finally, the candidates change the nature of their efforts after the debates conclude, which now seems to be in early October, and focus instead on convincing their own partisans to remain loyal and to actually cast votes. The time of this final drive, aimed at accomplishing the goal of "getting out the vote," comprises the fifth period and now consists mostly of the month of October.

In my previous works mentioned above, I demonstrated that presidential candidates altered their strategies in order to respond to the changing exigencies that resulted from these different time periods. I also described how television news media responded to these candidate actions by shifting their attention to different themes and issues (Dover, 1994, 1998, 2002; also see Vanderbilt Television News Archive, 2006). My research was limited to television news, however, and did not include any references to advertising. My findings suggest that candidates should also alter the themes of their televised advertising in order to respond to the different political demands that arise from these five distinct time periods. I intend to show that the two major candidates in the election of 2004, incumbent George W. Bush and challenger John Kerry made these alterations.

Research Questions

The above discussion about incumbency, advertising, and campaign periods raises four questions that I seek to answer through the remainder of this book. First, do strong incumbents rely more on advertising themes about past deeds, future plans, and general goals than other incumbents and all challengers? The findings of the cited writers suggest the answer is yes. These incumbents had successful first terms and could use their accomplishments to justify reelection. One can see an example of this in Nixon's ad, *Russia*, from 1972. The emphasis was on Nixon's successful efforts at reducing tensions with the nation's greatest adversary. Second, do weak incumbents rely more on advertising themes about personal character, leadership abilities, and ideals than other incumbents and all challengers? Once again, the cited writings suggest the answer should also be yes. Ford's ad from the 1972 campaign had references to such personal characteristics as "courage to say no," "make hard decisions," and "open administration." Third, do surrogate incumbents differ from all challengers in their emphasis on either policy or character related themes? The answer here should be no. Surrogate incumbents seem to act more like challengers than incumbents, as the ad about Hubert Humphrey from the 1968 election, *Ahead of His Time*, suggests. The ad talked about Humphrey's entire public career over several decades rather than simply the four most recent years he had spent as vice president. Finally, do presidential candidates alter their advertising themes during the various time periods of the campaign year in order to adapt to the needs that arise from changing political contexts? As the works of Kaid, Trent and Friedenberg, and Benoit show, all candidates use a variety of ads throughout their campaigns, some positive, others negative in tone. One should also expect them to change their particular mix of ads throughout the campaign year.

Plan of the Book

Seven chapters follow this one with the next three focusing on the advertising strategies of the candidates who comprised each of the election categories. Chapter Two looks at elections with strong incumbents; Chapter Three directs attention to elections with weak incumbents, and Chapter Four is about elections with surrogate incumbents. These chapters follow a similar format. Each begins with an explanation of the recurring and unique features of the elections within that category and then follows with a description and evaluation of the advertising strategies employed by the two most recent incumbents and challengers who competed in this election category prior to 2004. The two strong incumbents were Ronald Reagan (1984) and Bill Clinton (1996) while their challengers were Walter Mondale and Robert Dole. Jimmy Carter (1980) and George Bush (1992) were the last two weak incumbents while their rivals were Ronald Reagan and Robert Dole. Finally, George Bush (1988) and Albert Gore Jr. (2000) were the last two vice presidents who attempted to succeed a retiring incumbent and they were opposed by Michael Dukakis and George W. Bush respectively.

This particular combination of elections provides an opportunity to direct the observation to recent campaigns while controlling for whatever effects may exist because of interactions between partisanship with incumbency. It is timely in that these six elections are the ones immediately preceding that of 2004. It controls for interactions in that each subset contains one Republican and one Democratic incumbent; Reagan (R) and Clinton (D) as strong incumbents, Ford (R) and Carter (D) as weak, and Bush (R) and Gore (D) as vice presidential surrogates.

The findings of these chapters are applied to the election of 2004, which is discussed in the three chapters, Five, Six, and Seven, that follow. The election of 2004 was unusual in that the political strength of Bush was ambiguous throughout the year. It was never quite clear of whether he was a strong or a weak incumbent. His approval rating rarely varied more than a few points from the fifty percent range (Gallup Poll, 2006). Partisans interpreted Bush's record differently. Republicans saw him as a strong incumbent deserving of another term and acted accordingly while Democrats considered Bush a weak incumbent who would be removed from office after one controversial term. Bush won a highly competitive election, but his popular and electoral vote margins were the smallest of any successful incumbent in more than a century. In retrospect, he was the weakest strong incumbent of recent times. Perhaps he engaged in a self-fulfilling prophesy; his advertising was similar to that of other strong incumbents and very much unlike that of weak incumbents.

A second issue discussed in these three chapters is the way in which the candidates varied the themes of their televised advertising during the five time periods of the campaign. The dates of those periods were; the nomination battle (January-March); post-nomination events (April-May); the national convention period (June-August); the early general election weeks (September); and post-debate period (October). Chapter Five focuses on the campaign for the Democratic nomination with emphasis given to John Kerry, his eventual running mate John Edwards, and to a few of his major rivals in this ten candidate battle. Chapter Six directs attention to Bush campaign throughout the entire year, while Chapter Seven looks at Kerry during the post-nomination periods from April through November. The final chapter, Eight, summarizes and interprets the findings of Chapters Two through Seven.

The ads used in this book, including those discussed in this chapter, were obtained from two different types of sources. One source consists of published videotapes of the most important ads used in the elections prior to 2004. Devlin has published twelve such tapes that contain ads he depicts as the most important in particular categories. The categories involve individual elections, such as 1996, or specific types of ads, such as long, short, or negative, that were used by candidates in elections ranging from 1952 through 2000. The *London International Advertising Awards* has published a similar, although less numerous, set of tapes that also focus on individual elections and includes the leading ads of various decades, such as the 1980's. These two publishers selected essentially the same ads for inclusion in their tapes. A second source, one used here only with respect to the election of 2004, is a collection of ads published on candidate websites. Each candidate published all of his televised ads on a campaign website. In addition, the Political Communication Laboratory of Stanford University published the same ads on its website relating to the 2004 campaign. I selected the seven ads discussed above in this chapter (relating to the elections of 1960 through 1976) for inclusion because they appear to be good examples of particular types of ads. In addition, I have used all ads published on any of the videotapes with respect to the elections of 1980 through 2000 and every ad that was contained on a candidate websites for the election of 2004.

The advertising analyzed here is limited to ads that were actually used by the campaign organizations of the various candidates. It excludes ads used by other groups such at Swift Boat Veterans for Truth or MoveOn.org in the 2004 election. While these groups, and many others as well, advertised extensively in recent campaigns, their messages are beyond the scope of this book. This book focuses on the videostyles of incumbents and challengers in a variety of recurring political contexts. While the ads of independent groups may be important, controversial, and even demanding of response, they are beyond the personal control of the candidates and are therefore not included in an analysis of the advertising themes used by incumbents and challengers.

CHAPTER 2

ELECTIONS WITH STRONG INCUMBENTS: 1984 and 1996

GENERAL OVERVIEW

Five presidential elections during the last half of the twentieth century (and an additional one during the first decade of the twenty-first century) concluded with the reelection of the incumbent. The outcomes of these elections were not random, however. Instead, they form a unique pattern with recurring features that are likely to be repeated on more than a few occasions during the coming decades. The twentieth century elections occurred in 1956, 1964, 1972, 1984, and 1996. The intervals between them varied from eight to twelve years, an average occurrence of about one such election per decade. The most important features of these elections were the victories of the incumbent presidents by popular and electoral vote margins considerably larger than the victory margins acquired by the winners of nearly all other presidential elections in the history of the United States. Moreover, these results were distinct from the outcomes of other, non-presidential, elections during those same years. Only rarely has the reelection of a strong incumbent president contributed to any important gains by his political party in other public offices (see Abramson, Aldrich, and Rhode, 1986, 1998; Ceaser and Busch, 1997; CQ Press, 2005; Germond and Witcover, 1985; Nelson, 1985, 1997; Pomper, 1985, 1997, and White, 1965, 1973, for detailed explanations of the leading events, contexts, and outcomes of the elections of 1964, 1972, 1984, and 1996).

A second major feature of all five elections is that each of them individually formed the middle point of a cycle of three elections relating to the successes and failures of the political party of the incumbent president. The cycles related to these elections are characterized by an initial election where the nominee of the opposition party wins the presidency after undergoing a highly competitive nomination and general election campaign, a second election four years later when the incumbent wins a second term after expanding his political following into a formidable coalition, and a third where the surrogate of the incumbent loses or barely wins the presidency when the incumbent retires. The presidential party lost four of the five elections that occurred at the end of these cycles, winning only in 1988.

With respect to the individual elections and cycles, Dwight D. Eisenhower won the nomination of the Republican Party in 1952 after a spirited battle with several other aspirants, the most notable of which was Senator Robert Taft (Ohio). Eisenhower then defeated the Democratic candidate, Governor Adlai Stevenson Jr. (Illinois) by a popular vote margin of 55.1 to 44.4 percent. Eisenhower's win brought twenty years of Democratic Party control of the presidency to an end. The high point of this election cycle occurred in 1956 when Eisenhower won reelection by once again defeating Stevenson and by doing so with an even larger vote margin than before, 57.4 to 42.0 percent. His victory was more personal than partisan, however, as the Republicans lost seats in both houses of the Democratic controlled Congress. This electoral cycle ended in 1960 when Eisenhower retired and the nominee of the Democratic Party, John F. Kennedy, won the election over the vice president Richard Nixon.

The victorious Democrats followed a similar script with a three election cycle of gains and declines. Kennedy attained the nomination of his party in 1960 only after a lengthy battle with Senators Lyndon Johnson (Texas), Hubert Humphrey (Minnesota), Stuart Symington (Missouri), and Stevenson. His struggles in the general election against Richard Nixon were even more intense as he won the closest election of the twentieth century, 49.72 percent to 49.55 percent. This election was characterized by the first televised candidate debates and strong reservations by many voters about Kennedy's Roman Catholic religion.

Kennedy enjoyed high personal popularity during his three years in office, particularly after the Cuban Missile Crisis in October, 1962, and appeared headed for reelection when he was assassinated in November, 1963. His successor, Lyndon Johnson, recorded one of the greatest electoral triumphs in American history when he defeated Senator Barry Goldwater (Arizona) by a margin of 60.8 percent to 38.5 percent of the vote. Unlike the Republicans of 1956, the Democrats gained a significant number of seats in Congress in 1964 and were able to use them to enact much of their program. This was the one exception to the pattern in that the presidential party recorded major gains in Congress when winning a second term.

The Democratic Party suffered a major decline in support over the four years following Johnson's victory. The party was badly divided in 1968 over the conduct of the Vietnam War and lost the election to Richard Nixon. This defeat occurred after Lyndon Johnson announced his decision to retire following setbacks in Vietnam and an unimpressive showing in the New Hampshire primary, the assassination of Senator Robert Kennedy (New York), and the televising of disruptive demonstrations from a controversial national convention in Chicago.

Richard Nixon became the third strong incumbent of the late twentieth century to win reelection. Once again, the new presidential party, in this instance the Republicans, saw its fortunes grow and decline in a cycle similar to those of the two just described. After losing to Kennedy in 1960, Nixon returned to his home state of California and ran for the governorship in 1962. He also lost, but the setback was more severe than his defeat for the presidency. Many political observers considered Nixon finished as a credible candidate for a future national campaign. Nixon struggled for years to make a political comeback and did so only after defeating a variety of formidable members of his party for the presidential nomination in 1968, including Governors Nelson Rockefeller (New York) and Ronald Reagan (California). He defeated the Democratic nominee and vice president Hubert Humphrey and third party candidate former Governor George Wallace (Alabama) in the second closest election of the twentieth century. Nixon attained 43.4 percent of the vote while Humphrey finished with 42.7.

Nixon eventually won the support of his two intra-party rivals Rockefeller and Reagan and scored a massive reelection triumph in 1972 by defeating the Democratic nominee Senator George McGovern (South Dakota) by a popular vote margin similar to that of Johnson, 60.7 to 37.5 percent. He also carried the electoral votes of a record 49 states, losing only Massachusetts and the District of Columbia. While sweeping, Nixon's victory was also more personal than partisan because the Republican Party failed to make any significant gains in either chamber of the Democratic controlled Congress. The pattern of decline that follows strong incumbent elections also occurred once again, this time helped by the Watergate scandal. Nixon was forced to resign his office in August, 1974 because of his involvement in the scandal. The Republicans suffered major losses in congressional seats in 1974 and Nixon's successor as president, Gerald Ford, lost the 1976 election to former Governor Jimmy Carter (Georgia).

Carter proved to be a weak incumbent and was defeated in 1980 by Reagan in his bid for a second term. Reagan's triumph began yet another cycle of gains and losses over the course of three elections by the presidential party, although this cycle was unusual in that it ended with the presidential party extending its tenure in office to twelve years. Reagan won the presidency in 1980 after two failed attempts at attaining the Republican nomination. He lost to Nixon in 1968 and to Ford in 1976, and then suffered what appeared to be a major, and perhaps fatal, setback in early 1980 when he lost the Iowa caucuses to George Bush. Reagan quickly regained his lead, however, and by May had forced his six rivals to abandon their efforts. He even selected his strongest rival, Bush, as his running mate. Reagan's other rivals were Senators Robert Dole (Kansas) and Howard Baker (Tennessee), former Governor John Connally (Texas), and two congressmen from Illinois, John Anderson and Philip Crane. After losing the nomination, Anderson ran for president as an independent candidate in the general election. Reagan defeated both Carter and Anderson with a majority of the popular vote, 50.7 percent, compared to Carter's 41.0 percent, and the electoral votes of 44 states.

Reagan's tenure in office followed the same script as those of Eisenhower, Kennedy/Johnson, and Nixon/Ford. He built a formidable personal following and won reelection to a second term in 1984 with a 58.8 percent to 40.6 percent majority of the popular vote against his Democratic rival, former vice president Walter Mondale. He also won the electoral votes of 49 states, losing only Minnesota and the District of Columbia. As with other strong incumbents before him, Reagan also failed to translate his personal successes into gains for his party. He had led his party to significant congressional gains in his initial victory in 1980 when the Republicans took control of the Senate for the first time in 26 years while recording major additions in the House of Representatives. These gains marked the peak of Republican successes during Reagan's time, however. Republicans lost seats in Congress in every subsequent election during Reagan's eight years in office, including 1984. They even lost their majority of the Senate in 1986.

The Republican Party also lost voter support during the final years of the Reagan presidency. The designated successor to the party nomination, George Bush, trailed his Democratic rival, Governor Michael Dukakis (Massachusetts), in public opinion surveys for several months during the early months of 1988 (Gallup Poll, 2006). Bush eventually gained the lead in August and subsequently won the election with 53.4 percent of the popular vote. This percentage was far less than what Reagan had won in 1984, however. Moreover, Bush was only a one term president as he lost his bid for a second term in 1992.

The most recent occurrence of the three election cycle of strong incumbency happened with Bill Clinton. Clinton sought the presidency in 1992 and initially competed in a battle with five rivals for the Democratic nomination. He defeated them through a series of primaries, with Senators Paul Tsongas (Massachusetts), Tom Harkin (Iowa), and Robert Kerrey (Nebraska) being his most formidable opponents. He was also opposed by one former governor and one active one, Jerry Brown (California) and Douglas Wilder (Virginia) respectively. After clinching the nomination in May and officially securing it at the national convention in July, Clinton campaigned against the incumbent Bush and a well financed independent candidate, Ross Perot, in an unusual three candidate general election campaign. Clinton was actually trailing both Bush and Perot in May but seized the lead in July and defeated his rivals by attaining 42.3 percent of the popular vote, while Bush and Perot garnered 37.4 and 18.9 percent respectively.

Clinton enjoyed a number of successes and failures over the next four years, including the enactment of his taxing and spending policies and the defeat of his health care reforms. His party suffered major losses in Congress in 1994, however, and Clinton then faced strong challenges over the next few years from an aggressive conservative majority. Clinton fought back, expanded his personal following, and attained a second term with 49.2 percent of the popular vote over the Republican nominee Robert Dole and independent Perot. Dole attained 40.7 percent of the popular vote.

The pattern of electoral decline that characterized the tenures of the previous four strong incumbents occurred once again. Clinton encountered major troubles during his second term, was impeached but not convicted, and saw his party's eight point margin in the 1996 popular vote decline to virtually nothing in 2000 when his vice president and political surrogate Albert Gore Jr. lost a highly disputed election to Governor George W. Bush (Texas).

This electoral pattern, where the nominee of the opposition party wins the presidency after a competitive campaign and close election; expands his following over the next four years in ways that culminate in a successful, but often very personal, reelection effort; and then sees his party lose the next election when he retires, supports the proposition that modern day presidential elections are candidate centered campaigns and that the incumbent is the most important and influential of all candidates. With this in mind, my purpose in this chapter is to illustrate how the televised advertising of presidential candidates in elections with strong incumbents reflects the recurring circumstances of the campaigns that comprise this category and which derive from the particular vantage points of the individual candidates. I show that strong incumbents use advertising strategies with positive (acclaims) related ads that emphasize the policy accomplishments of their first terms and goals for their seconds and negative (attack) ads that depict their challengers as threats to those same accomplishments and goals. Challengers tend to encounter great difficulties in competing effectively against such incumbents. They frequently employ advertising strategies that lack defenses of the last time their party occupied the presidency. Such ads do not address the strongest arguments strong incumbents can make in support of their reelection; that they have brought about valuable changes from the recent past and now want voters to reward them with reelection. Such arguments tend to prevail.

I focus attention on the last two of these elections that predated the one of 2004, those of 1984 and 1996. In particular, I show how the two incumbents of these years, Ronald Reagan and Bill Clinton, their general election opponents, Walter Mondale and Robert Dole, and the variety of candidates who sought the nomination of the opposition party presented themselves to the American electorate in the manner described above.

The incumbents of 1984 and 1996, Reagan and Clinton, were both unopposed for renomination. Both had united their partisans in support of their quests for second terms prior to the onset of the election year, accomplishments that proved unusually valuable as events of the campaign years unfolded. This unity enabled the incumbents to begin their reelection quests early in the campaign year while the opposition party was forced to devote about two-thirds of those same years to simply determining the identities of its nominees. In both election years, the opposition party encountered difficult circumstances. A strong and popular incumbent was seeking an additional term in office and was already campaigning and enjoying favorable media coverage for his actions in office. Meanwhile, this party had no clear and obvious leader who could unite it immediately. As a result, it had to undergo a lengthy campaign for its nomination that involved numerous little known candidates fighting against one another in a battle of attrition that lasted for several months.

Over the last several decades, television new media have structured their coverage of contested nomination campaigns around the actions of only two major candidates. They have assigned predetermined roles, those of front-runner and leading adversary, to these two candidates, and have reported about how each of the two candidates has fulfilled the expectations of his particular role (Dover, 1994, 1998, 2002). Seven candidates sought the Democratic nomination in 1984 but Walter Mondale clearly filled the front-runner role from the beginning. He took an early lead, as measured by his successes at raising money, acquiring endorsements from prominent party leaders, and generating high support for the party's supporters as shown in public opinion surveys (Gallup Poll, 2006). He had relied upon his previous service as vice president to attain this lead. His presence on two national tickets (1976 and 1980) and his four years as vice president had provided Mondale with opportunities to generate some very powerful support from the Democratic Party's activist community. As the media designated front-runner, Mondale was the central political actor in the unfolding mediated drama of the nomination campaign.

There was no obvious leading adversary, however. In response, each one of Mondale's opponents initially sought this designation. During the months preceding the first electoral tests of the campaign, the Iowa caucuses and the New Hampshire primary, Mondale's rivals and television news media together helped create a political context where the outcomes of these tests would provide the identity of that adversary. After this identification had been made, the campaign could then develop into a struggle between the two role playing finalists. The aspirants for this role were Senators John Glenn (Ohio), Alan Cranston (California), Ernest Hollings (South Carolina), and Gary Hart (Colorado), former Senator George McGovern (South Dakota), and Reverend Jesse Jackson. Mondale won the Iowa caucuses with about 45 percent of the vote while Hart finished second with about 15 percent. Rather than describe this outcome as a strong Mondale victory, television news media focused much of their attention on Hart because of his second place finish (Winebrenner, 1998).

The added media coverage enabled Hart to expand both his efforts and prospects considerably. He rapidly gained support from Democrats in all parts of the nation but most importantly from those planning to vote in New Hampshire. One week after his Iowa placing, Hart won the New Hampshire primary while Mondale finished second. The Hart victory contributed to the sudden withdrawal of all the remaining rivals of Mondale except for Jackson from the race within a few days. Hart failed to repeat his successes in most states, however. After a time consuming battle that lasted until the final primaries had concluded in early June, Mondale emerged with a majority of the national convention delegates supporting his nomination. He secured it at the party's national convention in July.

The Republican campaign in 1996 was quite similar in that the opposition party also devoted the first two-thirds of the election year to determining its nominee. The campaign attracted a number of candidates, with Robert Dole serving as the front-runner at the beginning of the year. Dole had been a major figure in the Republican Party for more than a quarter of a century. He had served as the national chairman of the party in the early 1970s, was the vice presidential nominee in 1976, had unsuccessfully run for the presidential nomination in 1980 and 1988, and had been the party leader in the Senate since 1985. He had extensive support from many of the party's most important leaders and activists. His rivals were numerous, but none had strong followings. They included Senators Richard Lugar (Indiana) and Phil Gramm (Texas), former governor Lamar Alexander (Tennessee), commentator Pat Buchanan, and businessman Steve Forbes. This campaign also developed into a battle of attrition. Dole won the first electoral test, Iowa, and finished a close second to Buchanan in New Hampshire. This outcome helped transform Buchanan into the media designated leading adversary for a few weeks. Dole did not lose another state, however, and by the end of March, Buchanan and the remaining candidates had concluded they could not win and withdrew. Dole had secured the nomination but he was financially exhausted. He had spent nearly all of his money and could not attain a significant amount of new funding until the federal monies he would receive as a party nominee became available after the end of the national conventions. This would happen in July. As had happened with the Democrats in 1984, the nominee of the opposition party in 1996 was unable to compete directly with the incumbent president until over two-thirds of the election year had ended.

INCUMBENTS

Perhaps more than any other categories of incumbents, those who were successful in winning second terms differed from all other candidates in the content of their televised advertising. The strong incumbents had an advantage not possessed by other candidates; they were unopposed for renomination within their own parties. This unopposed status provided the strong incumbents with a valuable political advantage; they could devote the initial stages of the election year to campaigning directly for reelection while their rivals from the opposition party were forced to spend that same time competing for a nomination. With such an advantage, the strong incumbents employed advertising strategies that emphasized the accomplishments of their first terms, the goals they wanted to pursue if reelected, and the values that guided their past and future actions. While occasionally employing attack ads, the strong incumbents relied far more on acclaims when making their televised appeals. As Benoit's work shows, they did so at a rate far in excess of all other categories of candidates.

Reagan

Ronald Reagan began the 1984 campaign with the usual advantages of a strong incumbent; voters gave him very high approval ratings and his party was united behind his effort for reelection. Reagan had attained this standing because of widespread public perceptions that his initial term in office had been successful. Reagan owed his popularity to a combination of several factors. He had brought about some far reaching tax cuts in 1981 while simultaneously increasing defense spending. This combination stimulated the economy and led to a few years of prosperity, although this would prove to be short lived and eventually drive his successor, George Bush, from office in 1992. In addition, Reagan was far more aggressive, in word and occasionally in deed, with the Soviet Union and other American adversaries. This came after the nation had lost the Vietnam War and had been humiliated with the Iranian hostage crisis. This combination of economic and foreign policy successes, when coupled with Reagan's optimism and penchant for patriotic homilies, resulted in high approval ratings. Republicans spoke of the "Reagan Revolution," and believed that a new period of national leadership had arrived, one that would result in many years of Republican control of government.

The opposition Democrats were in political trouble at the beginning of 1984. They had lost control of the Senate to the Republicans in 1980 and did not appear to have any realistic chances of regaining a majority anytime soon. While they still had numerical control of the House of Representatives, they all too often lost key votes in that chamber to a coalition of Republicans and conservative members of their own party. They were also unable to offer an alternative to Reagan's conservative agenda. Moreover, and perhaps most important of all, they lacked an obvious and unifying leader as the campaign began who could provide the party with a sense of direction and mount a credible challenge to Reagan for national leadership.

As a result of this combination of circumstances, Reagan was free to advertise the various features of his own candidacy early in the year although he was limited in that he could not make any personalized attacks against a specific Democrat until late summer. One of the most effective efforts the campaign employed during the early months of the year, and at a time when the rival Democrats were still struggling to determine the identity of their presidential candidate, involved Reagan's visit to France in June, 1984 for the fortieth anniversary of the Allied landing in Normandy (D-Day). Reagan used this opportunity to employ the symbolic dimensions of the presidency and project imagery where he appeared as a unifying national spokesman. Reagan's appearance and speech were reported extensively by news media and later illustrated by his campaign organization through a widely distributed film. While Reagan could look upon June 6 as a day of national honor, his two leading Democratic rivals, Walter Mondale and Gary Hart, did not enjoy such an opportunity. They spent this same time fighting against one another in a bitter California primary that was also scheduled for early June.

The ad *Normandy Excerpt*, which was drawn from the campaign film mentioned above, showed Reagan addressing a group of aged veterans who had attended the ceremonies. His words were patriotic and laudatory of the contributions the veterans had made and were supported by combat imagery, emotionally moving scenes of the veterans in attendance and of Ronald and Nancy Reagan touring a cemetery of war dead. Reagan saluted the veterans and described them as products of the freest society in history.

The Reagan campaign also employed the first versions of its signature ad from 1984, *Morning in America*, during the nomination period. The ad involved a narrator with upbeat but non specific remarks about the improvements of the Reagan years. "This is America, spring of 84 . . . and this is America . . . and this is America . . . and this . . . and this . . . and this," he said, with pauses interspersed throughout this opening sentence. This audio was supported by upbeat and often nostalgic imagery which included scenes of a meadow and farmhouse, of children frolicking at Easter, of elderly people walking along a sidewalk in a peaceful neighborhood, of happy families, of the Grand Canyon, and of new building construction. The accompanying audio portion emphasized the accomplishments of the Reagan years, "Just four years ago people were saying its problems were too big and too difficult to be handled by any one president. Yet what are we seeing now? Jobs are coming back, housing is coming back, and for the first time in a long time, hope for the future is coming back. And isn't it interesting that no one anywhere is saying the job of president is too big for one person? President Reagan, he's doing what he was elected to do." While the ad contained no direct attacks against specific individuals, it implied that voters had picked Reagan to reverse the trends of the recent, and Democratic, past.

Two additional themes complemented this same message during the general election campaign; Reagan's successes with national security and his opposition to the higher taxes he attempted to associate with Mondale. With respect to the upbeat theme of successes, the ad *America's Back* began with a scene of a child riding a bicycle and included imagery of a family moving into a new home, the sale of a new car, factory workers heading to their jobs, and of a building construction site. It concluded with a picture of Reagan and the American flag with a slogan that linked the accomplishments of the past four years with the symbolic legitimacy of the presidential office, "President Reagan, Leadership that's Working." The narrative began, "During the past year, thousands of families have moved into new homes that once seemed out of reach. People are buying new cars they once thought they couldn't afford. Workers are returning to factories that just four years ago were closed." It continued by attributing these changes to Reagan, "And America is back with a sense of pride people thought we'd never feel again. Now that our country is turning around, why would we ever turn back?"

The *Morning in America* theme and the implicit threat that Mondale made to it resurfaced once again in *Prouder, Stronger, Better*. This ad also emphasized Reagan's accomplishments within the context of emotionally upbeat and nostalgic imagery. The narrator remarked, "Its morning again in America." This was followed with imagery of a small ship sailing in a harbor, people crossing a busy downtown street, a cowboy working on a farm, a car stopping in front of an older house, a marriage ceremony, an older man raising the American flag, and children looking upwards (perhaps at the flag) in awe. "Today more men and women will go to work than ever before in our country's history," the narrative continued. "With interest rates and inflation down, more people are buying new homes and our new families can have confidence in the future. America today is prouder, and stronger, and better. Why would we want to return to where we were less than four short years ago?"

The interrelated themes of nostalgia for a simpler and smaller town America and the successes of Reagan's policies resurfaced in an ad about Reagan's Mid-western train tour. Following a decades old tradition, Reagan toured several states, including Ohio, by train. The imagery began with an older man closing his barber shop and was followed by scenes of younger men leaving a factory, and people waving small American flags while standing besides the railroad tracks (*Train*). "On a Friday just a few weeks ago," the narrative began, "the barber shop closed three hours early. The mill shut its doors at noon. And all across the state people were taking time out for something special, a train carry-ing the fortieth president of the United States and bringing with it a new spirit of accomplishment and optimism, and pride." The narrator then linked the imagery to Reagan, "Because in the past three and a half years, things have been looking up in the country. Today, the economy is up and taxes and inflation are down. Americans are working and so is America. So while some folks might have come so they could tell their grandchildren they saw President Reagan, most of them just stopped by to say thanks."

Reagan's supporters frequently called him the "Great Communicator." Reagan put his skills to work in the ad *Inflation*. This was similar to *Morning in America*, only this time Reagan was the narrator. He spoke from a podium, but much of the imagery was of scenes from his nostalgic country. It focused on unused and rusting farm equipment, a closed factory, and then to optimistic scenes of people working. Reagan began, "This was America in 1980, a nation that wasn't working. Interest rates were at an all time high. Inflation was at its highest in 65 years." He then spoke of his successes, "So we rolled up our sleeves and showed that working together there's nothing we can't do. Today interest rates are down. Inflation is down. Americans are working again. And so is America. And we'll carry on unafraid and unashamed and unsurpassed."

While accepting the Democratic nomination, Mondale stated that a tax in-crease was necessary and that he would seek one. He added that Reagan would also have to seek one. Despite his opposition in 1984, Reagan signed revenue legislation in 1985 that raised some taxes. In opposing tax increases during the election year, however, Reagan attempted to create distinctions between public services and goods supported by taxation, and the government as a tax consum-ing entity not necessarily linked to them. Three ads demonstrate this pattern.

Two of them involved comparisons of the candidates; the candidates com-pared to one another or Mondale compared to himself. In *Reaganomics and Mondalenomics* a narrator compares the two candidates by stating repeatedly that Mondale has only one position, more taxes. "Here's the difference between the two ways of dealing with the nation's economy," he begins. "With Reaganomics you cut taxes, with Mondalenomics, you raise taxes." This theme continues, "With Reaganomics you cut deficits through growth and less government spending, with Mondalenomics, you raise taxes. With Reaganomics you create incentives that will move us all forward, with Mondalenomics, you raise taxes. They both work, the difference is Reaganomics works for you, Mondalenomics works against you."

A second comparative ad looked at inconsistencies in Mondale's positions, although the time difference between his stands was not mentioned. The ad, *Side by Side*, contained two images of Mondale, one smiling and one frowning. The narrative went, "How do two presidential candidates stand on important issues. Candidate Mondale has promised to reduce government spending but Senator Mondale voted to increase government spending twelve years in a row." The camera focused on each of Mondale's images as the narrator spoke. The ad continued, "Candidate Mondale has promised a strong national defense but Senator Mondale voted to weaken defenses eighteen times. Of course there's one area where they agree. They both stand for higher taxes." Mondale had served in the Senate from 1964 to 1976.

A third tax ad clearly separated the uses of tax money from its collection. In *Tax Vignettes*, a narrator spoke of possible tax increases while his words were supported by imagery of people whose facial expressions indicated their strong opposition to higher taxes. The imagery involved a man working at a road construction site, a woman spreading peanut butter from a nearly empty jar, a farmer loading hay into a truck, and firefighters battling a blaze. The narrator remarked, "Walter Mondale thinks it would be nice if you put in some more overtime and helped pay for his promises with your taxes. What do you think?" The ad then moved to the image of the woman with the narrator adding, "Walter Mondale thinks you can squeeze some more tax money out of your household budget. What do you think?" The remainder of the narration consisted of, "Walter Mondale thinks if you stay out in the fields a little more each day, you can pay the higher taxes he needs for his promises. What do you think? Walter Mondale thinks if you work a little harder and get into a little higher tax bracket, you'll be able to pay the higher taxes he needs for all his promises. What do you think? Vote for President Reagan. For one thing his leadership is working. And for another, you have better things to do with your money than pay for Walter Mondale's promises." The ad does not link increased taxes to the funding of any particular governmental programs, including national security. While opposing higher taxes, Reagan used other ads to emphasize his accomplishments (higher spending?) in defending the nation from unmentioned enemies.

The national security ads focused on how Reagan had increased the nation's strength during the past four years and implicitly questioned the willingness of the Democrats to defend the nation through the use of military force. A prevailing theme was peace through strength. In one such ad, *Peace*, Reagan spoke with supporting imagery of children. It involved scenes of a small girl looking out from a home front porch, a boy getting a haircut, and other children playing with bubbles, or a dog, or swimming. Reagan said "In my lifetime we faced four wars. And I want our children never to have to face another. A president's most important job is to secure peace for our children." With this, Reagan moved on to the increased defense spending that had marked his first term. "But it takes a strong nation to build a peace that lasts. And I believe that America is stronger and more secure today. Thanks to the determination of our people. America is prepared for peace."

In *Roosevelt Room*, another ad emphasizing Reagan's advocacy of more defense spending to bring about greater national security, a narrator introduces the "President of the United States" while a scene of the White House appears on television screens. Reagan is then shown in the Oval Office where he begins talking while images of several flags are displayed from the nearby Roosevelt Room. Reagan says, "Just across the hall here in the White House is the Roosevelt Room. And draped from each flag are battle streamers signifying every battle campaign fought since the Revolutionary War." He continues by focusing on the need for military strength, "My fondest hope for this presidency is that the people of America give us the continued opportunity to pursue a peace so strong and so lasting that we'd never again have to add a streamer to those flags."

The most effective Reagan attack ad that justified higher defense spending while implicitly questioning the political judgment of Mondale and the Democrats was *Bear*. The imagery was of a bear walking through a forest while the narrator used the bear as a metaphor for security threats. The narrator said, "There's a bear in the woods. For some people the bear is easy to see. Others don't see it at all. Some people say the bear is tame; others say it's vicious and dangerous. Since no one can really be sure who's right, isn't it smart to be as strong as the bear? If there is a bear."

Reagan linked the symbolism of the presidency with his optimistic vision of the future. In *Your Future* he spoke about children while standing in front of the White House "The kind of future our young people will have is something you never forget when you live here," he began. "Their security, their job opportunities, and the dreams they'll take into the next century all begin with what we do today. When we work hard to insure a strong economy with inflation and taxes under control we're taking care of tomorrow. And in this magnificent house, nothing could be more important than that."

Reagan concluded the advertising component of his campaign with a five minute appeal during the final days of the campaign (*Unity*). He focused on his ideals and once again emphasized the major accomplishments of his first term. Seated in front of a fireplace, Reagan began, "There's been something special in this campaign. In the bright eyes of our young, I see America coming together again. They are what this election is all about. They deserve a tomorrow when they can fly as high as their talents will take them. We're coming together again and building together again. And across this shining land, we are hoping to get together again. How can anyone doubt that our best days are yet to come?" Reagan's best day was on the immediate horizon as he recorded one of the most sweeping reelection triumphs in American history just days after this appeal.

Clinton

Clinton's approach in 1996 was similar to Reagan's in that he was unopposed for renomination while the opposition party also had to undergo a contested battle to determine its standard bearer. There was an important difference this time, however. The newly created practice of front-loading primary elections had altered the timeline for concluding nomination campaigns and thereby influenced the advertising strategy of the strong incumbent. Since the early 1950s, New Hampshire has enjoyed the distinction of being the first state to hold a primary in a presidential election year. Other states did not challenge this unique distinction during the 1950s and 1960s, but began doing so in 1972 by scheduling their primaries on either the same day as New Hampshire or perhaps even earlier. In response, New Hampshire enacted a law that required the state to hold its primary one week before any other state held a primary and empowered the governor to schedule the vote on a date that would conform to this requirement (Busch, 1997).

Prior to 1972, New Hampshire routinely conducted its presidential primary on the second Tuesday in March but in particular this year it began a process of scheduling its primary on earlier dates in response to challenges from other states. In 1972 Florida scheduled its primary for the same day as New Hampshire, so New Hampshire simply moved its primary one week earlier to the first Tuesday in March. Challenges from other states in subsequent years have encouraged New Hampshire to move its primary to the last Tuesday in February, and in 2004, to the last Tuesday in January. Seven states decided to hold primaries on the first Tuesday in February in this most recent election year. While some states strived to compete directly with New Hampshire for valued dates, others have opted to have their primaries take place shortly afterwards in hopes that candidates and national media would show greater interest in them. This practice is now called front-loading. In 2000, eleven states held primaries on the first Tuesday in March on a day that media depicted as "Super Tuesday." The front-loading of primaries is so widespread that nomination campaigns are usually over by mid-March rather than just beginning).

Such were the circumstances in 1996. Although he did face some stiff competition, Robert Dole had been the front-runner for his party's nomination at the beginning of 1996 and then drove his final rivals from the race by the end of March. While the front-loading practice had clearly helped Dole secure his nomination early, it had also forced him to spend most of his campaign finances. He had only limited funds available until his formal nomination as the Republican National Convention in July made his eligible to receive federal funding. Clinton took advantage of this situation and began an extensive television advertising campaign. He fired numerous attacks against Dole's record at a time when Dole's financial condition made responding very difficult. Unlike Reagan, Clinton had an actual rival against whom he could direct his advertising strategy.

The Clinton campaign relied upon two major themes in its televised advertising during the nomination period. First, there was some emphasis on the accomplishments of the first term that were presented in upbeat and confident ways with imagery that relied on the trappings and power of the presidential office. Second, the campaign employed a number of attack ads that pointed out how Dole had opposed the major goals of Clinton's first term, and of how Dole was a threat to dismantle or damage many popular domestic programs. An important component of this second theme was an attempt to link Dole to the controversial Republican Speaker of the House of Representatives, Newt Gingrich (Georgia). Gingrich had become Speaker in January, 1995 and had emerged as the leading Republican spokesman for the congressional branch of the national party. He had also been quite vocal during a partial shutdown of governmental agencies in late 1995 as part of a battle with Bill Clinton over federal spending. Clinton developed a fairly strong lead over Dole in public opinion polls during this time (Gallup Poll, 2006).

Clinton's advertising differed from Reagan's in the sense that it contained virtually no appeals relating to national security. The nearest any of his ads came to the security issue was when they focused on domestic law and order. The Clinton campaign used the issue of gun control as a major part of its appeal on personal security matters. One ad, *Victims*, contained imagery and an accompanying narrative about several people who had been shot and killed with assault weapons. The narrative that accompanied the individual pictures started with the remarks, "an officer killed in the line of duty, a father gunned down at work, a student shot at school, a mother murdered in cold blood, victims, killed with deadly assault weapons." Afterwards, Clinton's accomplishments directed at improving security were highlighted. "Bill Clinton did something no president has ever been able to accomplish, he passed and signed a tough law to ban deadly assault weapons," the narrator told the audience. Clinton then appeared and spoke directly and forcefully to the television audience. "Deadly assault weapons off our streets, one hundred thousand more police on the streets, expand the death penalty. That's how we'll protect America."

The Clinton campaign emphasized other accomplishments of the first term while outlining the goals for a second in the ad *Cherish*. Here, Clinton was shown speaking before Congress and the nation in his most recent State of the Union Address. With the phrase "America's Future" shown repeatedly, viewers heard Clinton making references to such topics as children, families, affordable health insurance, tuition tax credits, protection of Medicare and Medicaid, and welfare reform. Each of these specific references was accompanied by a visual image of individual people related to the reference. Included were college students studying in a library and an older woman seated next to a child.

One of the more innovative features of the Clinton advertising strategy was a series of ads attacking Dole's record and promises while simultaneously emphasizing the goals and accomplishments of the Clinton presidency. L. Patrick Devlin described this comparative approach as the most effective component of Clinton's advertising strategy (Devlin, 1997). Each of the ads had a similar format; Dole would be shown in black and white imagery with a narrator making the attacks. After the narrator had concluded his remarks about Dole, Clinton would then appear while being shown in colors substantially brighter than those used for depicting Dole. The narrator would then contrast the accomplishments and goals of the two candidates. Two such examples can be seen in the ads *Gamble* and *Nobody*.

In *Gamble*, the Clinton campaign attempted to make the argument that Dole was a major threat to the new prosperity the nation was enjoying. The ad started with a narrator remarking, "America's economy is coming back." It continued with the narrator uttering short sentences accompanied with imagery of people and circumstances related to the remarks. "Ten million new jobs, the narrator continued. "We make more autos than Japan. Higher minimum wage. Now Bob Dole endangers it all with a risky last minute scheme that will balloon the deficit, raise interest rates, harm the economy." With this threat established, the ad then brings forth the importance of Clinton's role as president and outlines his plans for the future. The narrator continues, again accompanied by scenes of people that corresponded to the remarks, "President Clinton's plan; tax cuts for families, college tuition tax credits, health insurance you don't lose changing jobs, welfare reform, growth." It ends with some comparative phrasing that would recur in numerous variations during the campaign, "President Clinton, meeting our challenges; Bob Dole, gambling with our future." The personal references, to the "President" and to his rival "Bob," clearly placed the incumbent in a more statesmanlike role than the challenger and sought to create a distinction between the importances of the two candidates. A dichotomy between the political standing of the incumbent "President" and the challenger "Bob" was a constant theme of Clinton's general election advertising strategy.

A second ad contrasting Dole's threat to Clinton's policy goals was entitled *Nobody*. This was an attempt to juxtapose Dole with Gingrich and convince viewers that Dole and Gingrich together were serious threats to many of the nation's most popular domestic programs. The imagery usually revolved around photographs where Dole and Gingrich were shown standing next to one another at places in or around the U.S. Capitol building. The photographs were always in black and white and illustrated Dole as standing directly behind or either next to and slightly behind Gingrich. This imagery would be accompanied with scenes of Clinton appearing in various parts of the White House, such as the Oval Office, or outside the building. In this ad, the initial imagery is of the Oval Office and is followed with scenes of individual people that corresponded to the issues referred to by the narrator. At various times, the narrator referred to three major political actors; Clinton, Dole, and Dole's newly acquired "running mate," Gingrich. With a scene of the president's desk, the narrator begins by stating, "The Oval Office." With this, he follows, "If Dole sits here and Gingrich runs Congress, what could happen? Medicare slashed, women's right to choose gone, education, school drug programs cut, and a risky 550 billion dollar plan balloons the deficit, raises interest rates, hurts the economy." The imagery of the individual types of people mentioned here is also in black and white. The narrator then moves to the solution with Clinton now shown and the imagery of people changing to bright colors. "President Clinton says balance the budget, cut taxes for families, college tuition, stands up to Dole and Gingrich. But if Dole wins and Gingrich runs Congress, they'll be nobody there to stop them."

Clinton's advertising strategy in the general election was similar to the one he employed during the primaries. It coupled the accomplishments of the first Clinton term and an overview of goals for a second one with attacks on Dole and Gingrich for "their" opposition to them. The accomplishments theme was exhibited in several ways, with crime control being among the strongest issues worthy of mention. There was emphasis on the passage of the "Brady Bill," a law which prohibited the importing and sale of certain assault weapons. The crime control related ads also spoke of Clinton's support for the death penalty and about the enactment of the Community Oriented Policing Services (COPS) program that provided funding for 100,000 new local police officers. In *Seconds*, James Brady talked about the importance of the new gun laws while in other ads Clinton was frequently shown in the company of numerous uniformed police officers.

Clinton developed ads related to the future goals theme that were similar in several ways to those employed by Reagan. They were patriotic and upbeat, had imagery of individual people in a variety of nostalgic settings, and talked about how the successes of the past four years would be extended into the immediate future. In one, entitled *Next Century*, Clinton spoke against a backdrop of images of the American flag, families, older people, children, cheering crowds, people at work or in churches, and himself in the White House. Clinton began the narration by remarking, "Let me say to you that I am honored to have been given the opportunity to stand up for the values and the interests of ordinary Americans." While the imagery continuing, Clinton added, "My job as president if to take care of the American people, and I have done my best to take good care of this country. We are safer, we are more secure, we are more prosperous, but in the end what we stand for, the values we embrace and the things we fight for will shape the future that we will all live with. If we hold out our hands in cooperation and always stand up for what we know is right." Clinton ended the narrative with imagery were he was initially shown speaking to an audience and then later standing outside the White House with the Washington Monument appearing in the horizon. His final and upbeat remarks were, "This country's future will be even brighter that it's brilliant past. It is our responsibility to make that happen."

A similar futuristic ad employed this same theme and style, although this time a narrator rather than Clinton did the speaking. The imagery in the ad *Spirit* began with a full screen view of the American flag and then moved on to a scene of the Golden Gate Bridge. This was followed with images of farms, cities, the space shuttle, homes, children, families, the elderly, and finally, Clinton himself. The narrator began with the phrase, "the spirit of America." He continued by remarking, "You can see it in how far we've come but also in where we're going, toward a future where government is smaller and our economy even stronger. Where families are secure and our children cared for and where the work ethic is alive and well. This is the America, not of our dreams, but of our making." The narrator concluded by emphasizing the slogan the Clinton campaign had employed throughout the year, "President Clinton, meeting our challenges and protecting our values."

As it had acted throughout the primaries, the Clinton campaign also directed a substantial amount of it general election advertising to the theme of contrasting Clinton's accomplishments, goals, and values with Dole's opposition to them. One ad, *King*, emphasized Clinton's anti-drug record, including his advocacy of more school programs, border agents, criminal arrests, hiring of additional police, and his opposition to tobacco marketing directed at children while attacking Dole's congressional votes against supporting all of them. Other ads, including *Running, Real Record*, and others of similar theme and imagery, talked about Clinton's goals of expanding a variety of domestic spending programs such as college tuition tax credits, recession related increases in unemployment benefits, expanded family medical leave, protection of Medicare and Medicaid, job training for welfare recipients, middle class tax cuts, campaign finance reform, and targeted stimulus for economic growth. These were always accompanied with attacks that pointed out how Dole, and of course his associate, the ubiquitous Newt Gingrich, had opposed every one of them over the past four years. In *Parents*, after two parents were shown talking favorably of the Family and Medical Leave Law that had been enacted during Clinton's first term, a female narrator reminded voters that Dole had opposed this program.

Other anti-Dole ads focused almost exclusively on Dole and his positions rather than contrasting him with Clinton. The ads would direct attention to popular issues, such as Medicare, point out Dole's opposition or threats to them, link him once again with Gingrich, and conclude with a slogan such as, "Bob Dole, Wrong in the Past, Wrong for our Future." One example, actually entitled *Wrong in the Past*, spoke negatively about Dole's voting record over the several decades he had served in Congress. There were references to his opposition to the enactment of Medicare, student financial aid, federal spending on vaccines, drug control programs, and the family leave law. In continuing to contrast the status of the two candidates, the Clinton campaign depicted the adversaries as "President Clinton" and "Bob Dole." One candidate was the statesmanlike leader of the nation while the other was simply another politician who was trying to attain what the statesman had already accomplished.

The Clinton advertising strategy exhibited a number of features that appear to be recurring in the campaigns of strong incumbent presidents. Like all incumbents, Clinton used the trappings and power of the presidential office to present himself to the nation as an accomplished leader while emphasizing the continuation of his goals and values for a second term. He complemented the images and issues component of his advertising with a strong set of attack ads that sought to depict his opponent as an obstacle to the achievement of those goals and values.

CHALLENGERS

The two general election challengers of Reagan and Clinton, in these instances Walter Mondale and Robert Dole, faced several related difficulties in fashioning their advertising strategies. Both began their campaigns with the immediate necessity of securing the nomination of their own parties while facing a number of competitors for that role, some of who were quite formidable. This competition forced them to direct their initial advertising to their own partisans rather than to the general electorate and to downplay the upcoming rivalry with the incumbent. The strong incumbent, precisely because he lacked competition for his nomination, was free to begin his general election campaign immediately while the challengers were unable to respond. The challengers also faced an additional problem that derived from the contested nature of their nomination campaigns. Important differences exist in the composition of the nomination and general electorates. Voters in the nomination electorates are far more ideologically distinct, that is, Democrats more liberal and Republicans more conservative, than voters in the general electorate. Each challenger needed to make ideologically distinct appeals to unite his partisans in order to win the nomination, but he then had to downplay some of that distinctiveness in order win the general election. He needed a strategy that would enable him to retain the loyalty of his own partisans while allowing him realistic opportunities for making successful appeals to other voters who did not share the ideological perspectives of his most intense partisan supporters. This section looks at how Mondale and Dole addressed their needs in the nomination and general elections of their respective campaign years. In order to provide both consistency and context, I also direct attention to their leading rivals for their respective nominations.

Mondale and the Democrats

Despite the fact that he had served a term as vice president, Walter Mondale began his quest for office with the same problem that all other challengers ultimately encounter; many voters were still quite unfamiliar with him. As a result, he needed to devote a substantial portion of his initial advertising efforts to the task of becoming better known. The most important problem that he encountered derived from his own experiences. The office which now provided him with this opportunity to run for president and which had helped make him the front-runner for the nomination was the same office that could undermine his chances in the general election. He had been Jimmy Carter's vice president. This made him very popular among the most prominent leaders and activists of the Democratic Party but it could lead to rejection from the majority of voters who did not consider themselves to be Democrats.

Mondale's most important biographical ad was a lengthy piece entitled *America for Mondale*. He also employed shorter versions of this same ad on different occasions. Mondale narrated much of these ads while relying on a narrator for some portions of them. He began by telling the viewers about his "small town background of growing up and living in Minnesota and of the values he had acquired from these experiences." The ads included imagery of outdoor scenes from the forested regions of his home state. The narrator referred to Mondale's public life, including his military service, and his many years in public office as the Attorney General of Minnesota, U.S. Senator, and Vice President. This was followed with an emphasis on issues. Here, Mondale spoke in a variety of different contexts, sometimes acting as the narrator, other times speaking directly to the audience, and at other times addressing unidentified listeners from a podium. He talked about his interest in tax equity and of redistributing the tax burden from people of ordinary income to the wealthy, of how he wanted to strengthen the national economy, of his particular concerns for farmers and workers, and of the needs to increase international trade. Mondale also emphasized his background in foreign affairs and spoke of the need for arms control. He summed these experiences by telling his audience that he was ready to be president.

While he placed some emphasis on his experiences as vice president, Mondale clearly did not attempt to make this the defining feature of his background in public life. Instead, he treated his years in the vice presidency more as a part of a much broader public career that, when linked with the vice presidency, qualified him for the presidency. While his four year term had helped provide him with some background to be president, as he implied in the slogan that he "was ready to be president," it had not been the only relevant experience. Mondale was trying to breech a problem that periodically occurs in another category of presidential elections, those in which the incumbent party is represented by a surrogate, the vice president, rather than the actual incumbent. As described more thoroughly in Chapter 4, occupancy of the vice presidential office is a double edged political sword, it both helps and hinders a presidential campaign. Mondale had to introduce himself to voters in such a way that he appeared as experienced and qualified but where he did not convey the view that his primary motive for seeking office was to restore a previous administration to power. His message was that many years of varied experiences had made him ready to be president and that he would use that experience to address a number of redistributive issues related to economics.

In the most important presidential debate in the election of 1980, Ronald Reagan concluded his presentation by asking the members of the viewing audience of whether they were better off now than they had been four years earlier. Many people clearly said no to the question and responded by voting for Reagan. Four years later, Reagan was telling his audiences they were better off now and that he was responsible for their enhanced well being. Without attempting to tell these same voters that he had served as the vice president of the administration they had voted out of office, Mondale directed his issue related advertising to the limitations of the Reagan policies while promising to make needed changes.

The fiscal policies of the Reagan administration that had been implemented over the previous four years had led to lower taxes and a stronger and more prosperous economy, but they had also caused hardship for many people and posed long term threats to the nation's economic well being. The reduced revenues that resulted from tax cuts were offset by increases in national security spending, particularly for more technologically advanced communications and weapons systems. This combination of tax cuts and higher spending had served to triple the size of the annual deficit during the Reagan years (Wildavsky and Caiden, 2004). Mondale directed some of his advertising to the effects of these changes. He promised to reduce the size of the deficit in half within four years while blaming much of its recent increase on Reagan's policies, he talked frequently about the needs of farmers and workers and of the importance of expanding international trade. Mondale addressed these same issues during the general election campaign but did so with much greater frequency. The two major ads Mondale employed during the nomination campaign for attacking the Reagan record and advancing his proposed changes were *Trade* and *Deficit*. Despite these efforts, Mondale rarely attacked Reagan during the nomination period, however. His major attack ads were directed at his major rival for the nomination, Gary Hart.

Hart's second place finish in the Iowa caucuses soon translated into increased media coverage of his efforts and helped expand interest in his campaign. With this added exposure, Hart won the New Hampshire primary and appeared as if he might even defeat Mondale in other primaries and win the nomination. Hart's appeal was strongest among the younger Democrats, among nonpartisan voters who chose to cast ballots in the several state primaries that allowed nonpartisans to vote, among suburban residents, and in the Western states such as California. Mondale ran stronger in Southern states, among racial minorities, and with older Democrats and unionized factory workers. While Mondale emphasized the traditional Democratic positions that were popular with his constituency, Hart focused his attention on themes that would resonate with less traditional voters.

Gary Hart proved to be a formidable challenger for Mondale. After a spirited contest that lasted through the conclusion of the last primaries in June, he garnered the support of about 1,400 of the 4,000 delegates who voted for president at the Democratic National Convention. Hart campaigned on the themes of his own personal independence from "special interests," of how the nation needed a new and different choice, and on the importance that future changes should be based on "new ideas." Quite frequently, Hart spoke directly to his television audience rather than relying upon a narrator. In one ad, *Proud Democrat*, Hart told his audience that he was independent from both special interests and Washington insiders and then emphasized that Democrats needed a choice between past failures and a future guided by the public interest. In *Chicago*, and other ads with a similar theme, Hart said voters needed to decide between the past of old promises and a future of government without strings and to choose between government run by political bosses and one led by a new generation of leaders. His candidacy represented the national interest rather than the special interest, Hart concluded.

Hart employed this same theme of independence and new leadership is his attack ads. Most of these were directed at Mondale, although a few were also aimed at Reagan. In *Cake* and *PAC* the narrator focused on contributions from special interests and questioned whether a candidate who was as indebted to them as Mondale seemed to be, could lead in the national interest. The leading theme here was that Mondale was controlled by special, but unnamed, interests, and this contrasted with the claims of independence and new leadership that Hart used to emphasize his own candidacy.

In addition, Hart also attacked Mondale, and in this instance, Reagan as well, over the former vice president's support for Reagan's policies in Central America. In the ads *Central America* and *Leadership* Hart attempted to link his opposition to Reagan's foreign policies with the phrasing of many of his ads where he said he would seek to bring about new and courageous leadership.

Hart's rise as a formidable rival encouraged Mondale to make him a target of attack ads. In doing so, Mondale criticized Hart for his past actions and tried to link some of Hart's more controversial positions to his claim of new ideas. Some of the attacks focused on Hart's vote against the federally guaranteed loan to the beleaguered Chrysler Corporation that eventually saved the firm from bankruptcy and on his proposal for an oil import tax during a time of rising fuel prices (*New Ideas*). Another ad, *American Jobs,* contained imagery of idle factory machinery with the narrator telling viewers Hart's proposals would eliminate industrial jobs and increase unemployment. Mondale also questioned Hart's competence to lead the nation in a crisis. The ad *Hotline* used imagery of a red telephone with a narrator telling viewers that the telephone, which symbolized the grave necessity that the president might be forced to order a nuclear retaliation against a foreign nation, should not be in untested hands. The ad continued by telling viewers that Mondale was experienced in foreign and military matters and that this was the most important personal difference between Mondale and Hart.

Hart was not Mondale's only nomination rival, but he did remain in the race for a much longer period of time than the others. Most of the others saw their candidacies end after defeats in one or perhaps two of the earliest primaries. Alan Cranston had several ads (*First Day* and *Still Bald*) where he talked directly to his television audience while developing two themes; peace, which was to be attained through a nuclear arms freeze; and full employment. George McGovern emphasized (*Conscience*) that a vote for him would also be a vote for conscience since it would force the eventual Democratic nominee, presumably not himself, to adopt certain stands that he otherwise might have ignored. John Glenn directed attention to the theme of personal qualities and leadership skills. In *Pursuit of Peace*, Glenn told viewers that he had seen the horrors of combat through his extensive background in the military and this would help him keep the nation out of war.

Mondale entered the general election campaign trailing Reagan by substantial margins in all national polls. He had only a few weeks available for reversing a lead that Reagan had built over a period of three and one half years. This task proved insurmountable. Reagan remained popular throughout the remainder of the campaign and gave Mondale no significant opportunities for any gains. The Mondale advertising strategy continued to emphasize the major themes of Mondale's personal background, key issues, and the shortcomings of the Reagan presidency. With respect to issues, Mondale focused most of his attention on economics and as he had done during the nomination period, spoke about people who had been hurt by the domestic policies of the Reagan years. One memorable ad that attacked Reagan and drew attention to Mondale's major economic themes was *Roller Coaster*. Here, a narrator talked about the Reagan economic legacy while the ad included imagery of a roller coaster moving slowly uphill in a metaphorical image of the present, 1984. The Reagan economic record was described as having been built on a "mountain of record debt." The ad ended with the roller coaster reaching the peak of this "mountain" and then beginning its frightening and rapid descent downward in what the imagery designated as 1985.

Other Mondale ads also used metaphorical references comparable to the mountain of record debt. In *Limo*, an ad that directed attention to the charge that corporations and the rich were getting huge tax breaks, well healed lobbyists were shown getting into expensive cars while the narrator told voters they could stop this "free ride" by voting for Mondale. Mondale used another metaphorical reference in relation to his foreign policy approaches. In an effort to attack the Reagan goal of expensive space based weapons and to show how useless they would ultimately prove to be, the ad *Hole* had imagery of a family digging a hole in their yard while the narrator told of how Reagan was opposed to nuclear arms control and that he was digging the nation into a hole. A similar ad, *Computer*, focused specifically on space weapons, had imagery of how computers would be in control and would eventually make all decisions relating to war and peace. Finally, *Debate* included a scene from the first national debate of the year in which Reagan seemed confused when attempting to answer a question about his "Star Wars" weapons system. After viewers could see Reagan stumbling while attempting to explain his own policies, their attention was directed to Mondale who spoke of the need for controlling nuclear weapons.

Mondale's ads related to domestic policies included substantial imagery of people of various backgrounds and ages appearing with him, or with his running mate Geraldine Ferraro (*You've Made us Proud*), while a narrator would emphasize the theme of economic opportunities. There were references to the difficulty that elderly people faced in paying for health care and food (*Elderly*) and of how Reagan was trying to reduce Medicare and unemployment benefits while seeking more tax breaks for millionaires (*Ticket*). Other ads advocated arms control (*Teach*) and increased funding for college educational opportunities (*Cincinnati*). Central to Mondale's strategy was the theme of economic decency versus self-interest. He linked his candidacy with the former by advocating a number of redistributive efforts by the national government while depicting opposition to them as the misguided self-interest represented by Reagan (*Truth*).

The Mondale strategy, when viewed within the context of where a strong and popular incumbent was running for a second term by emphasizing what many voters considered to be a positive record of accomplishments, while clearly focused and often interesting, was generally ineffective. The election was a referendum on Reagan and Reagan passed overwhelmingly. Mondale directed his strategy at retaining the votes of traditional Democrats by talking about how Reagan's taxing and spending programs posed serious threats to the governmental programs upon which they relied. He failed to convince many voters to support him other than those who were already committed to the traditional issue stands of the Democratic Party. He attempted to illustrate that the upbeat and patriotic themes advanced by the Reagan presidency posed long term threats to the nation's well being but he made little headway against the barrage of *Morning in America* style ads that Reagan used to convince voters of the accomplishments of his first term. Mondale's themes, when coupled with his personal background and years of political experience, had been particularly effective during the nomination campaign but were of limited value in the battle against Reagan. Mondale used essentially the same themes when making appeals to the general electorate as he had used in appealing to Democrats. His appeals did not resonate with this larger component of voters.

Dole and the Republicans

Robert Dole faced many of the same obstacles in 1996 that Mondale encountered, although his rival Bill Clinton did not enjoy the same level of popularity as Reagan. Dole also had the problem that he too needed to devote most of his financial resources and advertising strategy to winning the nomination. This need prevented him from responding to Clinton effectively until the conclusion of the national conventions in mid-summer. He was simply unable to counter the aggressive advertising campaign of the strong incumbent during the nomination period.

Like other challengers, Dole also used biographical, issue, and attack ads to advance his cause. He did so in both of his campaigns, one for the Republican nomination where he faced eleven rivals, and in the general election where he opposed Bill Clinton. Despite the large number of candidates for the nomination, the race rapidly narrowed to only four leading contenders; Dole, Lamar Alexander, Pat Buchanan, and Steve Forbes. Dole used his attack ads only against these three.

His biographical ads focused on his personal background and emphasized how childhood experiences in Kansas and military service in the Army during the Second World War had helped form his character. Dole had suffered serious battlefield injuries while fighting in Italy, injuries that required months of hospitalization and which eventually left him with only partial use of his right arm. In an ad entitled *An American Hero*, Dole's wife Elizabeth spoke of his commitment to family and country. She was followed by an anonymous narrator who provided more specific details of Dole's experiences. The narrator said these experiences had given Dole the values that had guided his life during his earlier years. The narrator concluded by adding that Dole understood the price of being an American and that he had the personal character to lead the nation.

Dole also emphasized his personal character as a factor in national leadership in another biographical ad, *Midwest Values*. Here, Dole speaks of how the values that he acquired from his childhood and early adult life taught him to put trust in God and not in government. A narrator then told the audience that Dole has a conservative agenda, and possessed the character and courage to lead the nation.

The most widely employed theme in the Dole advertising strategy was an emphasis on a set of interrelated goals depicted as a "conservative agenda." Dole did not limit his efforts to a mere commentary on issues but tried to link his goals with his own personal qualities by implying that his character and courage were the essential factors that would bring the agenda to fruition. The conservative agenda, which was usually described by a narrator rather than by Dole himself, would change America by bringing about a balanced budget, a middle class and pro-family tax cut, reductions in both welfare spending and in the size of government, presidential appointments of more conservative federal judges, and the enactment of stronger sentencing laws (*Balanced Budget*). There was one irony of this approach, however. Dole rarely focused very much attention on the one personal, and clearly political, factor that would prove crucial in helping him bring about all of it, his extensive service in Congress.

Dole was a man of Congress. He had been elected to the House of Representatives in 1960 and to the Senate in 1968. He had 36 years of congressional experience when he sought the Republican nomination in 1996, including sixteen of those in various leadership roles. He had served as the chairman of the Senate Finance Committee and as both the Majority and Minority Leader of the Senate. Despite this extensive background, Dole did not attempt to convince voters that his governmental experiences were of very much importance. Instead, he seemed far more interested in an advertising strategy that was inherently anti-governmental. Rather than trying to convince people that government was an institution that could, with the right leadership, help improve the nation's public life, Dole implicitly advanced the theme that government was a problem that needed to be curtailed by limiting its political reach and financial capabilities. This theme was a factor in the Republican Party nomination campaigns because of Reagan's successful use of it in recent elections. Dole would unite his own partisans by using it this time but he would fall short in expanding his base of support during the general election.

The Republican campaign in 1996 developed on two very different fronts. It began with Dole clearly identified as the front-runner who was most likely to win the nomination. This status had been conferred on Dole by media observers who were impressed at his successes in raising money, in acquiring endorsements from prominent elected officials, and in garnering more support from Republican voters as measured in public opinion polls (Dover, 1998). Dole's decades as a party leader had provided him with numerous opportunities for meeting with and gaining the support of local and state party officials and activists. In contrast, Dole's rivals had only limited personal contact with party leaders.

The second front involved the battles in the states with the earliest delegate selection votes, Iowa and New Hampshire. Dole's rivals focused most of their efforts and political resources in these two states in the hope that success in at least one state, and hopefully in both, would translate into greater name recognition and momentum and make them the leading adversary of the front-runner.

These hoped for successes, in turn, would help advance their candidacies in other states where their prospects seemed more limited. Despite months of campaigning, all of Dole's rivals failed. Dole won in Iowa and finished a close second to Buchanan in New Hampshire. After the vote in New Hampshire, Dole's rivals rapidly faded from competition. Nonetheless, they did pose major threats to his candidacy during the first weeks of 1996. Dole clearly needed to respond to them at a time when Clinton was emphasizing his accomplishments and goals and building a strong case for a second term.

The strongest rival Dole faced, at least from the perspective of televised advertising, was Forbes, although Forbes failed to win a single primary. Forbes decided against relying on federal funding, thus freeing himself from legal spending restrictions. In 1976 the U.S. Supreme Court ruled, in *Buckley vs. Valeo*, that campaign spending was a form of free speech and that Congress could not limit the expenditures of candidates for public office. Congress responding by amending the campaign finance law requiring candidates to abide by the expenditure limits in order to receive federal funding. By refusing funding, Forbes was freed of these restrictions and could spend as much of his own personal financial fortune as he wished. In all, he spent about $25 million, mostly on television advertising, in Iowa and New Hampshire. This spending was so pervasive that Dole had little choice but to respond to Forbes.

Forbes saturated the airwaves with so much advertising that national news media assumed he was a major candidate and increased coverage of his efforts. Their cue came in mid-January when Dole started using attack ads against him. Forbes provided little biographical information, although he served as the narrator in many of his ads. Instead, he devoted much of his effort to calling for the enactment of a "flat tax" or attacking his opponents for their failure to support it. This plan would eliminate the progressive features of the income tax and assess all persons the same percentage rate while eliminating most deductions. While this may look fair, such a proposal fails to take into account the variety of other taxes, such as payroll (Social Security), consumption (sales), or property, that are not subject to the flat tax concept. This shortcoming provided the other candidates with an opportunity to attack Forbes for offering tax proposals that could be harmful to certain categories of voters.

Forbes ridiculed the current tax system with ads that spoke of the large staffing of the Internal Revenue Service (*Army*) to the fact that the federal tax code contained far more words than either the American constitution or the Bible (*Words*). He also advocated the creation of medical savings accounts as part of his tax plans (*Health Care*). His attack ads included references to Dole's support for congressional pensions, spending programs, and for some tax increases, such as Social Security during the early 1980s (*Blue, Pensions*). Forbes attacked Gramm and Alexander for their actions of supporting tax increases in Congress and in Tennessee respectively (*Less, Not More*).

In response, Dole attacked Forbes' public record, or perhaps one might say; the lack of a record. Forbes had never held an elective office, although he had held an appointive one during the Reagan administration. Dole's ads questioned the major claims that Forbes had raised, even with respect to Forbes' personal qualifications to serve as president. They said Forbes was "untested" and had "risky ideas" related to welfare benefits for illegal aliens, tax proposals that would increase the size of the deficit, and opposition to mandatory prison sentences for three time offenders (*Tested*). While the ads directly focused on the ideas that Forbes raised, they also served a second purpose in raising doubts about the candidate since Forbes seemed to be "untested and risky."

Dole used the "untested leadership and risky ideas" theme in many anti-Forbes ads. These ads focused on such charges that Forbes would "end Social Security as we know it (*Security*)," although viewers were never told how that would happen or of how we actually "know" Social Security. Dole also attacked the flat tax scheme with accusations that Forbes was advancing a plan that would actually raise taxes (*Deficits Versus Cuts*). This ad also focused on Dole's plan to balance the budget and bring about taxing and spending cuts. There were other attacks on Forbes's past experiences in appointive federal office and in his actions as a business executive. The attacks focused on the presence of high salaried employees in the government office (*Gravy Train*) and on how Forbes had discriminated on the basis of age by forcing older, higher paid workers to retire from his privately owned business (*Stop the Presses*). This latter ad said Forbes had been sued by a 65 year old woman over such a practice.

Although he directed the vast majority of his attacks against Forbes, Dole did not ignore Buchanan and Alexander. He attacked Buchanan over remarks about women's rights and the use of nuclear weapons (*Crossfire*) and Alexander for his actions as governor of Tennessee. Alexander tried to create an image as being an outsider from Washington, D.C. He campaigned in a red flannel shirt and frequently spoke of his experiences in state government. Dole's ads raised questions about Alexander's record as governor and of his support for higher taxes and increased state spending and even referred to the former governor a liberal (*The Great Pretender*).

Before one concludes that Dole devoted his time to attacking others rather than justifying his own candidacy, these attacks were made in response to attacks by Buchanan and Alexander. Buchanan's ads accused Dole of voting for numerous tax increases and expansions in the federal debt limit and said he personally eligible for a $2 million pension under a retirement law he had helped enact (*Bob*).

While Alexander did not direct many specific attacks toward Dole, the general theme of his campaign, that he was an outsider to national government, implied that Dole was a major part of the problem that Alexander indicated he was qualified to resolve.

Buchanan had centered his appeal on issues related to economics and race. With economics, he attacked policies that had encouraged the loss of American jobs to other nations. In *Louisiana Trade* Buchanan specifically mentioned the harmful effects of the North American Free Trade Agreement (NAFTA) of 1993. A similar ad, *Alaska*, blasted federal bureaucrats over restrictive land policies. Buchanan said he would permit more oil drilling and logging in national wildlife areas and forests. He also favored stronger efforts aimed at stopping illegal immigrants from entering this nation and the use of affirmative action programs. In the ad *Immigration,* Buchanan claimed that illegal immigrants come here in order to commit crimes and use public services. He then accused liberal judges of encouraging this behavior while calling for term limits for all federal judges. Buchanan criticized affirmative action and racial quotas in hiring and attempted to link them to the economic difficulties facing the nation (*Affirmative Action*). He also attacked his rivals over their lack of commitment to reducing taxes (*No New Taxes*).

As part of his attempt to create an image of the Washington D.C. outsider, complete with the red flannel shirt mentioned above, Alexander directed his issue ads to matters usually associated with state government. He spoke of his efforts at improving Tennessee's economy and schools while reducing taxes during his tenure as governor. The central theme of his issue stands was his opposition to the national government's role in much of domestic policy. In the ad *New Hampshire Aim,* Alexander said that the answer to problems was not in Washington but in our communities, churches, families and neighborhood schools. He promised more freedom from Washington and the assumption of greater personal responsibility by individual people. He also talked about specific issues, such as telling voters that reductions of both taxes and business regulations would produce more jobs, and that increased community citizenship would lead to better schools (*Mud Balls, Future, New Leadership*). Alexander differed from his rivals in that he relied less on attack advertising, although he did use some. Instead, he linked attacks with his efforts at image creation. His ads described Dole as a Washington insider, Forbes as a Wall Street insider, and himself as an outsider (*New Hampshire Switch*).

The remaining candidates fared so poorly that their campaigns were already over or nearly over by the time Iowa and New Hampshire voted. Richard Lugar, Phil Gramm, and Pete Wilson had only limited opportunities for presenting themselves through televised advertising. All three concentrated on biographies and issues. Lugar focused his ads on personal experience and trust, particularly with respect to foreign policy (*Dignity*). Gramm spoke of his background with particular attention to personal integrity. One ad, (*I Know Who I Am*) described how he had once been Democratic congressman who resigned from office because he disagreed with his party's positions on taxes and spending. Gramm was reelected as a Republican. He also referred to his long time opposition to tax increases. Wilson spoke of his opposition to illegal immigration and advocacy of more stringent criminal sentencing laws while he had served as governor of California (*Courage*).

As had occurred with Mondale, Dole trailed far behind the strong incumbent in national public opinion surveys by the time he won his party's nomination. And like Mondale, Dole failed to reduce that gap. Dole continued to rely upon biographical ads that emphasized his background while linking it with a new slogan of "a better man for a better America," as the campaign moved into its general election phase (*Do Better*). Many of his ads were similar to those often used by weak incumbents; an emphasis on leadership skills and personal integrity. By using such an approach, Dole drew attention to questions of personal integrity and implicitly attacked Clinton over his controversial moral lapses.

Dole's ads also included imagery of the American flag, of families, and of his wife Elizabeth talking about his background in Russell, Kansas. Mrs. Dole said her husband could be trusted to do what was right, and that he would not make any promises he could not keep (*Elizabeth, From the Heart*). In addition, Dole continued raising essentially the same policy concerns he had advanced during the primaries but this time coupled them with character related attacks against Clinton. He focused on taxing and spending by advocating a fifteen percent reduction in the federal income tax (*Plan, The Stakes*). He linked this with a series of attacks against Clinton for failing to reduce taxes and for increasing government spending on domestic issues while accomplishing little of consequence (*Truth on Spending*). Dole also employed the character theme while attacking Clinton on issues of drug use among teenagers (*At Stake*), ethics and corruption (*Riady*), and broken promises about taxes and health care (*Sorry Taxes, Fool*). One ad, *Too Late*, included footage of Clinton remarking about how he had once tried marijuana but had not inhaled while similar ads had imagery of newspaper headlines related to Clinton's personal scandals (*Riady*).

Despite these themes, Dole had the dilemma that all challengers of strong incumbents ultimately encounter; the election was a referendum on the incumbent who was widely perceived as having been successful in his first term. Dole continued to trail Clinton throughout the campaign and eventually lost the election. He did make some modest gains in the polls during late October, however, and avoided losing by a double digit margin. With the help of Ross Perot who ran as the candidate of the Reform Party this time, Clinton failed to attain a majority of the popular vote, garnering 49.2 percent. This was the weakest showing by a winning incumbent president since Harry Truman in 1948. Dole and Perot respectively attained 40.8 and 7.8 percent of the vote.

Perot

The Perot effort in 1996 paled in comparison with that of four years earlier. Perot's support declined from the 18.9 percent of the vote he had attained in 1992 to less than half of that in 1996. Moreover, the Perot advertising efforts reflected this decline. The major theme in his 1996 televised advertising was his exclusion from the presidential debates. Perot had been included in 1992. Several neutral observers and media critics thought he had done well, perhaps even winning one of the debates. A new debate commission, jointly controlled by the Republican and Democratic parties, had been formed to operate the debates in 1996. The commission limited participation to nominees of only the two major parties but did agree to allow other candidates to take part if they had the support of at least ten percent of the electorate as measured in a nationwide poll. This policy created an insurmountable obstacle for minor party candidates. Their exclusion encouraged voters to ignore them and ultimately reduced their support. They would have to be included in the debates in order to expand their support but they could not participate because of the lack of support. Perot devoted most of his advertising to urging voters to demand that he should have been included in the debates (*Commission, What Are They Afraid Of?* and *Where's Ross?*). Despite his efforts, he was not included.

CHAPTER 3

ELECTIONS WITH WEAK INCUMBENTS: 1980 AND 1992

GENERAL OVERVIEW

Despite the extensive institutional and rhetorical advantages incumbent presidents enjoy when the seek reelection; they are not necessarily assured of certain victory. It is possible that incumbents can fail in their quests for second terms. In fact, three have been defeated during the same past half century in which five incumbents have won. Moreover, a fourth seemed headed for defeat when he withdraw before the nomination campaign concluded. The three who failed were Gerald Ford (1976), Jimmy Carter (1980), and George Bush (1992) while the president who withdrew early was Lyndon Johnson (1968). The outcomes of these four elections, as occurred with the ones discussed in the previous chapter, were not random events. Instead, they also exhibit enough similar characteristics to warrant inclusion is a category of television age elections that are both unique in relation to other elections and likely to occur again. I depict the ones that fall into this category as elections with weak incumbents (see Abramson, Aldrich and Rhode, 1982 and 1994; Ceaser and Busch, 1993; CQ Press, 2005; Germond and Witcover, 1981, 1993; Nelson, 1993; Pomper, 1981, 1993; White, 1969,

1981; and Witcover, 1977, for detailed explanations of the leading events, contexts, and outcomes of the elections of 1968, 1976, 1980, and 1992).

Unlike elections with strong incumbents, the ones in this latter category do not necessarily fit neatly into the midpoint of twelve year electoral cycles. They are more likely to occur after the presidential party has been in office for any number of consecutive terms, although one necessary prerequisite is that the incumbent himself can only have served one term. Without this prerequisite, the incumbent could not seek reelection. One of the elections, 1980, actually occurred after the presidential party, Democratic in this instance, had been in office for only one term. The others happened at different times in the partisan cycle, however. The one in 1976 took place after the presidential party had been in office for eight years but it happened under very unusual circumstances. The strong incumbent of the previous election, Richard Nixon, had resigned in 1974 and was succeeded by Ford. Although Ford was the incumbent in 1976, he had been president for only two years. In contrast, Bush extended the Republican control of the presidency to twelve years by winning the election of 1988. Bush lost in 1992 while trying to extend that partisan tenure to four consecutive terms. Finally, Johnson's circumstances in 1968 were similar to those of Ford and Bush. Like Ford, Johnson had become president after a vacancy, but like Bush, he had extended his party's tenure in office by winning the previous election. Johnson had been president for five years in 1968 but was eligible for another term.

Perhaps the most significant recurring feature in each of these elections was that the incumbent was in serious political trouble at the onset of the campaign. He had not enjoyed the policy successes or related public adoration as had the strong incumbents. Moreover, television news media tended to depict him less in a leadership or Rose Garden role and more as a beleaguered politician struggling to defeat his rivals in a battle for reelection (Dover, 1994). The incumbents compensated for these differences in public imagery by emphasizing the superiority of their personal character and the depth of their leadership skills. Thus far, such a strategy has not led to a reelection victory.

Gerald Ford is the only person to become president without having been elected on a national ticket. He was nominated for vice president in September, 1973 by Richard Nixon after the resignation of Vice President Spiro Agnew. Ford, who had spent the previous 25 years as a member of the House of Representatives, took office in December after confirmation by Congress in accordance with Amendment 25 of the U.S. Constitution. He became president eight months later when Nixon resigned. These experiences contributed to his political weaknesses. Ford had only limited support from Republican leaders and activists. Ford angered many people, Republicans included, when he pardoned Nixon for any role the former president might have played in the Watergate scandal. Afterwards, the vulnerable Ford faced a spirited challenge for the Republican nomination by former governor Ronald Reagan (California).

The two candidates battled inconclusively for months through the primaries with Ford eventually winning the nomination in August by a close vote at a divisive national convention. Meanwhile, the opposition party, Democratic, effectively resolved its nomination battle months earlier when former governor Jimmy Carter (Georgia) defeated various rivals in the primaries. Carter was nominated in July at a united and enthusiastic national convention. As a result, Ford entered the general election campaign at a serious disadvantage. He had devoted the greater part of the election year fighting to secure the nomination and had not been able to focus attention on his Democratic rival. The opposition party believed it had a promising chance of victory, so it united relatively early around a challenger who appear to offer hopes of electoral success. Ford trailed Carter in public opinion surveys throughout the next few months and eventually lost the election by a popular vote margin of 50.1 to 48.0 percent (Gallup Poll, 2006).

Only four years later Carter became the second weak incumbent of past half century to lose a reelection bid. As had occurred with Ford, Carter also began his quest for a second term while encountering serious political trouble. While he had been stronger then Ford when initially taking office, he did have the backing of a unified party and an election victory, Carter soon began a steady decline in popularity. His support diminished to where less than one voter in four approved of his performance in office (Gallup Poll, 2006). The causes of Carter's problems were complex. The national economy limped along after being hit by an unusual combination of high unemployment, inflation, interest rates, and gasoline prices while new threats arose in the international scene. The Iranian hostage crisis, the Soviet invasion of Afghanistan, and new difficulties with Cuba had contributed to Carter's decline. He had even lost the support of many of his own partisans. This was seen in the fact that he ultimately attracted two rivals for the Democratic nomination, Senator Edward Kennedy (Massachusetts) who proved to be formidable, and former governor Jerry Brown (California).

Carter and Kennedy fought one another throughout the primaries without resolution. Carter had clearly come out ahead of Kennedy, acquiring the support of about two-thirds of the national convention delegates, but Kennedy had won a number of crucial states, including both California and New York. After an intense procedural vote where Kennedy could not bring about certain rules changes, Carter attained the nomination. Nonetheless, he encountered essentially the same problems that Ford had faced in 1976. He had already spent most of the year seeking his party's nomination while his rival, Ronald Reagan, had secured his nomination early and with relative ease. Reagan had been nominated by a united Republican Party that was very optimistic about its electoral chances. The campaign followed much the same script as that of 1976. The weak incumbent emphasized his character and personal leadership skills only to lose to the challenger. Carter acquired 41.0 percent of the popular vote and the electoral votes of six states and the District of Columbia. Reagan, in contrast, carried 44 states and 50.9 percent of the popular vote. Congressman John Anderson (Illinois), who had unsuccessfully sought the Republican nomination, ran as a nonpartisan and garnered 6.6 percent of the vote.

The election of 1992 followed this familiar pattern. The incumbent, in this instance Bush, was also in political trouble at the beginning of the campaign.

Bush's troubles were of recent origin, however. His personal popularity had been at a record level, an 88 percent approval rate in the Gallup Poll, in early 1991 because of the American victory in the Gulf War. Bush's standing declined sharply after this, however, as many voters were dissatisfied with the performance of the American economy and believed that Bush was failing to make the necessary corrections (Gallup Poll, 2006). The nation was involved in an economic recession at the time. In addition, Bush had angered many of his own partisans by reneging on an important campaign promise he had made in 1988, of opposing any new tax increases. While accepting the Republican nomination that year, Bush uttered the controversial words that would help him win an initial term but which would also contribute to his subsequent loss in 1992, "Read my lips, no new taxes." In order to reach an accord with the Democratic congress in late 1990, Bush had agreed to a number of tax increases in exchange for some spending reductions. Conservatives, including Pat Buchanan, were furious.

Buchanan ran against Bush in five Republican primaries of which New Hampshire was the first. He attacked Bush on a number of leading issues but directed most of his furor at Bush's failure to honor his tax cut pledge. He even ran advertising that contained imagery of Bush actually making the pledge. Buchanan also opposed Bush in South Dakota, Colorado, Georgia, and Maryland. His share of the vote ranged from a low of 30 percent in Georgia to a high of 37 percent in New Hampshire. Although he did not win in any place, Buchanan exposed the extent of Bush's weaknesses among Republicans. These results helped encourage Texas businessman Ross Perot to enter the campaign as a moderate to conservative independent candidate.

Perot may have spent as much as $100 million on his efforts, with much of it going to an unusual approach in televised advertising. This approach is discussed in some detail later in this chapter. Meanwhile, the opposition Democrats, optimistic about victory, acted very similarly to the opposition parties in the earlier elections with weak incumbents. It kept discord to a minimum and unity to a maximum and united very quickly behind a strong candidate who emerged early in the primary election season, in this instance Governor Bill Clinton (Arkansas). While he had not needed to devote most of the campaign year to winning the nomination of his own party as had been the case with Ford and Carter, Bush encountered a problem similar to theirs. He had to spend much of the year trying to win the support of many Republican and/or conservative voters who were angry at him and attracted to Perot. Like other weak incumbents, he failed.

The decision by Lyndon Johnson to abandon his efforts toward seeking a second term eliminated the election of 1968 from the weak incumbent category and instead made it an election with a surrogate incumbent. This election will be discussed more extensively in the next chapter. Prior to Johnson's withdrawal, however, the 1968 campaign was conforming to the patterns of weak incumbent elections, so I discuss those specific features of the campaign at this time. Like other weak incumbents, Johnson was also in serious political trouble at the beginning of the election year. While many voters were critical of his policies relating to race relations, the most significant difficulty he faced was opposition from within his own party relating to the war in Vietnam. He encountered a strong challenge to his renomination hopes in the New Hampshire primary from Senator Eugene McCarthy (Minnesota). The result was close, although Johnson won, but he attained less than 50 percent the Democratic vote. This was not a good showing for an incumbent. Encouraged by these results, Senator Robert Kennedy (New York) entered the race. This move, coupled with the fact that he now faced both an intense battle for the Democratic nomination and the prospect that he would then have to fight a unified and optimistic Republican Party under the leadership of Richard Nixon convinced Johnson to announce, on the last day of March, that he would not be a candidate for reelection.

In summary from the above description, elections with weak incumbents are characterized by several recurring features. The incumbent is in political trouble at the beginning of the election year. He has not had the policy successes that can readily translate into strong personal popularity. As a consequence, he must devote a substantial amount of the campaign year to securing the support of his own partisans. The incumbent pursues this requisite need by either defeating one or more rivals in a contested struggle for his party's nomination or, if he has already secured the nomination, by striving to attain the support of many of his party's members who may be tempted to vote for another candidate in the general election. Defeat of these intra-party rivals and even the ultimate contesting of the general election often encourage the incumbent to rely upon positive advertising that emphasizes his personal character and leadership skills rather than his policy accomplishments and on negative advertising that strives to raise doubts about the character and leadership skills of his rivals. The challenger conducts a campaign that tries to mobilize its partisan constituency while exploiting the incumbent's political weaknesses.

In this chapter, I direct attention to the manner in which weak incumbents and their challengers, both for the nominations and in the general elections, implemented advertising strategies that addressed their most important political needs. As I did in the previous chapter, I direct attention to the last two elections that fit into this category, those of 1980 and 1992. I describe how the weak incumbents, Carter and Bush, fought to secure the support of their partisans; of how their opposition party rivals in the general elections, Reagan and Clinton, united their partisans and challenged sitting presidents; and how two independent candidates, Anderson and Perot, contributed to the defeat of the weak incumbents.

The nomination campaigns in both of these elections followed similar, and clearly recurring rather than random, scripts. Two major candidates, the incumbent and his one challenger, sought the nomination of the presidential party while a wide variety of contenders aspired for the top spot on the national ticket of the opposition party. There are two reasons for this pattern. One, a credible challenge to an incumbent president within his own party is an extremely difficult undertaking and may compromise the future chances of the challenger for a party leadership role. Such an endeavor should cause many of the most prominent leaders of this party to hesitate, even if they are dissatisfied with the incumbent's actions. Robert Kennedy exhibited this pattern quite well. He was a major critic of the Johnson administration during the two years preceding the

1968 election, but initially declined against opposing Johnson for the nomination. He changed his mind after McCarthy's strong showing in New Hampshire illustrated the weakness of Johnson's position. This difficulty in challenging an incumbent encourages the incumbent's intra-party detractors to unite behind the one candidate who actually chooses to make a challenge. In 1980, Edward Kennedy emerged as the one major rival of the incumbent, Carter, while Buchanan filled that same role in 1992 when he ran against Bush.

The second reason relates to the unique circumstances facing the opposition party. American politics lacks any useful institutional methods for designating the national leader of the opposition party before the actual election year. While the president is clearly the leader of his party, the constitutional devices of separation of powers and federalism creates powerful obstacles that prevent the opposition party from having one unifying leader. The leader emerges during the nomination phase of an election and officially becomes the leader when nominated at the national convention. This limitation has the effect of encouraging numerous aspirants to seek the presidency and compete for that position in the public forum offered by primaries.

Seven Republicans sought the nomination of their party in 1980. Ronald Reagan was clearly the front-runner at the beginning of the campaign. He had been a presidential candidate twice before (1968, 1976), was a major spokesman for the conservative ideology shared by most Republicans, and had emerged as the strongest candidate after Gerald Ford lost the election of 1976. Reagan did not win the nomination without a battle, however. Two of his rivals proved troublesome. These were George Bush, who had served in a variety of appointive offices during the Nixon and Ford administrations, and John Anderson, who was running as an ideologically moderate candidate in a party where few of that breed still exist. Bush actually defeated Reagan in Iowa, and finished second to him in New Hampshire. Bush won several more primaries in the weeks that followed, but he lost far more of them to Reagan. He withdrew in May and was eventually nominated for vice president. Anderson did not win a single primary but he did finish quite well in several Northeastern and Midwestern states that permitted independents to vote in partisan primaries. He attracted the support of numerous moderate and liberal nonpartisan voters. After realizing that many of his supporters were not Republicans, Anderson stopped his nomination quest and then sought the presidency in the general election as an independent. In addition, Reagan faced challenges from four additional Republicans, but none ran well in any primary and all concluded their efforts shortly after the primaries began. The list included two major congressional leaders, Senators Howard Baker (Tennessee) and Robert Dole (Kansas), Congressman Philip Crane (Illinois), and former governor John Connally (Texas).

The battle for the Democratic nomination in 1992 was similar to the Republican one of 1980. The winner, Bill Clinton, faced challenges from five other Democrats and eventually forced each of them to abandon his efforts after one or more dismal primary showings. His strongest rival was former Senator Paul Tsongas (Massachusetts) who won the initial vote of this year, New Hampshire, and several other primaries in the Northeast. Tsongas withdrew in late March after being overwhelmed by Clinton in such major states as Florida, Texas, Illinois, and Michigan. In addition to Tsongas, Clinton faced challenges from two Senators from Midwestern farm states, Tom Harkin (Iowa) and Robert Kerrey (Nebraska), and from one current and one former governor. The current governor was Thomas Wilder (Virginia) while the former one was Jerry Brown (California). Wilder was the first of Clinton's rivals to depart the race, as he did so before the first primary; the two senators were the next to leave, although each won an early test, Harkin in Iowa and Kerrey in South Dakota. Tsongas followed after losing the four major states mentioned above, while Brown continued his efforts through the national convention. He managed to win the support of a limited number of delegates, however.

INCUMBENTS

While strong incumbents use advertising strategies where they emphasize their first term accomplishments and promise to continue them after reelection, weak incumbents compensate for their political weaknesses with themes about their personal character, leadership skills, and ideals. They also differ from strong incumbents in that they need to devote the early months of the campaign year to securing the support of their own partisans during contested primary campaigns. This latter need temporarily prevents them from concentrating their advertising on any actual or potential rivals in the upcoming general election. As Benoit's findings indicate, weak incumbents differ from all other candidates in that they have divided the themes of their advertising about evenly between references to character and policy. In this section of the chapter, I demonstrate how the weak incumbents of 1980 and 1992, Carter and Bush, relied on this strategy in their failed reelection bids.

Carter

Jimmy Carter launched his campaign for reelection in late 1979 while facing a major challenge for the Democratic nomination from Edward Kennedy. Some polls indicated that Kennedy might have been able to defeat Carter (Gallup Poll, 2006). The battle between these two changed significantly, however, when a hostile mob of Iranians seized control of the American embassy in Teheran and held 52 Americans hostage. The sudden entry of an international crisis into a campaign that had previously focused almost exclusively on domestic and economic issues clearly helped Carter and hurt Kennedy. The crisis helped transform foreign policy and the threat of one or more international crises into important topics for discussion in the ensuing campaign and directed more attention to the personal characteristics of the two candidates.

While the crisis ultimately contributed to Carter's defeat by Reagan in the general election, it appears to have aided him in his nomination struggle with Kennedy. It brought two matters to public attention that influenced the course of the campaign dialogue; Carter's recent successes earlier in 1979 at facilitating the signing of the Camp David Accords between Israel, Egypt, and the United States, and Kennedy's accident at Chappaquiddick Island in 1969 that had resulted in the controversial death of his female passenger. Carter appeared to have been successful as a statesman at Camp David when he mediated a resolution to long standing differences between two of the most powerful nations in the Middle East. The leaders of these nations, Anwar Sadat (Egypt) and Menachem Begin (Israel), would ultimately win the Nobel Peace Prize for their actions. This experience suggested to many Democrats that Carter could handle an international crisis. In contrast, Kennedy had appeared disoriented, unsure of himself, and less than truthful in the days following his accident. Many people were unconvinced of the Kennedy's veracity in explaining his actions and in his denial of inappropriate behavior. His entry into the presidential campaign interjected these questions into the political debate relating both to his character and his abilities to respond effectively and honestly to a crisis. Carter dominated the debate and took the lead in public opinion surveys shortly after the beginning of the crisis. Carter had a problem, however. Many voters, including substantial numbers of Democrats, did not believe he had been a particularly successful president during his first term. To them, Carter may have possessed an admirable personal character, but he also lacked the accomplishments they expected from the standard bearer of their own party (Gallup Poll, 2006).

The ad *Things* provides an example of how Carter tried to deal with this problem. Here, a narrator talks about character while the television viewer is shown an image of a ballot containing the names of both Kennedy and Carter. At first, the ballot appears to be at a long distance from the viewer, but gradually moves closer throughout the ad. Eventually, an anonymous person is shown casting a vote for Carter. This imagery is followed by a picture of Carter covering the entire screen. One version of this ad was used in the Pennsylvania primary during the last week of April. The narrator emphasized the primacy of character over record when he stated the major question the Carter campaign wanted voters to consider, "A man brings two things to a presidential ballot. He brings his record and he brings himself. Who he is is frequently more important than what he's done." The narrator then talked about the importance of character and placed a burden on each voter to respond accordingly. "You the voter must weigh both record and character before deciding. Often it's not easy and you wind up asking, "is this the person I really want in the White House for the next four years?"" With the choices and questions now clearly presented, the narrator designated Carter rather than Kennedy as the right choice. The accompanying imagery showed a voter finally making a decision and casting a ballot for Carter. The narrator concluded by remarking about the primacy of character in the choices voters would make, "In 1976 the people of Pennsylvania sent a steady man of unquestioned character to the White House. On April 22nd you have a chance to keep him there."

Another example of this approach appeared in the ad, "Family." This ad focused attention on the president's family life and, by implication, the character he brings to public office. The imagery began with a distant scene of the White House and then focused on close up imagery of Carter with his wife Roselyn and daughter, Amy. The spoken component included statements from a narrator, remarks by Carter, and concluding comments from the narrator. The ad began with the narrator setting the context with initial remarks, "The White House is today the pivot point of some of the most important decisions in the world. It is also a home." The imagery shifted from scenes of the White House to ones involving the three members of the Carter family seated together. Carter now spoke, but he narrated rather than directly addressing the audience. "I don't think there's any way you can separate the responsibilities of a husband, a father, and a basic human being from that of being a president," he said. "What I do in the White House is maintain good family life, which I consider to be crucial to being a good president," Carter concluded. The narrator finished the ad by emphasizing Carter's personal attributes and attempted to link them with national leadership, "Husband, Father, President, he's done these three jobs with distinction." The final imagery was of an appeal shown on a full page, green background that read, "Re-Elect President Carter."

Carter did not disregard political issues during his nomination campaign, but he attempted to link them with his leadership abilities and personal character. In *Mideast*, he made this point with imagery of his meetings with Sadat and Begin while occasionally acting as his own narrator. He began by remarking, "To get peace in the Mideast is more important than my being reelected. And we've made everybody angry in the process at one time or another, but we've made steady progress." With this, a narrator spoke in tandem with imagery actual signing of the accords. He linked character with policy by stating, "In his quest for peace in the world, President Carter has not forgotten the words of Abraham Lincoln when he called the United States of America the last best hope on Earth." The narrator then linked policy with personal leadership with his closing remarks, "President Jimmy Carter, Peacemaker."

The character issue presented Kennedy with significant problems that he ultimately failed to overcome. He needed to develop an image of responsibility in order to confront the belief that he lacked the skills necessary for national leadership. He attempted to do this by emphasizing his many years of experience in the Senate in his biographical advertising and by linking that experience with the issues, mostly economic, that he advocated. In his introductory ad *Senate Effectiveness*, Kennedy spoke after a narrator had told viewers of how effective the Massachusetts Democrat had been as a Senator. In attempting to demonstrate the relationship between his congressional record, Kennedy said the president must lead Congress and set national goals. He continued emphasizing this theme in a number of other ads, including *Apollo*. Here, with imagery of the launch of an Apollo space flight, a narrator raised the question of whether the nation had lost its spirit to solve problems and meet challenges. He said we needed strong leadership. Kennedy followed the narrator and spoke about these themes. Kennedy's attack ads followed the same idea; a narrator said that if Carter were to win, our choices would be over. He added that we needed new choices and these would come from Kennedy (*Four More Years*). These themes were not enough to provide Kennedy with the major help he needed to defeat Carter, however.

Carter employed many of the same themes in the general election that he had used against Kennedy, although he directed them to a different opponent whose character was not as questionable as Kennedy's. He introduced a variety of new ads that focused more attention on his domestic accomplishments. Nonetheless, the focus was still heavily oriented toward personal leadership factors. In an attempt to emphasize the importance of his individual skills over those of Reagan, Carter used a series of ads, actually several different versions of the same one, which illustrated him performing in the job of president (*Oval Office*). He was shown working at his desk in the Oval Office in one version while in others viewers could see him walking up the exterior stairs of the White House during the early evening. In this latter ad (*Light*), the camera followed Carter's ascent of the stairs by focusing attention on a single lighted room on the second floor of the White House. Since this was the family living area, viewers were expected to conclude that Carter was taking his work home to continue with it at night.

When Carter was shown working at his desk in the Oval Office version of this ad, the narrator emphasized the importance of the individual person who holds the presidency when he said, "Each day many people come to the Oval Office with advice and information. But when it comes time to decide something, President Carter must decide alone." The narrator continued emphasizing the importance of personal decision making by a competent individual when he remarked, "No matter how many advisors and assistants, a president can never escape the responsibility of truly understanding an issue himself. This is the only way that a presidential decision can be made." With this, the narrator concluded by reminding the viewers of Carter's unique personal qualities, "And the only way this president has ever made one. President Carter."

The various ads that had shown Carter ascending the White House stairs and then working (at home) into the night (*Light*) reiterated this same theme of personal leadership but combined it with some emphasis on policy accomplishments. "In the past four years, working day and night," the narrator began, "President Jimmy Carter has hammered out America's first energy program, deregulated airlines and trucking, broke through to an agreement at Camp David." By this time, Carter had finished climbing the stairs and was now inside the family living area of the White House. "He cut down on federal employees and paperwork, strengthened NATO, brought real help to American cities, increased our defense capabilities, and kept this nation at peace," the narrator continued. The imagery was now of the White House at night with a light showing from one, and only one, window on the second floor. With this, the narrator concluded his remarks, "And he's not finished yet. President Carter."

The unresolved Iranian hostage crisis was troublesome for Carter, but the president's problems with foreign policy became even more difficult with the intervention of the Soviet Union into a civil war in Afghanistan. As seen in the next section of this chapter which describes the actions of the challengers of the weak incumbents, Ronald Reagan was making a major issue of the nation's defenses. Carter responded to these charges with the ad, *Commander*. The ad featured imagery of Carter speaking to reporters at a press briefing and then followed with scenes of several newly created weapons systems. Among the weapons that were displayed were a tank, an aircraft carrier, a missile being launched, a frigate, and a fighter aircraft. It concluded with imagery of Carter signing the Camp David Accords with Begin and Sadat. The speaking role was divided between Carter and a narrator. Carter began the ad by speaking at the press briefing. "My number one responsibility is to defend this country, to maintain its security, and I put a strong defense at the top of my priority list, and it's going to be maintained that way," he remarked. To whom Carter was addressing his remarks was not clear.

With this, the narrator spoke while Carter was shown watching the tank and then addressing the sailors on the aircraft carrier. As had occurred with so many of Carter's ads, this one also emphasized his personal characteristics. "It's good for the nation's security when the commander in chief is himself an experienced military man," the narrator began. "Jimmy Carter, Annapolis graduate, is just that." Carter was then shown speaking from the deck of the carrier to a large crowd of service personnel while accompanied by the ship's senior officers. "Your presence in the Indian Ocean and in the Arabian Sea is most crucial in that troubled region of the world and vital to all nations on earth," Carter remarked.

The ad continued with imagery of the remaining weapons systems mentioned above, but the theme of the narration changed from a maintenance of military strength to one of advancing peacemaking through diplomacy. Once again, the emphasis was on the personal leadership qualities that are essential for peacemaking. There was also an unspoken message here; the diplomatically successful Carter had such qualities while the tough talking and inexperienced Reagan certainly did not. The narrative continued, "Yet even an expenditure of $136 billion a year on the most modern weapons does not bring the final security. The final security comes only when nations eventually reach out to touch each other in their minds and hearts." The imagery was now of the signing of the Camp David Accords. The ad finished with the narrator linking the two complementary features of Carter's character that had been emphasized in the ad, "Jimmy Carter, a military man and a man of peace."

The Carter campaign employed other ads that also tried to link issues with character. Some contained narratives by individual voters, such as a farmer and a laborer, who spoke about how Carter's policies had improved their economic well being. They gave him personal credit for the improvements of recent years, including such policies as the federally backed financial bailout of the Chrysler Corporation (*Farmer, Akron*). Mary Tyler Moore spoke in one ad about Carter's contributions to issues that were of particular interest to women. She also talked about how Carter, as an individual, had worked hard to advance the rights of women (*Mary*). Finally, a woman in the audience at a Carter public address stood as if to ask a question but instead thanked him for his efforts as a peacemaker. Carter smiled as she praised his work (*Lorraine*).

There were, of course, a substantial number of ads whose primary purpose was to attack Reagan directly rather than implicitly. One of the major themes employed here was to raise doubts about Reagan's abilities to lead the nation in a number of areas, particularly foreign affairs and war. A second theme questioned Reagan's honesty and character by showing how his campaign promises and his past actions as governor of California were contradictory. With respect to the first theme, several versions of the same ad focused on the remarks about individual people who resided in various parts of California. Each of them, shown speaking to an unseen camera, talked about Reagan's lack of abilities and of how poorly they thought he had performed as governor of their state. Many of them referred to Reagan's lack of experience in foreign policy (*Street Concern, Street Hip*).

In ads related to the second anti-Reagan theme, the narrator talked about how Reagan had promised to cut taxes and reduce the size of government when he had first run for governor. The narrator then informed viewers of how Reagan had broken those promises and had actually increased taxes and the number of state employees while in office. After pointing out that Reagan had refused to acknowledge the accuracy of reports that proved these charges, the narrator concluded by questioning Reagan's honesty and character by remarking, "But can we trust the nation's future to a man who refuses to remember his own past (*Reagan Record*)?"

The attempt by the Carter campaign to contrast his leadership abilities and personal character with those of his opponent had work effectively during the battle with Kennedy because the two candidates agreed on many of the same policy objectives. Democrats were asked to determine which of two aspirants for the presidency would be the better person to implement policies about which most of them agreed. They decided that Carter was the one for the task. This strategy did not work as effectively when Carter faced Reagan, however. Policy differences were far more important in the general election, first, because of the broader nature of that electorate, and second, because Reagan and Carter offered ideologically distinct values relating to the direction the nation should take. A set of appeals limited to the theme that a unified nation should select a person of superior background and character to lead it simply did not resonate with an electorate that lacked the requisite ideological unity for such a theme to work.

Bush

The Bush advertising strategy was similar to Carter's in the sense that its most significant themes were personal qualities and leadership abilities. Policy accomplishments other than those relating to foreign affairs, and the Gulf War in particular, were given limited emphasis. The ads can be divided into three distinct time phases, with each one relating to a specific political need that Bush faced during the campaign. At the outset, Bush had to deal with the immediate reality of a strong conservative challenge from Pat Buchanan in the New Hampshire primary. He had to respond to both Buchanan as a significant rival and to the unique circumstances of this one specific state that had helped fuel the Buchanan challenge. Bush did so with two sets of ads, those emphasizing his policy goals and those attacking Buchanan. The personal qualities and leadership abilities theme was pervasive in both sets, with Bush shown to have them while Buchanan clearly did not.

New Hampshire marked the high point of the Buchanan effort. The television commentator attained 37 percent of the Republican vote, compared to only 53 percent for Bush, while the remainder of the vote was cast for others, some of whom were candidates in the Democratic primary. After this election, Buchanan opposed Bush in four more states but was unable to duplicate his New Hampshire showing, ran out of money, and withdrew from the race. With this, Bush then changed the themes of his ads as his campaign entered its second phase. Here, Bush was running against a yet to be named Democratic opponent. Unlike the strong incumbents who frequently use the late stages of the nomination period to speak of the accomplishments of their first term and their goals for the second, Bush, as a troubled and weak incumbent, responded instead to his political weaknesses by emphasizing his character and by attacking the Democrats as a party and as the leading cause of the troubles that had plagued his first term.

Once the Democrats had finally nominated Bill Clinton, the Bush campaign moved to the third phase of its efforts, the general election battle against a specific opponent from the opposition party and an independent candidate who was willing to spend millions of dollars of his own fortune on the campaign (Ross Perot). Bush employed an advertising strategy that used ads emphasizing that he was trustworthy and of good personal and moral character while adding that Clinton was lacking in both attributes. In addition, there were the usual attack ads, in this instance they told of how poorly the challenger had performed in his most recent political office. In this instance, that office was the governorship of Arkansas. The Bush campaign did not focus much of its attention on Perot, however, apparently seeing him as a temporary distraction whose support would decline as the campaign year advanced.

The national economy was in recession in 1992 and one of the hardest hit states was New Hampshire. Buchanan responded to these conditions by attacking Bush repeatedly over his economic and tax related polices. Bush dealt with this challenge in his annual State of the Union Address to Congress by advocating an economic program involving tax, welfare, tort, and educational changes that he said would strengthen the economy. The components of the plan were not new; Bush had been pursuing them throughout his term. He chose to reemphasize them in late January, however, and in doing so, demanded that Congress implement them by March 20th. There was virtually no chance that Congress would pass this plan but Bush's demand provided a ready scapegoat on whom he could blame the nation's economic troubles.

One can see an example of this approach in the ad, *Send a Message*. Bush employed numerous ads throughout the nomination and general election campaign where he used the symbolism of the presidency by speaking to voters from the Oval Office. In some ads he would be standing and talking directly to the television viewers while in others he would be seated at his desk reading or signing papers with a narrator speaking. In this particular ad, Bush stood and talked directly to the viewers. He began by remarking that "New Hampshire and our nation have been through tough times and I've given Congress a deadline of March 20th to pass my plan for economic growth." With this, he summarized his major goals, emphasizing that his plan "will cut taxes for families, encourage investments so business can create new jobs, and restore the values of homes and real estate. My plan will work without big government spending." There was one final plea aimed at placing the blame on his political opponents if the economy did not change, "But I need your help now to send a real message to Congress to get this job done."

In *Joined*, an ad with a similar theme, the initial imagery was military in nature and related to the successes of the recent Gulf War but it quickly changed to scenes where Bush was shown talking to a small group of people who were seated with him at a table. The narrator told the audience that "when President Bush led America to victory in Desert Storm and the Cold War, some opposed him." With this, the audio portion followed the themes of *Send a Message* with the narrator once again placing the major blame for New Hampshire's economic difficulties on the Democrats in Congress. The final scene focused on Bush delivering his State of the Union Address and demanding that Congress implement his economic plan by March 20th. The date Bush wanted was politically significant; it was about one month after the voters in New Hampshire would have cast their ballots. These Republican voters would no longer have a chance to retaliate against Bush for a broken promise.

Buchanan was unusually virulent in his challenge of Bush. He introduced himself, defined the nature of his candidacy and developed his issues primarily by attacking the Bush record. His favorite theme was taxation and of how Bush had broken his famous promise from the election of 1988 of "Read my lips, no more taxes." In *Broken Promises* a narrator attacked Bush's tax record while imagery showed the president actually making the promise. The narrator accused Bush of betraying our trust. He then asked viewers if we could afford four more years of broken promises and urged them to "send Bush a message." This same message of mistrust for Bush was also a theme in other Buchanan ads that also included imagery of the president making his tax pledge (*Protect, Check Your Socks, Behind the Mask*). Buchanan did not limit his attacks exclusively to the tax issue and trust, however. He criticized Bush over such issues as federal aid for pornographic art that glorified homosexuality and perverted Christianity (*Freedom to Abuse*), over the Internal Revenue Service practice of removing tax exemptions from churches if they had major political involvements (*Pay to Pray*), affirmative action and hiring quotas (*I Won't Sign*), and of how numerous administration officials had been registered lobbyists for foreign governments (*Foreign Agents*).

Buchanan's withdrawal took place prior to both the conclusion of the Democratic race and the entry of Ross Perot into the campaign as an independent candidate. With no specific general election opponents at this time, which was the early spring months, Bush directed his advertising almost exclusively to the theme of personal qualities and leadership abilities. This strategy is illustrated in the ad *Agenda*. The ad combined an overview of the major issues that Bush was advancing with imagery of him working in the Oval Office. Bush was the initial speaker and began with remarks related to goals and ideals, "If we can change the world we can change America." An anonymous narrator was responsible for the rest of the commentary, which then focused primarily on personal qualities rather than the goals that Bush had just outlined. "Perhaps no president in our history has shown the world such strong leadership," the narrator began, with emphasis clearly on Bush acting in the role of a talented world leader. At time stage of the campaign, Bush clearly needed to solidify his backing among those conservatives who had supported Buchanan and who might have voted for Perot if the Texas billionaire had chosen to seek office. This ad focused on the issues that were important to those people. The narrative added that, "Now he has an agenda to strengthen our economy and make America more competitive in the world." This summary was followed by short statements from the narrator about what Bush wanted to do with particular issues, "To change welfare and make the able bodied work. End fraudulent lawsuits that destroy businesses and drive up insurance rates. Rebuild our education system so it demands responsibility and results." In concluding, the narrator linked issues with personal abilities in the concluding remark, "President Bush, the future of America in the hands of experience." Finally, a similar ad with many of these same themes, including some imagery related foreign affairs and terrorism, concluded with the phrase, "This man, who has changed the world, will change America. President Bush, experience" (*The Leader*).

The Bush advertising strategy for the general election also revolved around the personal qualities and leadership abilities theme. Trust was central to many of the ads Bush used in this phase of the campaign. Trust was implicitly depicted here as a personal attribute that Bush possessed but which Clinton clearly lacked. There were, of course, many attack ads relating to Clinton, including those which questioned his performance as governor. Among them were attacks on Clinton's record of increasing various taxes in Arkansas. One ad, *Guess*, talked about how Clinton, rather than the state legislature, had increased taxes on general sales, beer, mobile homes and television cable service. This ad also implied that Clinton would seek new federal taxes. It did so by claiming that the new and expanded programs that Clinton was advocating would increase federal spending by $220 billion. The Bush campaign also attacked Clinton over the possible effects of his health care plans by claiming that such plans would increase government control of health care decisions, cut spending on Medicare and Medicaid, and cost about 700,000 jobs (*Healthcare*). No explanation was provided of how so many job losses would occur. The ads also labeled Clinton's plans as socialized medicine.

Central to virtually every attack against Clinton were comments by either narrators or seemingly ordinary voters about their inability to personally trust him. Examples of narrators' remarks include, "Now for Bill Clinton it's a question of avoiding the truth." This remark came at the end of an ad that used stark, black and white imagery of Clinton while raising questions about his avoidance of the military draft during the Vietnam War (*Trust*). Other ads also emphasized the theme of Clinton's untrustworthiness. "You can't trust Bill Clinton's economic plan (or you can't trust Clinton's health care plan)," were the concluding phrases by the female narrator in several ads that attacked Clinton's proposals on those issues (*Federal Taxes*). In a series of attack ads that followed the televised debates during September and October, the words, "on integrity," flashed onto the screen. After this opening, individual people would raise doubts about Clinton's trustworthiness with statements like, "If you're going to be president, you have to be honest;" or "I just don't trust Bill Clinton, I can't trust anything that he says," or "I don't think he tells the truth", or "I don't think he's honorable, and I don't think he's trustworthy" or "I wouldn't trust him at all to be commander in chief (*Debate, Cincinnati: Fred, Cincinnati: Barney, Peter*)."

With one set of ads raising questions about Clinton's trustworthiness and implying that he lacked the personal character to be president, other Bush campaign ads raised the theme of trust in defining Bush's own qualifications. In the ad *Crisis* the major theme was trustworthiness and its relation to the presidential role of commander in chief. The imagery was of several major crises of recent years, including scenes from the Gulf War, of Mikhail Gorbachev being released after a failed coup by old line communists against him in 1991, of Boris Yeltsin appearing before the anti-communist forces in Russia during these events and that eventually led to the fall of the Soviet Union, and of terrorists holding American embassy workers hostage in Iran in 1979. The narrative began with a recording of Bush addressing the nation at the beginning of the Gulf War, continued with excerpts of two newscasts, and then concluded with a narrator talking about character while the television viewer could see supporting imagery of the president's chair in the Oval Office.

"Just two hours ago allied air forces began an attack on military targets . . ." Bush was heard remarking at the outset of the ad. His words then faded as the voice of a female news reporter became dominant. "President Bush said today that he reassured Mr. Yeltsin that the United States will stand by democracy," the reporter said. Viewers then heard the voice of what appeared to be a second reporter, male in this instance, who stated, "If revolutionaries and terrorists are armed with nuclear and chemical weapons it may pose a new challenge to the president." These opening and related remarks and imagery were followed by the words of the ad's narrator whose comments were accompanied by imagery of the president's empty chair placed behind a desk in the Oval Office. In wording that directly addressed the issue of trust and implicitly linked it to Bush and not to Clinton or Perot, the narrator asked the question, "In a world where we're just one dictator away from the next major crisis, who do you most trust to be sitting in this chair?"

The Bush campaign concluded its advertising efforts during the final days of the election season by redirecting attention toward Bush and away from Clinton. It continued emphasizing the personal qualities and leadership abilities theme, however. In *Presidency*, Bush was shown speaking in conversational tones to a roomful of admiring people about his concept of the nation's highest office. "There are many times that the president alone must make the tough decisions that effect people's lives," Bush told his attentive listeners. "He's the commander in chief and I want you to think about that. He must have the resolve, the maturity, the moral authority to lead the nation in times of crisis," Bush continued. Once again, he hinted that he alone possessed the personal qualities needed for leadership. The ad lasted for two minutes, an unusually long time for a political message. It was used during the final days of the campaign and provided no other narrative than Bush speaking talking and no other imagery than the room full of people.

Bush reiterated the personal character theme several more times in this ad while implicitly suggesting that his opponents were not qualified for the presidency. "America must have a leader who understand the world and is prepared to act," Bush stated, "Leaders of other nations, people all over the world, judge America by the character of the president and the president's work must be good. The person that you choose to lead America must have certain qualities; decisiveness, honesty, integrity, consistency," followed. The implication, of course, was that Bush had these "certain qualities." In what appears as an implicit reference to Clinton, Bush added, "All of you know that the presidency is the most serious job in the world and you simply cannot put America's future at risk with a person who is wrong the job and with policies that are wrong for America." This last phrase linked the president's remarks with an attack slogan the Bush campaign had used earlier against Clinton. Several ads that were designed to raise doubts about Clinton's economic and health care plans, and his personal integrity, had concluded with the slogan, "wrong for you, wrong for America." Finally, *Presidency* concluded with a slogan whose primary purpose was to once again emphasize Bush's personal qualities and leadership abilities, "President Bush, Commander in Chief."

Bush encountered many of the same difficulties in the general election that Carter had faced twelve years earlier by choosing to concentrate his appeals on the character and qualifications theme. This strategy was useful during the nomination campaign when voters of the same party and of relatively similar ideological views were asked to choose a person to lead them in the pursuit of agreed upon goals. It did not work as well in a general election when voters were less ideologically unified and wanted more than merely an experienced individual with good character to lead them. Once again, this strategy proved to be ineffective for an incumbent president seeking reelection.

CHALLENGERS

Every challenger of an incumbent president needs to implement an advertising strategy that addresses certain fundamental requirements that arise from his unique vantage point. A challenger must compete in both phases of modern elections; he must defeat several other aspirants in a series of primaries in order to secure the nomination of his own party, and then he must compete effectively in the general election against an incumbent president. To win the nomination, a

challenger must implement an advertising strategy that addresses the three requisite needs discussed previously, 1) introduce himself to the voters, 2) develop
issues that define his candidacy, and 3) attack his rivals in order to protect his
own partisan base. These needs are universal for all challengers regardless of the
strength of the incumbent. The electoral context that challengers of weak incumbents face differs, however. The problem that challengers of strong incumbents encounter in combating the favorable imagery of successful first term accomplishments is not as pressing for the challengers of weak incumbents. Weak
incumbents have difficulties in speaking about their first terms, so they direct
their attention to character. This provides an opening for the challengers who
can now implement advertising strategies that call for change at a time when
many voters are quite susceptible to such themes. In this section, I demonstrate
how the challengers of the weak incumbents of 1980 and 1992, Ronald Reagan
and Bill Clinton, used these opportunities to win the presidency. In addition, I
review the advertising strategies of their rivals for their respective party nominations in order to provide some context for the demands of the nomination campaigns. Finally, these two elections were distinguished by the presence of formidable independent candidates in the general elections; John Anderson (1980)
and Ross Perot (1992). I also discuss their advertising strategies.

Reagan and the Republicans

    Ronald Reagan began his quest for the 1980 Republican nomination as the
clear front-runner in a field of seven candidates. This front-runner status had not
come easily for Reagan; he had acquired it only after thirteen years as a national
conservative leader and two failed campaigns for his party's presidential nomination. He had emerged as a national conservative leader in 1967 during the first
year of his initial term as governor of California. This year marked a transitional
time for conservatives. Their most prominent spokesman of the past few years,
Senator Barry Goldwater (Arizona), had lost the presidential election of 1964 by
such an overwhelming margin that many conservatives no longer saw him as an
effective leader. In response, some conservatives, including Goldwater, looked
to former vice president Richard Nixon as the best conservative hope for the
presidency while others searched for an alternative to the often moderate sounding Nixon. Reagan filled this void in his role as governor of the nation's largest
state. He rapidly emerged as a major critic of the policies of the Democratic administration and congress and of the 1960s counterculture behavior that conservatives often found so repulsive. By 1968, he had become a national leader of
such significance that many conservatives longed for him to make a presidential
bid. Reagan had a major problem in that far too many Republicans, including
even some of his admirers, saw Nixon as the better choice for that election.
Reagan's efforts were unusual in 1968 in that he did not contest any primaries
other than California, which he won without opposition. Instead, he kept hinting
at candidacy and eventually declared it within days of the Republican national

convention in July. He finished in third place on the only ballot, trailing Nixon and New York Governor Nelson Rockefeller. He had encouraged talk that he would become a member of a "dream" ticket of Rockefeller-Reagan. He called it Reagan-Rockefeller.

Reagan made a second presidential bid eight years later and proved to be a far more formidable candidate. He spent those intervening years building a stronger following within his own party. His status had increased so much that many Republicans saw him as the most likely successor of Nixon during the 1972 campaign. He was the front-runner among Republicans for the 1976 nomination according to several polls taken before Nixon's resignation from office in August, 1974 (Gallup Poll, 2006). Nixon's departure and the ascension of Gerald Ford to the presidency changed the dynamics of the 1976 campaign. Ford weakened his own prospects within one month after taking office with his pardon of Nixon for all Watergate related crimes. Reagan entered the race shortly afterwards. He won several primaries, including most of the ones in the Southeastern and Western states, and lost the nomination to Ford by slightly more than one hundred delegate votes out of approximately 2,200 that were cast at the Republican national convention. This strong showing, and his actions before 1976, made Reagan the front-runner for the 1980 nomination. He never lost that distinction. Reagan entered the 1980 campaign with more money, support in polls, and endorsements from prominent Republicans than any of his rivals.

These prior experiences freed Reagan from the need of devoting some of his advertising resources to introducing himself. Instead, he concentrated his efforts on two major issues that would define his candidacy throughout the year. One of Reagan's issues was national security. Relying upon the inability of Carter to bring about the conclusion of the Iranian hostage crisis and the recent Soviet invasion of Afghanistan, Reagan talked about the weaknesses of the American military arsenal compared to that of the Soviet Union. In the ad *Foreign Affairs*, which was accompanied with imagery of Soviet weapons, Reagan attacked current American weaknesses and emphasized that we needed to maintain peace through strength.

A second issue that Reagan emphasized, and which would eventually become one of the more defining features of his administration, was taxes and the pressing need to reduce them. In ads that relied upon both a narrator and Reagan himself occasionally serving as the speaker, Carter was attacked over the magnitude of the national tax burden with Reagan eventually adding that lower taxes would stimulate economic growth (*Carter*). The national economy had been hit by a combination of low growth, and high fuel prices, inflation, unemployment, and interest rates. Reagan used the theme that government was not the solution but was instead the problem.

With one notable exception, that being John Anderson, Reagan's opponents focused their advertising primarily on the need of introducing themselves. They used biographical ads that occasionally contained some references to tax related issues, but the personal aspects that qualified them for the presidency were central to their appeals. For example, Baker employed one ad containing imagery where he was seen talking to a small group of people about how he would attempt to increase personal savings with new tax incentives (*Savings*). In another ad, *Iranian Student*, Baker tried to show that he was a forceful leader when he used news footage of a young Middle Eastern man asking him a hostile question relating to Iran. Baker responded quite negatively to his questioner, although he his actions won the respect of his audience. He told the "student" he was more concerned about the fate of the hostages than about whatever matter the student was questioning.

Virtually since the nation's beginning, people have disagreed about what kind of experiences most qualifies someone for the presidency. Even if a correct answer to this question did exist, it is not self-evident. Often, candidates attempt to answer this unanswerable question by telling voters that they are the aspirants who have had the more qualifying experiences. Prior to taking office, most of our presidents had served as generals, congressmen, vice presidents, governors, or secretaries of state or war, and each of them emphasized the unique attributes such service had provided them. George Bush had held federal appointive offices for six years during the Nixon and Ford years and he attempted to convince voters that these qualified him for the presidency. He had been an envoy to China, the ambassador to the United Nations, and the Director of the Central Intelligence Agency. Bush employed ads with varied imagery of people in different settings with a narrator talking about how Bush would bring about new leadership and change (*Interior, Exterior*). They ended with a slogan designed to emphasize Bush's experiences, "A President we won't have to train."

While Reagan did encounter some opposition for the nomination, he actually had a fairly easy time winning it, at least when compared to challengers in other elections. Bush defeated him by a small margin in Iowa, but Reagan rebounded shortly afterwards with an overwhelming victory New Hampshire. He garnered a majority of the popular vote in this state and defeated Bush by a margin of more than 2 to 1. Reagan followed this success by winning nearly every one of the remaining primaries and caucuses. Two of his major rivals, Baker and Dole, abruptly terminated their activities after losing New Hampshire. Bush continued with his efforts until early May, but withdrew after a series of losses led him to believe that if he remained in the race he would eliminate himself from consideration for the vice presidential nomination. One candidate who decided against withdrawing was Anderson. While he did abandon his quest for the Republican nomination, Anderson quickly emerged as an independent challenger in the general election.

Anderson's advertising strategy during the primaries differed from that of the other Republican candidates. Instead of relying on a narrator and supportive imagery to make his case, Anderson spoke directly to his television audience about the issues he wanted to advance and of the difference his presidency would make. In one ad, Anderson told the viewers that he wanted to buy their votes, not with money, but with ideas that challenged them to think. He then outlined the ideas that would encourage thinking; his opposition to a tax cut the nation could not afford, the idea that we could not solve our energy problems by drilling more oil wells, and that we needed to make some sacrifices in order to balance the federal budget. He also promised to talk about national problems before rather than after the election (*Buy Votes*). In another ad, *Secret Solo*, Anderson stated that Reagan's promises to increase military spending and increase taxes were irresponsible. He concluded nearly all of his advertising with a slogan that provided a rationale for his unusual candidacy, "The Anderson Difference."

Anderson continued with this approach in his general election campaign, although he relied more on narrators this time. In his major biographical ad, *Independent*, Anderson's narrator talked about the candidate's background in Congress and of the years he had spent fighting for fiscal responsibility and social justice. Anderson then spoke directly to his television audience and warned then that the election of either a Democrat or a Republican would mean a continuation of politics as usual. He told them that because he was a political independent he would place the needs of the country above those of a party. In addition, Anderson used footage from an endorsement Gerald Ford had made for him several years earlier. Ford described Anderson as smart and told viewers the Illinois congressman always voted his conscience (*Fact*).

Ronald Reagan entered the general election with an enviable position. With Bush's withdrawal in May, Reagan became the unofficial nominee of the Republican Party. He officially attained that designation; and a running mate in Bush as well, at a unified Republican convention in July. Meanwhile, the Democrats failed to resolve their leadership struggle until mid-August when Carter finally defeated Kennedy at his party's convention. These time differences gave Reagan three additional months to take his campaign before a national electorate rather than merely limiting it to a partisan segment of all voters. The Anderson campaign also helped Reagan in that it posed a far greater threat to Carter and Mondale than to the Republican ticket. Although Anderson was a Republican, he was also a liberal. He was attracting more support from disenchanted Democrats than from Republicans. In responding to this threat, Carter refused to participate in any debates unless Anderson was excluded. This demand did not eliminate the debates from the campaign, however. Reagan and Anderson engaged in one debate without Carter and both attacked him for his absence. Eventually, Carter realized that he could not avoid any debates. He finally agreed to a debate with Reagan, and with Anderson excluded, to take place one week before the election. In the estimation of most observers, Reagan won the debate when he asked viewers to answer the question, "Are you better off now than you were four years ago?"

Reagan used the three necessary challenger themes in his advertising strategy; introduction, overview of issues, and attacks against his opponent. A biographical film that was shown initially at the Republican convention and used later in the campaign illustrates how Reagan combined a personal introduction with positions on selected domestic issues. A narrator began the documentary by speaking about Reagan's pre-political career. He emphasized such matters as Reagan's childhood life in Illinois, background from a small Midwestern city, professional experiences as a radio announcer for the Chicago Cubs baseball team and a career as an actor, and finally, union leadership as president of the Screen Actors' Guild. This led into an overview of Reagan's political accomplishments during his two terms as California governor. The narrator also emphasized several of Reagan's accomplishments as union president. This was mentioned in order to appeal to members of a traditional Democratic constituency. Reagan, the narrator said, had brought about better wages and working conditions for the actors and had removed the influences of organized crime from the union leadership. As governor of California, Reagan was said to have turned a financial deficit into a surplus, cut taxes, and improved the quality of life in his state, with working people specifically mentioned. The narrator concluded by telling the audience that Reagan will do the same for the nation that he has done for California (*Documentary, Record*).

A second category of issues Reagan emphasized related to foreign affairs. In light of the troubles with Iran and Afghanistan, the ads suggested that the solution to the nation's current foreign related problems was increased military strength and preparedness. In one ad, labeled *Peace*, Reagan spoke directly to the television audience and spoke about how a strong military was necessary for maintaining peace. Tyrants do not attack when nations are strong, Reagan told his viewing audience. He said they attack only when nations are weak. An implication that came from this message was that difficulties resulted from military weaknesses rather than bad policy choices. While this ad was oriented more toward policies than attacks, it did raise questions about Carter's actions. Other Reagan ads attacked Carter directly.

In *Flip-flop Economy* the Reagan campaign employed a fairly usual approach in attacking the incumbent by using two contradictory images where the rival was shown smiling or frowning while the narrator talked about contradictions in policy. In this instance, the contrasts focused on the promises Carter had made in 1976 (smiling) and the harsh realities of inflation, taxes, and deficits that existed in 1980 (frowning). Reagan also used footage of the attacks that Kennedy had made against Carter during the primaries related to inflation and the nation's economic performance (*Kennedy Inflation*). Finally, Carter's refusal to debate was the focus of some ads. In one instance, an elderly woman spoke about his refusal debate, attacked his record, and then added that the nation could not afford four more years of Carter as president (*Podium*).

The Reagan advertising strategy worked in the sense that it developed the theme that the challenger was a qualified alternative to the troubled incumbent. As a result, Reagan beat Carter by ten percentage points in the popular vote and carried the electoral votes of 44 states.

Clinton and the Democrats

Like Reagan twelve years earlier, Bill Clinton had excellent prospects in 1992 for winning the presidency if he could attain the nomination of his own party. He began the election year as the front-runner for the nomination. He had acquired this role by raising more money, garnering more endorsements from party leaders and elected officials, and attaining greater public support as measured in opinion surveys than any of his opponents. The campaign for the Democratic nomination began in early 1991, shortly after the conclusion of the Gulf War. At the time, George Bush seemed unbeatable, but that changed as the year advanced. The national economy was in recession and many people saw Bush as unable or unwilling to confront domestic issues. Bush's popularity dropped steadily throughout 1991 to the point that he appeared venerable at year's end. These weaknesses encouraged challengers to emerge from within Bush's own party (Buchanan) and from his conservative to moderate constituency (Perot). A political context such as this provided Democrats with an excellent opportunity for an election victory.

Clinton emerged as a national political actor in the years immediately prior to 1992. His elective offices had been limited to state government in Arkansas; two years as the state's attorney general and twelve more as governor. Unlike most states at the time, Arkansas did not have an eight year limit on gubernatorial tenure. As a result, Clinton had the unusual distinction of being the nation's senior governor with twelve years of service and it's youngest at age 46. These circumstances elevated Clinton into a leadership role among Democratic governors and helped him develop support for a presidential bid.

The campaign for the Democratic nomination differed from those of other recent years. One major candidate, Senator Tom Harkin, was from Iowa, the site of the first caucuses. Since a Harkin victory seemed certain, the other candidates bypassed the state and concentrated on the New Hampshire primary which was held one week after the Iowa vote. Clinton introduced himself in New Hampshire with an early version of his major biographical film, *The Man from Hope*. The title used the name of the small Arkansas town where Clinton was born into a metaphor for the promises (hopes) of the campaign and the candidate. A narrator told the audience about Clinton's background in Hope and later in Hot Springs, Arkansas. He described the many financial hardships Clinton had encountered early in his life; the personal successes Clinton had generated for himself such as meeting President John F. Kennedy while serving as a member of Boys Nation; education at Georgetown University and selection as a Rhodes Scholar; and several years of service in Arkansas state government.

Clinton was unusually effective as a communicator, as his detractors were to learn, much to their dismay, over the next eight years. He relied on this strength in many of his ads by speaking directly to his audience rather than relying upon a narrator. In *Plan*, an ad used mainly in New Hampshire, Clinton said the nation was in trouble and pointed out that during the 1980's "the rich had gotten richer and the poor had become poorer, the middle class had declined, and no politicians had taken responsibility." He then told his audience that he had a comprehensive plan to get the economy moving again. His plan would start with a middle class tax cut but would include some tax increases on the rich. It would implement national health insurance, and improve education and international trade. Clinton concluded by saying that he would put government on the side of the "forgotten middle class."

Clinton employed this same style and message content in other ads. He would speak directly to his audience about issues related to their economic well being and of how he planned to represent the interests of the middle class. In the ad *Restore*, he said he would "restore the American dream" by improving "what matters;" economics, education, taxes, and jobs. On other occasions, he spoke of his accomplishments in Arkansas on these same issues and health care, adding that working on them had been "the story of his life" (*Eleven Years*). On other occasions Clinton would not make eye contact with his audience, instead focusing on a "person" who seemed to be just out of the camera's range (*People Plan*). He continued with the same general economic related themes, however, emphasizing that he was fighting for the forgotten middle class and that we must "put people first" and "invest in people." He spoke about the economic issues that defined his campaign; jobs, health care, a middle class tax cut, and improved education and international trade (*Fighting*). Finally, Clinton used a narrator in other issue related ads that reiterated these same appeals while he interacted with various people (*New Covenant*).

The Clinton campaign also employed some attack ads, some of which were directed against his Democratic rivals while others were aimed at the Bush administration. With respect to his Democratic rivals, one ad questioned the tax proposals Tsongas was advancing by claiming that Clinton's plan would put people first (*Time*). Another ad pointed out the contradictions in Brown's promises to refuse money from political action committees compared to his previous acceptance of them (*Which*). The attacks directed at Republicans illustrated people had suffered economically over the past twelve years and pointed out how Clinton's promises would alleviate their difficulties (*Casualties*).

Clinton faced another problem, how to deal with the stories about sexual trysts that were rapidly entering the campaign dialogue. He dealt with this problem in two ways; with advertising, and by appearing with his wife Hillary for an interview on the television show *60 Minutes*. An ad designed to counter the rumors said Republican operatives were behind the controversy about his alleged affair with the Little Rock, Arkansas nightclub singer Gennifer Flowers (*Fact*). The interview, which took place immediately after the Super Bowl football game, was highly watched and appeared to have halted the declines in voter support that had been troubling the Clinton campaign in recent days.

Tsongas won New Hampshire, but Clinton salvaged a second place finish. In remarks after the vote, Clinton referred to himself as the "comeback kid." He then started winning primaries, drove Harkin and Kerrey from the race by early March, Tsongas by the end of the month, and reduced Brown to the status of a minor candidate by mid-April. With these victories, Clinton became the unofficial nominee of his party at about the same time of year as Reagan had become in 1980.

While Brown was the last of Clinton's rivals to quit the race, Tsongas clearly proved to be the most formidable. After his New Hampshire victory, the former Massachusetts senator ran strongly in several additional primaries in the Northeastern states. He won in Maryland and Massachusetts but then lost to Clinton in four major states; Michigan, Illinois, Texas, and Florida before withdrawing. Tsongas employed ads that emphasized his personal courage and his previous efforts at opposing special interests. In one ad, *Swim*, Tsongas was shown diving into and then swimming in a pool while a narrator told viewers about how Tsongas had fought against the odds and had beaten corrupt politicians. Tsongas remarked that he was not afraid to "swim against the current" and would fight the Bush economic policies.

The major theme in Tsongas' issue related ads was a collection of economic promises coupled with the assertion that Tsongas was not a captive of "special interests." In *This is Paul Tsongas*, a narrator claimed that Tsongas was not the candidate of Washington insiders but was instead "a candidate of ideas who would get the country moving again." Most of the issue related ads relied heavily on a narrator telling voters that Tsongas was "willing to take on Bush on economic ideas," that "leadership is getting the tough jobs done," and that "people who know Tsongas knows he tells it straight" (*Leadership, Old Politics*). The ads also included a promise that Tsongas would declare an economic emergency and promote new investments and jobs in order to bring about a recovery. Tsongas' attack ads were aimed primarily at Clinton over his tax cut proposals and record in Arkansas. With imagery of coins tossed into the air, a narrator in one ad and Tsongas in another, talked about how Clinton's tax proposals would provide a cut of only 97 cents per day to many people (*Change, Difference*). In addition, there were ads questioning Clinton's claim that he had reduced taxes as governor (*Straight Answers*).

The five Democratic candidates shared few differences in their promises, but they varied greatly in the styles and contents of their televised messages. Clinton directed many of his ads to economic issues while Tsongas frequently linked his to his personal independence. In contrast, Kerrey often referred to his experiences in Vietnam where he had lost a leg in combat and of how that related to his goals in public life. He used his medical experiences as an opening for promises about improving health care. After the introductions in a variety of ads that focused on his war record and injuries, Kerrey would tell voters how he had been helped by American medicine and that he was personally committed to bringing it about for everyone. He referred to how lives can be shattered by medical costs and warned that voters should not accept the counterfeit plans of others (*Shattered, Firefight, Cause*). There was a problem with such an approach, however, in that some voters might wonder if a war injury could compromise Kerrey's ability to act. He addressed this in an ad related to foreign trade where he employed hockey related metaphors and imagery. At the outset of the ad *Net*, Kerrey walked across the ice to an unguarded net while telling viewers that our economy was like the net. "We leave ours open while others guard theirs," he said. He talked about how Bush's trade policies had cost jobs and then promised that Japan "will learn that this president can play defense."

Harkin also spoke about economics, but he often used imagery of closed factories and unemployed people to make his points. He used ads where he was shown speaking to audiences of working people in various settings, including a closed factory, about the need to "Build a New American," of the failures of Bush's "trickle down economics," and of the need to "put people back to work" (*Work, Builder, Echoes*). Harkin also spoke of his efforts in Congress in assisting the handicapped and those disabled by work related injuries. In one ad, his brother Frank, who was deaf, spoke to the audience by using sign language, which was translated for viewers, about such efforts (*Frank*).

Perhaps more than any other candidate, Brown used the theme in which outsiders should unite behind his candidacy and take back the government from special interests. After using introductory ads, including one which talked of his experiences of working for Mother Teresa (*Care*), Brown directed his attention to the "take back" theme. In an excerpt from a documentary he had used for fundraising, he spoke of how George Washington had inspired his troops at Valley Forge to stay in the Army beyond their enlistments in order to save and then advance the revolution. Brown referred to these people as "winter soldiers" and added that all of us needed to become such soldiers and take back our country. His campaign slogan was "Take Back America."

Clinton also relied on the introduction, issues, and attack themes in his general election advertising strategy. The introductory ads were variations of *The Man from Hope*, with Clinton promising changes that would "bring hope to the American dream." He had a much greater variety of styles and topics in his issue and attack ads. Some issue ads focused on broad economic promises, others on specific policy concerns, while others were vague on details but upbeat in their imagery and enthusiasm. In *Change*, a narrator talked about how Clinton had brought economic growth to Arkansas and would invest in education, training, and jobs as president. Other economic ads that relied on a narrator for speaking focused on how Clinton had kept taxes low and had moved 17,000 people from welfare to work during his twelve years as Arkansas governor; and of how numerous financial experts, including Noble Prize winners, supported Clinton's economic plan (*Steady, Even*). Clinton spoke in some issue ads, saying that he "will end welfare as we know it," and that he would work on education, training, jobs, and health care as parts of his program to "put people first" (*Second Chance, Rebuild America*). His final issue ads had imagery of people, Clinton speaking to audiences while emphasizing changes and promising to get the country moving again, and attempting to create solidarity behind his efforts by claiming "if you have hope, you're not alone" (*You're Not Alone*). While these ads were quite upbeat and offered a variety of new programs, there was a serious problem that Clinton and the Democrats needed to overcome.

The Democrats had won seven of the nine presidential elections held from 1932 to 1964 but then lost five of the next six. Many critics had attributed this turn of fortune to the party's lack of interest in non-economic issues, particularly crime and governmental cost. In an effort to broaden his appeal beyond economic issues and recruit new supporters, Clinton addressed these concerns by saying he would work to control crime, supported the death penalty, and he had balanced twelve consecutive budgets in Arkansas while cutting $140 billion in spending (*Leaders*).

The Clinton campaign devoted a substantial amount of its advertising efforts to attacking Bush over his failed promises and his weak performance once in office. In *Curtains*, a narrator pointed out how economic conditions had become worse since 1988 while the ad included imagery of Bush promising thirty million new jobs and then denying that the national economy was in recession. This theme was also emphasized in an ad about the economic conditions in Bush's home state of Texas (*Energy*). After referring to the promise of thirty million new jobs, the narrator said this was 29 million too short. He then pointed out that 160,000 jobs had been lost in the Texas energy industry during Bush's tenure as president. Other economic ads attacked Bush for job losses in the automobile industry and for approximately 1.4 million industrial jobs throughout the nation (*Industry*). There was also an ad that accused Bush of giving Japanese industries trade advantages while getting little in return. In this instance, the Bush administration had classified a truck as a car for import purposes (*Looking*). There were also ads about the recent closing of a textile factory in Tennessee with the firm moving its manufacturing activities to El Salvador. The ad included interviews with long time workers who had lost their jobs and concluding by holding Bush responsible for the 117,000 textile jobs that no longer existed throughout the South (*Morning*).

The attacks on Bush's economic record also focused on taxes. Bush had attacked Clinton, as shown previously, as favoring tax increases. In response, the Clinton campaign attacked Bush over his tax record and frequently used imagery of the 1988 slogan of "read my lips, no new taxes." One ad began with imagery of Bush making that promise and then reviewed how he had broken it by signing legislation that raised taxes on the middle class while reducing them for the rich (*Promise*). There were also some tax related ads about Bush that were more personal in nature. One began with imagery from an ad that Bush had used to attack Clinton for advocating a tax increase (*Scary*). With this, the narrator talked about the tax and economic record of Bush and concluded with the claim that "nothing can be frightening then four more years of Bush." There were ads that even questioned Bush's own tax payments. One said he had lived, vacationed, and golfed in Maine while claiming residency in Texas and this had helped him "avoid" $165 million in taxes (*Maine*).

The Clinton advertising strategy worked because it denied Bush effective use of a major rhetorical device that Republican candidates frequently use to defeat Democrats; the threat of higher taxes if the Democrats win. Clinton made numerous promises about economic changes that could by implemented by an activist and more expensive government. Republicans rarely oppose popular government programs but they usually attack them indirectly by fighting against higher taxes. Clinton's advertising strategy allowed him to make expensive promises for policy changes but he then neutralized Bush's use of the tax issue with claims that Bush could not be trusted to keep promises on this matter.

Perot

The 1992 campaign involved an unusually strong showing by an independent candidate. Ross Perot used a videostyle that was unusual for a political campaign. Instead of relying primarily on short ads of thirty or sixty seconds duration with imagery and frequent uses of narrators, Perot spoke directly to the voters for extended periods of time and used charts and graphs as visual aids for making his case about the need for fundamental changes in government spending and taxation. In one example, Perot talked about the national debt. He attacked the nation's leaders, saying they had too many perks of office, had lost touch with ordinary people, and did not believe we were in a recession. Perot used charts about consumer spending, rates of production, and employment trends while advancing these charges (*Oops*).

Perot did not completely disregard the use of short ads, he had some, but the ones he used were not as central to his advertising strategy as they were to those of his rivals. The most frequently used type of short ad in the Perot campaign was that of a printed message rolling on the screen as the narrator spoke, often about the size of the national debt. In one such ad, *Children*, the message focused on how we were leaving a debt to our children and that we needed a proven businessman to balance the budget, expand the tax base and give the American dream back to our children. The narrative was complemented by imagery of children. A similar ad, *Storm*, contained imagery of a storm with wording about how the debt was a threatening storm. The debt was described as an ill wind that was destroying jobs and consuming $199 billion annually that could be used to create jobs. The ad concluded with the narrator remarking that the debt was not an act of nature was irresponsible, but not uncontrollable, "The choice is yours, the issue is the national debt."

The Perot campaign used other metaphor related ads that were similar in style. It used one with a ticking clock and a narrator talking about the threats posed by the national debt (*Time*). Another one relied upon medical imagery of heartbeat measurement with commentary about the critical condition of American health care. The narrator talked about how much we were spending on health care and of how little we were getting in return (*Healthcare*). There were also ads with falling rain and remarks about the failures of "trickle down economics," and of a skyscraper while a narrator spoke of the need for creating urban enterprise zones (*Trickle Down, Cities*).

Perot also attacked his two rivals. Without actually mentioning their names, he said Bush was responsible for the inability of the national government to respond to difficult economic conditions (*No More Voodoo*). Finally, and with supportive imagery that included a map of Arkansas with a chicken sketched inside it, Perot told voters of how the "Arkansas economic miracle" had indeed created many new jobs, but most of them were low paid ones in the poultry industry. If people did not want an economic future where they would support themselves by "plunking chickens," they should vote for him (*Chicken Feathers*). While he did not win the election or even come close to carrying any state, Perot ran stronger in the popular vote (18.9 percent) than any candidate from outside the two major political parties since Theodore Roosevelt in 1912. His efforts may well have contributed to Bush's defeat by providing an option other than supporting Clinton for conservative and moderate voters.

Chapter 4

ELECTIONS WITH SURROGATE INCUMBENTS: 1988 and 2000

GENERAL OVERVIEW

The incumbent president has sought another term of office in eight of the past thirteen national elections. Every election does not have an incumbent as a candidate, however. The constitutional provision limiting a president to only two terms has created the conditions for a third category of modern elections, those in which the incumbent is not available for reelection. There have been four instances over the past four decades when an election lacked an incumbent; 1960, 1968, 1988, and 2000. Three of these, 1968 excepted, were similar in that the incumbent was completing his second term and had to retire. The other, 1968, saw the incumbent of five years, Lyndon Johnson; announce in March of that year that he would not seek the additional term to which he was constitutionally eligible. All four elections have one significant feature in common; the presidential party nominated the sitting vice president as the potential successor of the retiring incumbent. These nominees included; Richard Nixon (1960), Hubert H. Humphrey (1968); George Bush (1988), and Albert Gore Jr. (2000). I depict those comprising this category as elections with surrogate incumbents (see Abramson, Aldrich, and Rhode, 1990, 2002; Ceaser and Busch, 2001; CQ Press, 2005; Germond and Witcover, 1989; Nelson, 1980, 2001; Pomper, 1989, 2001; and White, 1961, and 1969 for detailed explanations of the leading events, contexts, and outcomes of the elections of 1960, 1968, 1988, and 2000).

While these nominations appear to be commonplace and even unsurprising by today's standards, they are unique when compared to party choices of the nineteenth and early twentieth century. Vice presidents were rarely taken seriously as potential national leaders until Harry Truman assumed the presidency three months into Franklin D. Roosevelt's fourth term and led the nation through one of its most critical times, the concluding months of World War II and the onset of the Cold War (Goldstein, 1982). One can find support for the limited importance of the vice presidency as a stepping stone to higher office in the fact that only two vice presidents were candidates in general elections prior to 1960; John Adams (1796) and Martin Van Buren (1836). Nineteen elections before 1960 lacked incumbents. Today's practice of nominating the vice president as the potential successor of the retiring incumbent is not a result of political chance. Instead, it has resulted from widespread changes in the nature of the presidency itself, in the vice presidency, in the conduct of national campaigns, and in the expanding influence of mass media as the most powerful channel of political communication (Nelson, 1988).

In a previous work (2002), *Missed Opportunity: Gore, Incumbency, and Television in Election 2000,* I explained the reasons for the political rise of the modern vice presidency. I summarize those reasons here. Perhaps the most important reason accounting the significance of the vice presidency is the extensive growth in the scope of the presidency, as discussed earlier in Chapter One. The presidency, as an institution, did not begin in 1789 with the same powers that it possesses today. Instead, the office initially was very limited in power and expanded in scope over many decades primarily because of the efforts of individual presidents in responding to political exigencies (Cronin and Genovese, 1998). Political scientists often describe the president by a number of titles relating to his political and administrative responsibilities; party leader, chief legislator, commander in chief, chief diplomat, tribune of the people, leader of the free world, etc. The constitution does not provide for these roles, although it does not prohibit them either. The roles were created over the past two centuries.

Prior to 1940, presidential candidates did not select their vice presidential running mates. The running mates were chosen by the national conventions which looked at one factor only, how to balance the national ticket and win the election. Vice presidential candidates were chosen because they could help win the electoral votes of a specific state (Tally, 1992). For example, in 1844, the Democrats decided their presidential nominee, former House Speaker James K. Polk (Tennessee), needed a running mate from Pennsylvania. They confined their search to this one state and continued, despite some rejections, until George Dallas accepted. Such practices encouraged presidents to ignore their vice presidents after the election. Presidents even considered vice presidents as members of the legislative branch and required them to have their office in the Capitol

Building. The vice president was recognized as a member of the executive branch only after Eisenhower moved Nixon's office to the White House office complex during the 1950s and made Nixon into an integral member of his administration (Hatfield, 1997). Today, vice presidents spend much of their time campaigning for the president's reelection, explaining and defending presidential actions before mass media and the general public, representing the president at diplomatic settings, advising the president, and carrying out the administrative assignments the president gives them. These roles have transformed the vice president into the leading political surrogate of the president (Nelson, 1988). Several years of such behavior provides a vice president with a unique vantage point from which to seek the presidency when the incumbent retires. A vice president's own partisans nominate him because they approve of this surrogate role. The recurring nature of events in this context over the past four decades and the likelihood that they will happen again encourages me to describe elections when the incumbent retires as elections with surrogate incumbents.

The vice presidential office is a double edged sword for its occupants. It helps them unite their own partisans in their nomination quests and makes the quests all that much easier. The effects are limited, however, because the vice president is not the actual incumbent and he cannot employ the advantages of incumbency in winning the general election. The vice president is unable to pre-empt national television and announce his response to a major foreign crisis, he cannot sign bills into law at elaborate public ceremonies, and he cannot deliver the State of the Union Address at the beginning of the election year and attempt to create the agenda of political debate for the coming year. In essence, he is both an incumbent and challenger at the same time. He is a highly visible member of the administration but also appears to be an outsider (see Trent and Friedenberg, 2004). His advertising strategy should reflect this ambiguous circumstance. The surrogate incumbent is simultaneously both strong and weak. As a result, the four recent ones were involved in elections whose outcomes were different from elections involving incumbents. These four elections were among the most competitive and closest ones of recent times. The ones in 1960, 1968, and 2000 were the three closest elections of the past century with less than a one percent difference existing between the two leading candidates in the distribution of the popular vote.

In 1960, Dwight D. Eisenhower was retiring after two terms as president. He had won the two previous elections by large popular and electoral vote margins and was widely respected by much of the American public. Nixon had been Eisenhower's major political surrogate during those eight years and had helped define much of the partisan political role of the modern vice president. Eisenhower was not a career politician and was not particularly interested in fulfilling the presidential role of party leader. He left much of that role to Nixon. Nixon spoke frequently at Republican fund raising events, assisted candidates for congressional and state office, attacked Democrats on many occasions, and built a strong and loyal following among the nation's Republican leaders and activists. His support among Republicans was so extensive at the beginning of the campaign that no rivals, and there were some who wanted to become candidates, dared oppose Nixon for the nomination.

The Democrats were optimistic about their chances in 1960. The national economy was in recession and many people were worried that we were falling behind the Soviet Union in science, technology, and military power. This had contributed to a sweeping Democratic victory in the 1958 congressional elections. The opposition party had gained about forty seats in the House and fifteen in the Senate. With this, five major candidates stepped forward in pursuit of the nomination. After a spirited battle through several primaries and a dramatic first ballot vote, Senator John F. Kennedy (Massachusetts) defeated rivals Hubert H. Humphrey, Lyndon B. Johnson, Stuart Symington, and Adlai Stevenson. The Democrats were united behind Kennedy who selected his strongest rival Johnson as a running mate and who held out the promise of victory. The hoped for victory was there, although it was close. Voters saw Nixon and Kennedy as two very different representatives of the next generation of national leaders and were about evenly divided over their choice. Kennedy defeated Nixon by only .17 percent of the popular vote. Nixon was unable to translate Eisenhower's immense personal following into a successful bid for succession. The vice presidency had provided Nixon with an unusual opportunity to win the nomination, which he used very effectively, but it could not carry him all the way to the Oval Office; at least not yet.

The second recent election with a surrogate incumbent was in 1968 when Lyndon Johnson decided against seeking another term because of setbacks in Vietnam. As discussed previously, this election looked like it would involve the defeat of a weak incumbent until the latter part of March when Johnson announced to a national television audience that he would not seek another term. Two candidates were already in the race at the time of Johnson's withdrawal; Senators Eugene McCarthy (Minnesota) and Robert Kennedy (New York), while a third, vice president Hubert Humphrey would enter soon. The ensuing nomination battle was intense, involving the assassination of Kennedy in June, a divisive convention debate over Vietnam, and violence in the streets and nearby Grant Park between Chicago police and anti-war demonstrators. Humphrey won the nomination but entered the general election trailing far behind the Republican candidate, Richard Nixon, in all nationwide polls (Gallup Poll, 2006). While Kennedy's death led some people to doubt that Humphrey would have otherwise been the nominee, Humphrey did have the support of most of the Democratic Party's elected leaders and state chairman by mid-May. He had attained this support in much the same manner as Nixon had in 1960, by acting as the president's most important political surrogate from his position of vice president. Most Democratic leaders wanted Johnson for a second term; they found little difficulty in switching their loyalty to his surrogate Humphrey after the end of March. Humphrey had used the opportunities of the modern vice presidency to secure his party's nomination.

The Republican campaign of 1968 differed considerably from its Democratic counterpart. Nixon dispatched his main early rival, Governor George Romney (Michigan) in the New Hampshire primary and faced no significant opposition for several weeks. Nelson Rockefeller had been reluctant to enter the race after Romney's withdrawal but changed his mind and announced his candidacy in late April. Ronald Reagan followed with his announcement of candidacy several weeks later but neither man, acting either individually or together with the hint that the two of them would appear on the same ticket, could stop Nixon. After a first ballot victory and an early lead in the polls, Nixon held on and defeated Humphrey and independent candidate George Wallace. He attained 43.4 percent of the popular vote with Humphrey and Wallace getting 42.7 and 13.4 percent respectively.

The Humphrey campaign differed from those of the other three vice presidents; Nixon, Bush, and Gore. These three candidates ran for president upon the retirement of a two term incumbent and each promised to continue the policies of the outgoing administration. Humphrey was headed for defeat when voters saw him as the surrogate of the 1968 version of Lyndon Johnson. Only after Humphrey promised changes relating to Vietnam and then directed his appeals to the unfinished components of Johnson's domestic policy, did his campaign take off. In a sense, Humphrey almost succeeded in convincing voters to elect him as the major surrogate of the 1964 version of Lyndon Johnson, who was a strong incumbent.

This chapter follows the same format as the previous two; I direct attention to the advertising strategies of the candidates who sought the presidency in the two most recent elections which comprise the category I discuss. The last two elections with surrogate incumbents occurred in 1988 and 2000. These two were similar in several ways besides the fact that the vice president was the standard bearer of the presidential party. The two vice presidents, Bush and Gore, did not have the luxury of Nixon in winning an uncontested nomination but they also did not face the agony of Humphrey by winning a bitter one. Bush and Gore began their respective campaigns as the front-runners for their nominations, fought with one or more rivals in a few primaries, won nearly every contest, and secured victories by mid-March when their last remaining opponents abandoned their fleeting efforts.

Despite his eight years as Reagan's vice president and political surrogate, George Bush faced five rivals in his quest for the 1988 Republican nomination. His strongest was Senator Robert Dole (Kansas) who was minority leader in the upper chamber. Bush and Dole had similar biographies; both were approximately the same age, were combat veterans of the Second World War, were moderately conservative in ideology, and had many years of experience in the national government. They differed in one crucial feature, however, the locus of their political experiences. Dole's actions were concentrated exclusively in the legislative branch while nearly all of Bush's had taken place in the executive branch. This proved crucial in the final outcome. Dole struck first by winning the Iowa caucuses while Bush came in a weak third. Bush responded with three crucial wins over Bush in New Hampshire, South Carolina, and Illinois, results that encouraged Dole to abandon his efforts. Bush had the active support of the Republican governors of each of these three states. The acquisition of their backing would have been far more difficult if Bush had been unable to rely upon his surrogate role. He had worked with all three governors on many occasions during the previous years in generating policy and political support for the Reagan administration. The legislative branch had not provided comparable opportunities for Dole to generate this level of support.

There were four other aspirants for the nomination, but none of them fared particularly well. Each of them had dropped out of the race by mid-March. They were Reverend Pat Robertson who finished second in Iowa but who never had a decent showing in any other state; Congressman Jack Kemp (New York), former governor Pete Du Pont (Delaware), and retired general Alexander Haig. Haig quit after finishing last in Iowa, Du Pont ended his efforts when he ran poorly in New Hampshire, while Robertson and Kemp withdrew after finishing far behind Bush and Dole in South Carolina.

In its role as the opposition, the Democratic Party offered a much more competitive battle for its nomination. The winner was governor Michael Dukakis (Massachusetts) but he did not clinch a victory until mid-May, fully two months after Bush had become the de facto Republican choice. The outcomes in the initial states of Iowa and New Hampshire provided few clues relating to the identity of the ultimate winner. Dukakis came in third in Iowa, losing a narrow decision to Congressman Richard Gephardt (Missouri) and Senator Paul Simon (Illinois), and then recorded a strong victory in New Hampshire. Many observers saw these results as inconclusive in that voters may have been influenced by the presence of well known candidates from nearby states.

A new event, Super Tuesday, took place in mid-March. Sixteen states, mostly in the Southeast, had arranged for their primaries to take place on the same day in hopes that collectively they could influence the national outcome. This event was the creation of Democratic governors, but it turned out to be the political equivalent of a Frankenstein monster. Bush won every primary and took an insurmountable lead for his party's nomination, but four Democrats won contests this day and helped make their party's race even more confusing. The day's winners were Dukakis, Senator Albert Gore Jr. (Tennessee), and Reverend Jesse Jackson, who won five state apiece, and Gephardt who took one state. The losers were Simon, Jerry Brown and Gary Hart, who were a former governor and senator from California and Colorado respectively. The battle continued through other states such as Michigan, Wisconsin, and New York before Dukakis emerged as the front-runner and eventually drove his rivals from the race.

The general election campaign between Bush and Dukakis was quite competitive with the lead in the national polls changing hands on several occasions. Bush eventually won because of two important developments that are reflected in the advertising strategies of the candidates. These are discussed in more detail in the next two sections of this chapter. Bush relied upon the satisfaction that voters had with the Reagan administration and upon the inability of Dukakis to effectively introduce himself to the electorate to win. He linked his own candidacy with the statesmanlike imagery of Reagan and then defined Dukakis as a dangerous and incompetent politician who could not be trusted to act in the nation's best interest. Bush's margin of victory was solid but not overwhelming. He attained 53.4 percent of the vote compared to 45.6 percent for Dukakis.

The most recent surrogate incumbent election, 2000, was unusually close and is now one of those infrequent battles in which the winner of the popular vote finished second in the electoral vote and loses. This election was also unusual in the sense that it was not decided until six weeks after the election when the Supreme Court awarded Florida's 25 electoral votes to Bush after an unresolved vote counting dispute. The nomination and general election campaigns in 2000 were similar to those of 1988 in the sense that the vice president began as the front-runner and remained that way within the presidential party while many candidates sought the nomination of the opposition party. The battles were of only limited duration, however. Both of them ended in early March after the conclusion of eleven primaries of Super Tuesday.

Gore encountered relatively little trouble in winning the Democratic nomination. He attracted only one rival, former Senator Bill Bradley (New Jersey). Gore defeated Bradley by a margin of 63 to 35 percent in Iowa and by a much closer one, 52 to 48 percent in New Hampshire. The Bradley challenge faded afterwards, with Gore capturing all of the Super Tuesday primaries. Bradley withdrew from the race immediately. The Republican battle ended at the same time, although it was more contentious. Twelve candidates initially sought the nomination, but six proved to be so ineffective in raising funds that they each quit the race before the end of 1999. Four others were effectively gone after the Iowa and New Hampshire votes, if not before. Only one candidate, Senator John McCain (Arizona) proved to be a competitive rival to the overwhelming front-runner, Governor George W. Bush (Texas).

Bush began his efforts in March, 1999 and raised more money and endorsements than all of his rivals combined. He relied upon his father's contributors from past races, on the supporters who had backed him in his two campaigns for governor of Texas, and on over twenty Republican governors, including his brother in Florida. A majority of Republican voters supported Bush in every primary. McCain tried a different appeal, however. He ran well among independents who could vote in the Republican primaries in selected states. With strong showings among these people, McCain defeated Bush in New Hampshire and seven other states, but lost elsewhere, including in such major states as Ohio, New York, and California.

The general election campaign was competitive and very close with both candidates, Gore and Bush, failing to take command of the polls at any time. Eventually, both focused their efforts on about twelve battleground states where the outcome seemed in doubt. Even these were inconclusive, with the two candidates dividing the electoral votes of these states about evenly. Bush lost the popular vote by about one half of one percent, 48.4 to 47.9, and appears to have been helped in attaining his victory by the presence in the race of a third party candidate from the political left, Ralph Nader, and by the voting problems in Florida that inflicted far more damage on Gore than they did on him.

INCUMBENTS

Surrogate incumbents occupy an ambiguous political position when they seek the presidency. In one sense, they are unusually strong candidates who hold out the prospect of victory, but in another they appear relatively weak and threaten to end their party's tenure in office. As is true for all candidates, regardless of their particular vantage points in any given election, surrogate incumbents must divide their efforts into two distinct phases; winning the nomination and contesting the general election. The first phase, the nomination, is usually the easier of the two because the surrogate begins with an advantage over his rivals. His service as vice president has provided him with opportunities unavailable to the other candidates. He has already fulfilled one of the leading responsibilities of the modern vice presidency, representing the president at party gatherings, and he had done so over many years. Three of the four modern surrogates; Nixon, Bush, and Gore, had been vice president for eight years when they ran for president. All four vice presidents began the quests with widespread support within their own parties. They needed to implement advertising strategies where they linked their campaigns to the popularity of the retiring incumbent. The second phase is much more difficult, however. Incumbents almost always leave office with mixed legacies and this can influence the outcomes of general elections. Voters who do not respect an incumbent may transfer that disrespect to the surrogate while some of the incumbent's followers may see the surrogate as a political understudy undeserving of their respect. The surrogate needs an advertising strategy where he comes across as an independent political actor who will continue the policies of the retiring incumbent. Bush appears to have done so, while Gore clearly failed.

Bush

George Bush's televised advertising in the nomination campaign was aimed at accomplishing the three major needs of personal introduction, definition of issues, and attacks on opponents. In almost all instances Bush tried to link his candidacy to Reagan and present himself as a qualified replacement for a president who clearly was held in very high esteem by Republicans. Several ads directly addressed this theme. In *Inaugural*, the imagery included scenes of Bush taking the oath of office as vice president with the narrator telling the audience of Bush's background. The commentary focused on Bush's actions as a fighter pilot in the Second World War, of his years in private business as a Texas oilman, and about his governmental experiences prior to his tenure as vice president when he had served as a congressman, United Nations ambassador, Director of the Central Intelligence Agency, and envoy to China. A related ad, *Free World Leadership*, carried this theme into Bush's work as vice president and included imagery and a related narrative about his various meetings with a variety of world leaders while serving as vice president. These two ads concluded by summarizing Bush's unique qualifications for office that derived from his role as presidential surrogate with the slogan "George Bush, ready on day one to be a great president." This theme resurfaced in a variety of other introductory ads, including ones where Bush talked directly to the audience and in others where a narrator was the speaker. Both formats referred to Bush's personal and governmental experiences and strongly emphasized that his eight years as vice president had made him more qualified than any of the other candidates for the nation's highest office.

The advertising also linked Bush to Reagan even when the topics were issues or attacks. In *Strong Defense*, Bush told his audience about the need for a strong national defense and then emphasized how he had helped to bring it about through his personal combat experiences and political actions as a member of the Reagan administration. Attack ads were similar in content. Robert Dole rapidly emerged as Bush's major rival and therefore was the target of the attack ads. In one ad, *16 of 34*, a narrator spoke of how frequently Dole had voted against Reagan on leading issues, of how strongly Bush had backed Reagan, and then implied that Reagan had chosen Bush as vice president because of loyalty. Finally, the Bush campaign employed comparative ads with imagery and narratives about how hard Bush had worked on such issues as arms control and taxes and of how little Dole had accomplished on these same issues (*Period/ Straddle*). These ads also concluded with the slogan about Bush's readiness to be a great president.

In addition to emphasizing the three necessary themes as they related to themselves individually, Bush's rivals also needed to counter his claims that he possessed unique qualifications that derived from the vice presidency. One ad employing this theme was Dole's *Footprints*. Here, an individual, clearly symbolizing George Bush, was shown walking through the snow and following in the footsteps of a giant but leaving no actual footprints of his own. In addition to this subtle attack on Bush, Dole uses ads that were more explicit. The ad *Difference* had a narrator speaking about Dole's accomplishments as a congressional leader on taxes, social security, and arms control while contrasting this with Bush's lack of unique contributions on these same issues as vice president.

While Dole was able to address the question of Bush's tenure as vice president, the brevity of the nomination campaign actually prevented Bush's rivals, even Dole, from engaging in much more than personal introductions. There is a review in a previous chapter of Dole's introductory advertising from the 1996 campaign. His introductory ads in 1988 were similar to those of the latter campaign. Dole emphasized that a combination of his Midwestern background, Second World War combat activities, and years of service in Congress had provided him with the values and experiences that are needed for the presidency. He also employed issue ads that reflected the contradictions that existed within the Republican Party and the Reagan administration over the direction of government. One ad addressed the long time conservative goal of reducing government spending in order to control the size of the annual deficit and the rising interest rates that were a consequence of increased debt (*Difference/Dole/Bush*). Another spoke about expanding the strength of the nation's armed forces in order to deal more effectively with the Soviet Union (*Gorbachev*). Neither ad explicitly drew attention to the difficulty the nation might encounter in simultaneously pursuing two incompatible goals.

Haig, the first of Bush's rivals to depart from the race, talked about how his military experiences qualified him for office. In *Peace*, a narrator told the audience that twelve generals had been president but that no wars had begun while any of them were in office. Haig linked himself to this fact by saying that he had led troops in combat and could bring about peace. Perhaps suspecting that voters might consider a general to be different from them, Haig tried to show that he was "everyman," as Trent and Friedenberg noted, in an ad where he was eating pizza (*Pizza*).

Du Pont devoted much of his advertising to issues. He directed a number of attacks to the cost of farm subsidies and demanded their elimination. In *Scarecrow*, Du Pont used imagery of a sad scarecrow becoming happy when $26 billion in annual subsidies arrived. Kemp directed his ads at a variety of economically interrelated issues such as taxes, social security, job growth, and a balanced budget. The most widely used approach was for a narrator to tell viewers that Kemp, who was supported by imagery were he was meeting with people, could reduce the size of the deficit, reduce taxes, and balance the budget without threatening social security. Kemp's ads usually ended with the slogan, "If he wins, we all win" (*Bio, Deficit, Difference*).

Robertson was the only Republican other than Dole to offer Bush a challenge of consequence. He devoted a number of months to a major effort aimed at organizing Christian conservatives for large turnouts in the Iowa caucuses. It paid off, as Robertson finished in second place, behind Dole and ahead of Bush, but Robertson found little support elsewhere and his campaign soon ended. His ads were issue related and focused mainly opposition to federal financial aid to communist nations and on the need for reducing the tax burden on families (*Communists, Families*). Most of Robertson's ads concluded with his slogan of "Bring common sense back to government."

Bush entered the general election campaign of 1988 as a much stronger candidate than any of the other surrogates who have sought the presidency during the past few decades. Unlike Nixon, Humphrey, and Gore, he was actually leading his opposition party rival in the polls at the conclusion of the national conventions. Moreover, the other vice presidents failed to gain the lead at any time during their campaigns. Each of them did manage to narrow their gaps so that survey analysts proclaimed that the respective races were too close to call, however. In contrast, Bush had a lead that varied between five and ten percentage points, depending on which poll one views, in mid-August and he held on to it through the rest of the campaign. These results encouraged the survey analysts to forecast a Bush victory. Bush did not always lead in the polls, however. The early conclusion of the Republican nomination campaign, brought about by Dole's withdrawal in late March, deprived Bush of the intensive media coverage that accompanies such contests. As a result of his absence from national news and the corresponding attention still directed at Michael Dukakis and other Democrats, Bush fell behind his future rival in the polls for several months. He trailed Dukakis throughout May, June, and particularly during July. The Democrats held their national convention in this latter month. The poll results were only a temporary problem for Bush, however. He seized the lead in mid-August when the Republican convention provided him with an opportunity for intense media coverage and forced Dukakis temporarily out of the public eye. Afterwards, Dukakis was the candidate who needed to regain the lead (Gallup Poll, 2006).

An initial matter that needs addressing at this time is to determine why Bush was so much stronger than each of the other surrogates. Related to this is an explanation of why Bush was the only one to win. Bush had two strengths; the incumbent Ronald Reagan was popular, and both Reagan and Bush were relying upon that popularity to contest the election. Despite a recession during the first two years of his presidency and the Iran-Contra scandal during the final two, Reagan enjoyed high approval ratings for the American public throughout his eight years in office. The nation was at peace in 1988 and was relatively prosperous, although the massive budget deficits of the Reagan years posed a serious threat to that prosperity. Voters were not angry, and therefore many were quite likely to support the status quo. Dukakis, rather than Bush, had to confront the problem of convincing satisfied people to make a change. In contrast, the nation was in a recession in 1960, divided by a controversial war in 1968, and angered over personal misconduct of the president in 2000. The second strength that worked in Bush's favor was his willingness to link his candidacy to Reagan and in Reagan's eagerness to help him in that endeavor. As described above, Bush directed many televised ads to illustrating and explaining his actions as an integral member of the Reagan administration. The other surrogates either avoided (Gore and Humphrey) or downplayed (Nixon) their roles as presidential surrogates.

The closeness of the election of 1960 raised questions among Republicans of what they might have done differently to assist Nixon more effectively against Kennedy. One of their strongest conclusions was that Eisenhower should have campaigned more extensively for Nixon. Reagan was aware of this debate and wanted to make certain that he did all he could to advance his own vice president. He spent the last two weeks of the campaign making highly attended personal appearances on behalf of his vice president (Dover, 2002). Bush carried every state where Reagan spoke and some of them were very competitive.

Bush used three major themes in his general election advertising: biographical information, linkages to Reagan, and attacks against Dukakis. The biographical themes reemphasized the messages from earlier in the year; Bush's previous experience in the executive branch uniquely qualified him for the presidency. The Bush campaign used ads containing imagery of the White House with Bush telling the audience he was the man to sit at the president's desk; of Soviet Leader Mikhail Gorbachev while emphasizing Bush's foreign policy background; and of members of the Bush family (*I Am That Man, Gorbachev, Family*). These ads concluded with a slogan that reinforced the continuity of Bush's personal accomplishments with the fulfillment of his promises for the next four years, "Experienced Leadership for America's Future."

This slogan also was widely used in ads that linked Bush with Reagan. Much of the time, the emphasis was on foreign policy and national security. Bush reiterated Reagan's theme of "peace through strength" in a number of complimentary ads. In *Eliminating Nuclear Weapons*, a narrator focused on the peace component by talking about Bush's importance in helping Reagan bring about reductions in nuclear weapon stockpiles between the superpowers. The strength component appeared in *Gorbachev*. The narrator reminded viewers that the next president would have to deal with Gorbachev and a variety of foreign problems. Imagery of both the Soviet leader and of Bush with the military accompanied these remarks. The slogan appeared at the end of each of these ads.

Perhaps the most famous theme, or infamous depending upon one's point of view, in the Bush advertising campaign was the attack strategy employed against Dukakis. When he accepted the Democratic nomination, Dukakis told his cheering partisans that the campaign was about "competence, not ideology." The Bush ads questioned this competence by directing attention to several divisive social issues which they associated with Dukakis. The strategy was to depict Dukakis as a dangerous, irresponsible "liberal" who should not be entrusted with national leadership.

The most controversial ad was *Willie Horton*. This ad focused attention on the Massachusetts prisoner furlough program and on an unfortunate incident involving one of the inmates participating in it, Horton. Here, certain felons were eligible for short term releases, perhaps for several days or a weekend, and would then return to custody. While on such a release, Horton raped a woman. The ad questioned the need for such a program and implicitly blamed Dukakis for Horton's latest crimes. It included a picture of Horton, who was African-American. Many critics denounced the Bush campaign for pandering to racism. The Bush campaign did not actually use this ad; the ad had been created and distributed by a private group not associated with Bush. However, the Bush campaign supplemented it by running a number of crime related ads, including *Revolving Door*. Here, a narrator attacked the furlough program, talked of crimes committed by those using it, and employed stark black and white imagery of prisoners walking through a revolving door into and then out of prison.

The ad was strong on emotion and short on both facts and context. Massachusetts was not the sole place that had prisoner furlough programs and Horton was not the unique inmate who had committed crimes while participating. A number of federal convicts had committed crimes during the Reagan administration while they were on furlough. Dukakis should have countered the ad by raising these facts. In way of a personal story related to this policy and which illustrates how widespread it was, in 1987 I was employed as Assistant Professor at the University of Tennessee at Martin. Two inmates (robbery) from a nearby penitentiary used a furlough to visit the university, meet with me for academic advice, and register for classes. They returned to prison, were paroled several weeks later, then attended college, and eventually graduated.

Other attacks on Dukakis focused on the environment, taxes, and national defense. Supported by stark imagery of extensive pollution, the narrator in *Boston Harbor* told viewers that the harbor in Boston was the nations most polluted. He then referred to Dukakis' promise to do for the nation what he had done in Massachusetts. The imagery in *Tax Blizzard* was of numerous tax bills arriving at a home while the narrator told viewers of the numerous tax increases that had been implemented in Massachusetts under Dukakis. Finally, in an ad that exploited a communication failure of the Dukakis campaign, Bush used imagery from the Democrat's own advertising to attack him. In *Tank*, the narrator used scenes of Dukakis driving a tank and spoke of the weapons systems the governor had opposed. Dukakis looked more like the cartoon characters "Snoopy" or "Rocky the Squirrel" than a potential president. The Bush attack ads served their purpose; they questioned the competence of Dukakis and reinforced the view that the vice president had the requisite political experience for leading the nation.

Gore

Al Gore began his quest for the Democratic nomination in 2000 from a political vantage point similar to that of Bush in 1988. He enjoyed widespread support among his own partisans and was the overwhelming front-runner to win the nomination. In fact, he had an even easier time than Bush. Unlike Bush, who had five opponents and finished third in Iowa before winning every other state, Gore did not lose a single contest to his only rival, Bill Bradley. In fact, Bradley dropped out of the race in early March after losing all eleven primaries on "Super Tuesday." Despite the easy nomination triumph, Gore lost the election. Granted, his loss can, to some extent, be attributed to the problems in Florida. A more compelling explanation of the loss rests with Gore himself, however, and particularly in the manner in which he presented himself to voters. He did not seek office as the vice president. Instead, he ran as if he were simply another member of Congress, indistinguishable from any other candidate. Gore did not exploit his most useful asset; his eight years as the leading surrogate in an administration that many people, despite reservations about the moral character of Bill Clinton, considered successful on a wide range of foreign and domestic policy matters.

An example of this approach occurs in *Reporter*, the major biographical ad Gore used during the primaries. The ad begins with a narrator talking about Gore's background; "he was the son of a U.S. Senator but he chose to serve in Vietnam, he was a family man, and upon conclusion of his military service had started a career as a news reporter. It was in this latter context that Gore saw what was wrong in the nation and then changed his career and fought back." After a summary of Gore's major issues; working families, prescription drugs, health care, education, and the environment, the ad concluded with the slogan that was to be repeated in many subsequent ads, "Al Gore, fighting for us." Bill

Clinton did not exist in the imagery projected in this ad and the issues were not unique to the vantage point of the vice presidency.

Gore devoted most of his nomination advertising to the issues mentioned above. He usually concluded his ads with the slogan where he was "fighting for us." In *Champion*, which was aimed at working families, Gore was shown talking to a small audience about the president's responsibility to speak for all people, including those often "left behind." He directed attention to prescription drugs and health care in *Only*. Here, the narrator told viewers that Gore was "fighting" the major drug companies and Health Maintenance Organizations (HMO's) over the costs of prescription drugs and the provision of health care for families and children, that he advocated the enactment of a Patients' Bill of Rights, and was the only candidate in the race, of either party, committed to protecting Medicare. Gore also spoke of education. He emphasized his opposition to the use of vouchers and called them a threat to public education, said he was the only candidate to make education a priority, and pointed out that he had attained the endorsements of the major teachers' unions; the American Federation of Teachers and the National Education Association (*Teachers*). There were also ads relating to Gore and the environment. An experienced mountain climber once told viewers that Gore had scaled a peak with him. This illustrated Gore's determination to see things through, the climber remarked (*Frush*). In addition to these issue specific ads, Gore also employed ads lumping the various issues together while focusing primarily on the theme that he was fighting for all of them. Once again, the "fighter" did not attempt to link his ability to win these battles with his vantage point in the administration (*Momentum*).

The general election campaign of 2000 began in early March after Gore and George W. Bush had driven their last rivals from the field in the primaries of "Super Tuesday." The two candidates began attacking one another at this time. Gore used one ad that questioned the poor quality of Texas education and of how little Bush had accomplished in his six years as governor (*Turning*). Bush had made education one of his major issues and would lead efforts to enact the "No Child Left Behind" act after taking office.

The themes that Gore used in his nomination related advertising were actually quite similar to those employed by Bradley. Bradley also used a biographical introduction with imagery where he appeared as an outsider who entered governmental service to advance important causes. Bradley emphasized his experiences as a college and professional basketball player, as a Rhodes Scholar, and as a member of the Senate for eighteen years in his major biographical ad *Crystal City*. Gore had been a member of Congress for sixteen years, eight in each chamber, before becoming vice president. Using the slogan of "It can happen," Bradley supplemented this ad with a variety of appeals related to specific issues. Among them were health care, including his sponsorship of a law that required funding for 48 hours maternity stays in hospitals, and of a deplorable situation when a mother had to choose between food for her family and health care for her ill child. There were also ads focused on the issues of abortion, Bradley claimed he had always been pro-choice; campaign finance reform; racial equality, basketball great Michael Jordon endorsed Bradley and spoke about this issue; gun control; and visions of hope for the future (*Always, Agenda, Chicago, Real Risk, Positive Values*). These were many of the same issues of which Gore spoke. In addition to their similarity on major issues, both men referred to their backgrounds in non-governmental roles, such as basketball and news reporting, and of their years in Congress as qualifying them for the presidency. One ironic feature of the issue related ads that indicates how Gore did not exploit the opportunities provided by his office was that Bradley, the administrative outsider, spoke of how he had brought about a policy change, the maternity leave law (*Mom*), while the insider, Gore, took credit for no such accomplishments but instead spoke exclusively of his goals.

Gore's advertising strategy for the general election differed from what he employed for the nomination in one major way, the use of numerous attacks focused on Bush. With respect to biographical ads and issue related appeals, Gore restated much of what he had used previously. His leading biographical ad, *1969*, focused once again on his family background, including his father's opposition to the Vietnam War and of Gore's own service. It concluded with references to his positions on such issues as toxic wastes, his support for the Gulf War, and the other issues he had addressed during the primaries. The issue ads were also similar with some focusing on a variety of problems while others were directed toward specific matters. In *Bean Counter*, Gore was shown speaking to an outdoor audience while wearing a blue denim shirt. He blasted HMO's over their preeminent concerns with health care costs and said that we needed to return medical decisions to doctors and nurses. The ad *Ian* used the example of a disabled child who had been cut off from aid by an HMO. A narrator told viewers that Gore was "fighting" against HMO's and for a patients' bill of rights. Other issue related ads focused on education, including the need for school accountability, smaller class size, increased discipline, and more support for college tuition (*Accountability*). Once again, Gore was shown speaking to an outdoor audience while dressed casually. Although he did not link himself directly with Clinton, Gore did make some references to Clinton's policies. In one instance he said we needed to keep our economic prosperity, implying that a victory by Bush would pose a clear threat to it, but Gore failed to assert that the Clinton policies might have been partly responsible for its existence (*Interview*).

Gore used an advertising strategy that attacked Bush over many of his domestic policy accomplishments and promises, however. One such issue was prescription drugs. This was an issue of some importance in 2000. The cost of prescription drugs had increased far beyond the normal rate of inflation in recent years, thereby creating a financial burden on persons with fixed incomes such as retirees. In response, politicians called for governmental aid for the purchase of such drugs, rather than for price controls that might limit the cost. Gore called for the Medicare program to pay for the benefits while Bush advocated more financial incentives for HMO's to address the problem. Several Gore ads compared the two proposals and suggested that Gore's was the superior of the two (*Check*). The issue of governmental programs versus private HMO's surfaced again over the issue of health care for children. Gore's ads attacked Bush over the limited coverage his proposals would provide compared to the superior results they claimed would come from the ones Gore advanced (*Care*). Ads questioning Bush's opposition to a patients' bill of rights were also used as part of Gore's attempt to depict Bush as interested in HMO profits rather than public health (*Baby*).

Related to the health care issue was the question of changes in Social Security. Some governmental leaders have raised doubts about the long term financial viability of this retirement system while others have argued that the program is healthy and will remain so for many years to come. Bush advanced a proposal that would have allowed younger workers to invest some of their taxes in private securities where they could attain higher interest payments than existed in the current system. While the proposal sounded intriguing, it also raised a number of unanswered questions. What if the stock market declined in value and the worth of one's social security related investments fell accordingly? The social security system uses incoming receipts to pay benefits for retirees. Would the smaller receipts reduce the benefits for those people who have paid into the system for many years and have been expecting certain payoffs? In *2 promises*, a narrator attacked the dual and competing nature of Bush's proposals by pointing out that he could not keep his promises to younger workers for allowing private investments and to older workers that he would protect their investment. This ad used quotes from the business oriented newspaper Wall Street Journal to question the financial integrity of Bush's plan. A similar ad called attention to a misstatement Bush had made when he accused Gore of wanting to treat social security as if it were a government program. This was followed by another attack on the contradictory nature of Bush's promises (*Confused*).

The Gore campaign attacked Bush on a number of other domestic issues during the final weeks of the year, taxes in particular. Bush had promised a tax cut that would not reduce the size of the financial surplus that had developed during the final years of the Clinton administration and which had been projected to provide $2 trillion in surplus revenue over the next decade. Gore advocated using some of this surplus to finance his economic proposals and reduce the size of the national debt. His ads raised questions about the economic assumptions that Bush used to justify his proposals. One claimed that very little of the tax cut money would make its way to ordinary people while another one said that eight Noble prize winning economists believed that Bush's plan was unsound (*Doesn't*).

Gore also attacked Bush over his accomplishments in Texas with ads proclaiming the state trailed behind the nation in educational quality, environmental controls, and wage levels. One ad had the state where the viewers lived, Ohio for example, slowly morph into Texas as the narrator spoke of the poor quality of life in Bush's home state (*Morph*). Finally, the Gore ads attacked Bush for his environmental record. One accused him of planning to dump nuclear waste in Nevada while pointing out that Bush had received large financial contributions from the nuclear power industry (*Jackpot*).

Gore's effectiveness as a candidate will remain an unanswered question for many years to come because of the closeness and controversial nature of the election outcome. He captured the popular vote by a margin of one half of one percent (500,000 votes) and he might have won the Electoral College tally as well had there been no difficulties in Florida. Despite this uncertainty, Gore appears to have made a major mistake in not relying more on his vantage point of vice president to demonstrate continuity between the outcomes of the immediate past and his promises of leadership for the future. He defined himself and advanced issues and attacks in ways that appeared very similar to those of virtually any aspirant from Congress who seeks a nomination. He failed to use his greatest asset, surrogate of a successful incumbent.

CHALLENGERS

The lack of actual incumbents in certain elections and their replacement with surrogates influences the nomination campaigns of the presidential party, as shown in previous chapters. This influence is most noticeable with respect to the number of challengers who oppose the incumbent in his bid for renomination. Strong incumbents do not attract strong intra-party rivals while weak incumbents may attract one. The extent of competition surrogates encounter is less consistent; it has varied from only one challenger (Gore) to five (Bush). In contrast, the competition within the opposition party is unrelated to the strength or status of the incumbent. All incumbents, regardless of whether they are strong, weak, or surrogate, attract many rivals from the opposition party. This consistency occurs because the electoral structure of American politics does not provide sufficient opportunities for the opposition party to choose its leaders prior to the nomination campaign. Moreover, leaders of the opposition party are not always impressed with the strength of an incumbent and may be willing to offer a challenge that members of the incumbent's party would not consider. The number of candidates who sought the nomination of the opposition party in the four recent surrogate incumbent elections totaled five in 1960, four in 1968, eight in 1988 and twelve in 2000. This consistency in both the political contexts of nomination campaigns and in the number of available candidates for them encourages the candidates, most of whom are relatively unknown to much of the voting public, to devote most of their advertising resources to accomplishing the three essential tasks of introduction, definition of issues, and attacks on rivals. In this section, as with those in previous chapters, I look at the efforts of the two most recent opposition party challengers of surrogate incumbents; Michael Dukakis (1988) and George W. Bush (2000), and at the contexts from which they made their challenges.

Dukakis and the Democrats

Academic and media observers of American presidential elections frequently refer to the events that occur in the year immediately preceding a campaign as the "invisible primary." They use the word "invisible" to indicate that most of the leading events of this period are unpublicized and are of interest to only a limited number of people; political activists and themselves. Candidates spend most of this time raising money, generating endorsements from important party leaders, and developing campaign strategies and organizations. The invisible primary among Democrats in 1987 was unusual in several ways. First, a number of potential candidates that many Democratic activists had counted on to run for president decided against seeking office. Governors Bill Clinton (Arkansas) and Mario Cuomo (New York), Senators Sam Nunn (Georgia) and Charles Robb (Virginia), and Representative Patricia Schroeder (Colorado) initially hinted at candidacy but eventually declined. In addition, two leading candidates who entered the race eventually withdrew because of personal troubles. Former Senator Gary Hart (Colorado), a strong contender in 1984, began 1987 as the front-runner for the nomination. After a strong start, Hart withdrew when the circumstances of a sex scandal damaged his public standing and directed attention away from his policy proposals and more toward his character. Senator Joseph Biden (Delaware), whose initial support was weaker than Hart's, withdrew after failing to generate much support and then being criticized for plagiarizing a speech previously used by a British Labour Party leader. Hart eventually changed his mind and reentered the race, but never regained his front-runner standing. The race attracted seven candidates; Governor Michael Dukakis (Massachusetts), former Governor Bruce Babbitt (Arizona), Senators Albert Gore Jr. (Tennessee) and Paul Simon (Illinois), Congressman Richard Gephardt (Missouri), Reverend Jesse Jackson (Illinois), and Hart. Media pundits depicted this group as the "seven dwarfs."

Unlike the invisible primary, the actual campaign was far more ordinary. It eventually turned into a battle of attrition through the front-loaded primaries with Dukakis emerging as the clear winner by early May. The first state to vote, Iowa, was inconclusive with Gephardt, Simon, and Dukakis finishing closely in that order. Dukakis won the New Hampshire primary, but the proximity of his home state of Massachusetts led observers to downplay the significance of that win. The next showdown, "Super Tuesday," when seventeen states held primaries, was also inconclusive as Dukakis, Jackson, and Gore, divided the vote about equally among themselves. Simon and Gephardt recorded their first victories when they captured their respective home states. Despite these conflicting outcomes, there were some losers. Babbitt and Hart ran poorly everywhere and withdrew. The remaining candidates faced one another in the next round of primaries with the weaker performers usually quitting. The next to leave was Gephardt who dropped out after losing in Michigan. Simon withdrew after finishing fourth and last in Wisconsin, Gore then quit after finishing third and last in New York, while Jackson, who lost every primary after "Super Tuesday," remained in the race until the national convention, but he garnered the support of only about 1200 of the 4000 national convention delegates. Nearly every other delegate voted for Dukakis.

Dukakis, as was true of all other candidates, began the advertising component of his campaign by introducing himself through biographical ads. His tenure as governor was his most important qualifying feature. He had won an initial term in 1974 but had been defeated for reelection four years later in the Democratic primary. Dukakis ran for governor once again in 1982, defeated the incumbent in the primary, and won the general election. The second term was far more successful. The state's economy boomed and thereby provided Dukakis with an excellent opportunity for election to a third term in 1986. In his most important biographical ad, Dukakis used a narrator to inform viewers that his fellow governors had named him as the nation's best governor. After speaking of Dukakis's background as the son of immigrants, as a veteran, and as inspired by John F. Kennedy, the narrator talked of his accomplishments in Massachusetts. Included were references to fighting corruption, ending deficits, and creating jobs. Dukakis often claimed credit for the "Massachusetts Miracle," a technologically driven economic expansion (*Bio*).

The theme of economic accomplishments was also evident in other biographical related ads. Several ads featured prominent state leaders endorsing Dukakis while speaking favorably of his deeds. Tip O'Neill, a long time resident of Massachusetts who had retired as Speaker of the House two years earlier, said Dukakis had the strength, maturity, and record to be a great president. He added that Dukakis had created jobs while serving as governor, would continue to do so as president, and was strong on protecting Social Security (*Tip*). Other ads relied on a major labor union leader from the state to tell of how Dukakis had created 400,000 good paying jobs as governor and on a narrator speaking of how the recent revitalization of the state's economy would help children by providing them with future opportunities (*McIntyre, Little Miracles*).

While economics was his leading issue, Dukakis focused some attention on other matters. In an ad where he was also the narrator, Dukakis talked about safety threats from a proposed nuclear power plant in New Hampshire and of how he had personally blocked the project (*Seabrooke*). He also spoke of the plight of homeless people and of their need for adequate shelter (*Central America*). Dukakis rarely addressed foreign related matters, however, and when he did, he tended to link them with domestic concerns. In *Central America*, Dukakis spoke before an audience about the importance of domestic needs while the ad used several photographs to illustrate the carnage and destruction that had resulted from the Reagan administration's aid for the Contras in Nicaragua.

Finally, Dukakis relied on attacks, although such ads were less frequent than the biographical and issue related ones. Sometimes the attacks were directed at all of his rivals but at no one of them in particular, as in *Budget*. Here, a narrator, supported with imagery featuring the other candidates, spoke of how Dukakis, alone among the candidates, had balanced budgets, created jobs, cut taxes, and fought off the effects of a recession. Other ads focused on specific candidates, such as Gephardt, who was Dukakis's major rival in the earliest voting states. Ads attacked Gephardt for his financial contributions from political action committees and for his votes on economic matters (*List, Record Help*).

Gephardt and Simon contested Iowa, and in doing so, became the initial aspirants to face Dukakis. While both emphasized the three requisite themes of images, issues, and attacks, they differed in the rhetorical content of their messages. Gephardt directed more of his advertising to his major issue, class based economics, while Simon focused far more attention on his own personal character. Gephardt linked his biographical ads to his advocacy of the economic issues that were important in Midwestern states such as Iowa, the loss of industrial jobs to overseas locations. His ads spoke of his working class background in St. Louis and of how his father had been a wage earner. They continued with an overview of his public career as a city alderman in St. Louis and a member of the U.S. House from that same city (*Change*). The emphasis then shifted to economic and class related issues such as how Gephardt had helped close tax loopholes for the rich while providing tax relief for six million poor people, and of how he had strived to protect Social Security. In *Trade*, his strongest issue related ad, Gephardt spoke, while supported by imagery of automobile workers, of how hard Americans worked but of how South Korean tariffs had raised the price of American car imports in that nation beyond the reach of most people. He added that we would continue to defend South Korea in war because "that's the kind of people we are," but he would implement the same tariffs the South Korean Hyundai as they have on American made cars. This would raise the price of the Hyundai to $48,000, a price that clearly would reduce imports and boost the sales of American, and of course, Midwestern, made cars. Gephardt depicted himself as the defender of working people. In *Soul* he talked of how unnamed "others" wanted to leave workers and farmers behind. He then praised these workers for changing America and for giving the nation its soul. Gephardt used this same theme of defense of working people in his attack ads. In *Belgian Endive*, he attacked Dukakis on trade, taxes, jobs, and family farms and ridiculed the Massachusetts governor for a statement he had made urging farmers to diversify and grow Belgian endive.

Simon focused most of his ads on personal integrity. In *Bio*, he spoke about how he had become involved in politics in Southern Illinois and of how he had fought against the influences of organized crime. He supported the personal integrity theme with comments by people in government, including members of the U.S. Senate and the Illinois legislature, who spoke of Simon's honesty and of how they believed he would make a good president.

Babbitt and Hart also competed in Iowa, although they finished far behind Gephardt, Simon, and Dukakis. Babbitt employed a style similar to that of Simon, emphasizing his character, although he did not ignore issues. A narrator described him as a "different kind of candidate," who would "put America in charge again." The narration focused on Babbitt's past efforts in advancing civil rights, fighting poverty, and combating crime. Babbitt spoke in many of his ads while directing his attention to the need to make cuts in government spending, at increasing revenue, and in being honest with the American people. He said that people are begging for honesty and that honesty is the key to victory (*Bio*, *Guts*, *Turned Off*).

Despite his previous troubles, Hart focused almost exclusively on character. He tried to define character as willingness to be different to take on special interests, to continue a fight, to challenge old ways, and to make fundamental changes. Hart also said he would not accept contributions from interest groups.

His ads were similar in style and substance to those he had used earlier in the election of 1984 (*Character, Different*).

The last two rivals who faced Dukakis were Jackson and Gore, both of whom directed their initial efforts to the primaries of "Super Tuesday." Jackson proved to be the more formidable of the two. His ads emphasized his ability to accomplish difficult tasks on behalf of ordinary people. One ad dealt with an incident that had taken place several months earlier when Jackson had traveled to Syria and won the release of an American pilot who had been captured by the Syrian government (*Only One*). The ad *Iowa Farmer* featured a farmer who told viewers about how Jackson had helped his renegotiate his farm debt by talking to the banker. In *Stood*, a narrator told of how Jackson had stood with for family farmers, with parents and teachers on drugs, with senior citizens on health care and with other people on a variety of issues. In contrast, Gore directed much of his advertising to character. He emphasized how his Southern, family, military, and governmental background had given him the bedrock American values of family, hard work, patriotism, and honesty that prepared him for the presidency (*Bio, South*). He attacked his rivals on a variety of different issues, such as Dukakis on foreign policy, Gephardt on economics, and Jackson on experience (*Triple*).

The Democratic campaign was relatively free of rancor and concluded with the enthusiastic nomination of Dukakis and his running mate, Senator Lloyd Bentsen (Texas). The party had not enjoyed such unity since 1976, which was also the last time it had won the presidency. Moreover, public opinion polls gave Dukakis a substantial, in some surveys more than ten percentage points, lead over Bush (Gallup Poll, 2006). Dukakis had indeed united his partisans, but he had done so in the dangerous manner frequently employed by challengers. He held out the promise of victory by downplaying issues that had divided the party in previous, and losing, campaigns. In his acceptance speech, Dukakis told the convention delegates and the millions of viewers in the national television audience that the election was about competence, not ideology. One might ask; competence for what purpose? Dukakis did not provide an answer except for additional vague and generalized promises that he would bring about an economic "miracle" similar to his claims in Massachusetts.

In a more general sense, Dukakis did not embark upon a particularly unwise rhetorical strategy; his troubles came with its execution. Every general election challenger of a surrogate incumbent faces an unusual political dilemma that is unique to elections of this nature. His party has been out of power for some time, as mentioned earlier, perhaps as much as eight years, but is now optimistic about its chances for victory. The incumbent who defeated them in recent elections is retiring and is being replaced as party leader by a weaker surrogate. The opposition party wants to unite and win rather than divide and lose. Therefore, its activists are willing to downplay divisiveness and the ideological issues that might encourage it. Dukakis tried to appeal to this preference when he distinguished ideology and competence. His language was code for the prevalence of unity and electability over values. John F. Kennedy made a comparably coded promise in 1960 when he said he would "get this country moving again," while

George W. Bush would follow a similar course in 2000 by describing himself as a "compassionate conservative." The problem with this approach rests in the vagueness of the promises and the political qualifications of the person making them. While motivating to party activists, vaguely coded promises may leave undecided voters uneasy and lead them to question the challenger's personal competence to fulfill the rigors of the presidency. Each challenger in the surrogate incumbent elections lost ground in the polls during the final days of their respective campaigns. All four were ahead at various times during their campaigns, but only Kennedy and Nixon (1968) held their popular vote leads through the final vote counts. Dukakis and Bush (2000) lost their leads, however.

Dukakis started his general election advertising by reiterating this theme of unity and competence. In *New Era*, a narrator talked about the Massachusetts Miracle and claimed that under Dukakis, the state had 400,000 new jobs, higher overall incomes, and had controlled its deficit and balanced its budget. He also told viewers that the cause of this outcome "wasn't a miracle, it was leadership." The supporting imagery was of Dukakis addressing the Democratic convention where he was shown emphasizing the importance of unity by remarking that "we can accomplish much by working together." The unity and competence theme appeared in a number of other ads, although the concluding phrase was a slogan rather than personal remarks from Dukakis. The slogan, "the best America is yet to come," stated the same coded message, however. Some of the ads employing this style dealt with an overview of Dukakis's accomplishments as governor, about how the increase incomes in the state aided a young married couple, of upbeat imagery of happy people, and of Dukakis actually using the slogan in one of the televised debates (*Leadership/Responsibility*, *Two Paychecks*, *Anthem*).

These upbeat promises were not enough for Dukakis to maintain his lead in the polls for very long, however. Bush seized that lead in mid-August and held it through the rest of the campaign. The combination of televised attacks that exploited Dukakis' vagueness and voters' uncertainty with him, and Bush's successful attempts to link himself to the popular Reagan, both discussed earlier in this chapter, effectively compromised the Dukakis bid. One may question the ethics of the Bush campaign for the vehemence and often misleading nature of its attacks, but one must also place some of the blame on Dukakis for failing to understand and then address the problems that are inherent in a rhetorical strategy that is based on vague appeals to unity. Dukakis eventually responded to the attacks, but this effort was far too late.

The response centered on three general themes; direct attacks on Bush's record as vice president and his promises for future policies, raising doubts about the competence of Dan Quayle for executive office, and responding to Bush's attacks relating to Willie Horton and other issues. In *Plant Closing*, a narrator, supported with imagery of a closed factory, told of how Bush was opposed to laws that would require timely notification of factory shutdowns, of how Quayle, as a U.S. Senator, had voted against a proposed federal law to this effect, of how Bentsen had led the successful fight in the Senate to pass the proposal, and of how Dukakis had enacted and then implemented a similar law in Massachusetts. Other ads attacked Bush for his record on Social Security including his past votes against benefit increases, while others questioned his commitment to anti-drug programs aimed at juveniles (*Crunch, Effort*).

The effectiveness of the attacks questioning Quayle's abilities varied. *Oval Office* clearly delivered the message that Quayle may very well lack the qualifications associated with recent vice presidents while *Packaging* was so vague in its references that voters might have been more confused than enlightened. The first ad featured a narrator talking of how Harry Truman, Lyndon Johnson, and Gerald Ford had taken office in difficult times, after either a president had either died or resigned. It then referred to Bush's choice of "J. Danforth Quayle" as a potential chief executive. The use of this name, rather than "Dan Quayle" was designed to raise doubts about the common experiences of the Republican candidate while also suggesting that he was too wealthy and inexperienced for national leadership. The second ad focused on the comments of "Republican advertisers" who lamented Quayle's presence on the ticket.

Finally, but much too late, Dukakis responded to Bush's attacks. In *Furlough from Truth*, he told voters that he had ended the Massachusetts furlough program while adding that over 7,000 prisoners had participated in similar federal programs during the Reagan years. He talked about his commitment to various weapons systems in *Counterpunch* while questioning Bush's attack on his positions and by raising questions about Bush's defense record. The effect of these late ads was limited; Dukakis won thee electoral votes of only ten states and the District of Columbia.

Bush and the Republicans

George W. Bush was a most unusual candidate for the presidency in 2000. He was generally unknown to much of the voting public, a characteristic that is very common to nearly all challengers, but he possessed a staggering array of advantages that any surrogate incumbent would envy. His public career was limited in duration; he had been governor of Texas for only six years. Bush's personal involvements in his father's previous campaigns for president (1980, 1988, 1992) and vice president (1980, 1984), had provided him with valuable opportunities for meeting some of the leading contributors and activists within the Republican Party, however. The fact that he was the eldest son of the last Republican president and that his name was similar to his father's provided Bush with opportunities for media coverage and public interest that were rarely available for any of his rivals.

Bush entered a campaign that was characterized by an ambiguous political context. The nation was at peace and was enjoying a period of prosperity and high income. Even the national government was faring well; the incumbent Bill Clinton had brought about a balanced budget without causing major economic disruptions. These factors by themselves should have led to a strong victory by the incumbent party. Unfortunately for the Democrats, Clinton's sex scandals had raised doubts among enough voters that many party leaders were cautious about their chances at the beginning of the election campaign. The Republicans were bolstered in their optimism by recent election trends. They had ended forty years of Democratic control of the House of Representatives in 1994 by capturing 52 seats from their rivals. Moreover, the Republicans gained enough seats in the Senate to take control of that chamber as well. This victory eventually proved to be enduring as Republicans maintained control of both chambers of Congress through the final six years of the Clinton presidency. A presidential victory in 2000, which now seemed promising, would mean that Republicans would have control of all three major institutions of the national government; Presidency, Senate, and House, for the first time in nearly fifty years.

The nomination campaign began in the early months of 1999 when twelve candidates officially entered the race. Bush emerged as the front-runner by mid-year, however, on the strength of successes at garnering key endorsements and raising money. His most important endorsements came from his fellow Republican governors as more than twenty of them announced their support for his candidacy. Several of them were from major states such as New York, New Jersey, Ohio, Pennsylvania, Illinois, Michigan, Wisconsin, and Florida. Their support opened additional fundraising doors for Bush beyond what he had generated from his father's contributors and his supporters in Texas. By July 1, 1999, Bush had raised more money, approximately $35 million, than all of his eleven rivals combined. This success influenced the composition of the race as six of those rivals soon ended their under funded efforts. Those leaving were Dan Quayle, Elizabeth Dole, Lamar Alexander, Patrick Buchanan, Senator Bob Jones (New Hampshire), and Representative John Kasich (Ohio). Only one of Bush's remaining five rivals, Senator John McCain (Arizona) appeared to be a strong rival. Bush faced his other four rivals, McCain excluded, in Iowa and easily defeated them. The four; Steve Forbes, Orrin Hatch, Alan Keyes, and Gary Bauer, ceased to be of any consequence as candidates after the Iowa vote. McCain passed on Iowa, concentrated his efforts extensively in New Hampshire, and defeated Bush in that state by a margin of about seventeen percentage points. A field of twelve candidates had been reduced to only two.

Every presidential election has some unique features and 2000 was no exception. The first one that was relevant in 2000 occurred in the primaries. For several years, the Democratic National Committee (DNC) had strived to prevent the early scheduling of state primaries. These efforts were not always without effect. In 1988, for example, the DNC would not allow any states other than the few which had already acted before this particular election, to schedule primaries or caucuses before the second Tuesday in March. This ruling led to the creation of "Super Tuesday" when sixteen states held primaries on that particular day. This time, 2000, the DNC decided that no states other than Iowa and New Hampshire could hold their votes before the first Tuesday in March. Rules by the DNC are not binding on the Republican Party, of course, but primaries are conducted by state governments. Most legislatures have been unwilling to bear the expenses for two different primaries to be held on the specific days each party prefers.

Prior to 2000, most states had respected the DNC rules and had scheduled their primaries in accordance with the preferred dates.

This was not true in 2000, however. Several states with Republican controlled legislatures conducted primaries in February but allowed Democrats to hold party financed caucuses at later dates. This practice meant that several states would hold primaries where the only choices were the Republican candidates. Nonpartisans, and in some states, Democrats as well, could vote in most of these Republican primaries. South Carolina, Arizona, Michigan, Virginia, and Washington held Republican primaries during February, 2000. Bush and McCain faced one another in three of them, South Carolina, Michigan, and Virginia. A majority of Republicans supported Bush in each state but McCain, who had strong backing from nonpartisans and Democrats, tried to organize that backing in order to impress his fellow partisans that he could win the general election while Bush would likely fall short. All three contested primaries were close, with Bush winning in South Carolina and Virginia and with McCain taking Michigan. The next round of primaries came on "Super Tuesday" when eleven states voted. Most of these states, including the largest ones of California, New York, Ohio, Georgia, and Missouri, limited the ballot to Republicans. Bush defeated McCain in each of these states and took what appeared to be an insurmountable lead for the nomination. McCain withdrew two days later. It was his context, Bush directing his appeals to strong Republicans and McCain aiming his at nonpartisans and Democrats, and some Republicans of course, that defined the advertising strategies of these two Republican candidates.

Bush's biographical and issue related ads focused on his accomplishments in Texas and included promises that he would extend them to the national government. His most important biographical ad in the primaries, *Successful Leader*, involved a narrator talking about how Bush had cut taxes, controlled the growth of state government, reduced welfare, battled crime, and improved educational quality. The supporting imagery and slogan were of Bush campaigning for "A Fresh Start." The theme of personal character and of how it might qualify Bush for national leadership was not a central feature in biographical related advertising.

The slogan of a fresh start appeared as the concluding phrase in a variety of Bush's issue related ads. The two issues that generated the largest amount of advertising from the Bush campaign were education and taxation. Only the most unusual candidates would speak against education, and Bush clearly was not such a person; he supported public education. Candidates often differ in the content of the promises they make about education, however, and sometimes disguise the values they cherish when they describe their goals through the used of politically coded words. Bush used the codes that have been associated with conservative goals in recent years when he described his educational plans. In *Every Child*, a title that was incorporated into the name of his educational program, "No Child Left Behind," Bush advocated responsibility and accountability, an emphasis on reading and phonics, and more local control. While such words may appear neutral and unifying to many observers, they also mask controversial political goals. For liberals, accountability translates into mandatory and standardized testing with funding linked to the results of those tests. Calls for local control are often disguised appeals to segregationists and an emphasis on reading and responsibility means lower spending on remedial learning and social services for lower income children. Bush also used conservative code words when speaking about taxation. He promised to reduce taxes during this time of financial surpluses. Bush relied upon a rhetorical dichotomy that he alleged existed between the "government's money" and the "peoples' money." By advocating that the surplus should be returned to the people Bush was also indirectly opposing options to spend that money on collective goods or services such as Social Security, national defense, or health care. Bush emphasized this distinction in a variety of taxation related ads, including instances where he was speaking to reporters (*Real Time: Salem*), presenting his views during a televised debate (*Debate*), or performing as his own narrator in an ad which had extensive imagery of children (*America's Spirit*).

The competitiveness of the Bush-McCain primary battles encouraged both candidates to use attack ads. Bush focused his on two themes, taxes and campaign finance reform. In *Solid Values*, a narrator insisted that McCain's tax plans would increase the assessments on charities while providing only limited relief for most taxpayers. McCain had placed more emphasis on campaign finance reform than on any other issue. The Bush ads questioned his commitment to this idea by pointing out that a number of Washington D.C. lobbyists and "insiders," were playing active roles in McCain's campaign (*Promised*). Finally, the early conclusion of the nomination battle, it ended in mid-March, gave Bush an opportunity to focus attention toward the general election and his upcoming battle with Gore. He attacked Gore and Clinton over education and restated his conservative goals and slogan in *Challenging the Status Quo*.

In contrast to Bush, McCain put far more emphasis on the relationship between personal character and national leadership. One can see the difference by comparing the major biographical ads of the two candidates. *Ready to Lead* began with a narrator telling of McCain's military experiences in Vietnam where he had been a prisoner of war for over five years. It included imagery of McCain with Ronald Reagan and remarks by McCain where he attacked special interests and defended veterans. His slogan, which was also more character oriented than Bush's, was "Ready to Lead . . . Courage . . . Character." Also, Representative Lindsay Graham (South Carolina), to the theme of "Duty, Honor, and Country," spoke of how McCain's naval experiences would help him lead the nation. The McCain campaign used other biographical ads that emphasized this same theme. Some of these involved attempts to link McCain with Ronald Reagan in order to appeal to conservative Republicans. These ads would combine imagery of McCain's military experiences with scenes where he appeared with Reagan. McCain identified himself as a "Reagan Republican" with the message that he was ready to lead the nation with courage and character (*Reagan Conservative, Can Win, Leader*).

McCain emphasized a variety of issues in his ads, with campaign finance reform being the one that distinguished him most from Bush. He talked about his independence from special interests and of how he would direct his tax relief policies more toward the middle class rather than the rich, a group his often linked with Bush. He used another slogan here that contained an attack against special interests and privilege, "give me your vote and I'll give you back your government" (*Message to America*). McCain's attack ads focused on Bush's use of such ads and then reemphasized the Arizona senator's major issues. In *Wrong*, McCain, shown speaking to an audience, attacked Bush over his advertising and then he identified himself as a conservative reformer who would reduce taxes, save Social Security, and pay down the national debt. In *Trust*, a narrator questioned Bush's use of attack ads and raised the question of whether we wanted another politician in the White House we can't trust.

The fact that so many Republican candidates withdrew before the first primaries even occurred, or offered such limited competition to Bush and McCain if they had remained in the race, makes their advertising nearly insignificant. Forbes relied upon his private fortune rather than campaign contributions to fund his efforts and therefore offered a limited challenge to the major contenders. He introduced himself as a family man by using ads that contained imagery and comments from his wife and five daughters (*Family*). His major issues were opposition to taxes and government regulation of business and support for the enactment of individual retirement accounts to replace Social Security (*Lunch Counter, Social Security*). His major attack ads questioned Bush's tax cutting record in Texas (*Mary*). Of the others, Gary Bauer spoke of his support for families and of national security threats from China (*Newport, China Threat*); Alan Keyes focused on his opposition to income taxes, gun control, and abortion (*Rush, Kids, Second Amendment*), while Lamar Alexander attacked Bush with an ad in which Texas millionaires were bidding for the presidency at an auction (*Auction*).

The requisite general election need of the challengers of surrogate incumbents is to maintain the support of their own partisans while indicating to other voters they will make some important changes and are personally qualified for office. The Bush campaign relied heavily on appeals related to change but placed less emphasis on his personal ability to deliver. This is evident in *New Americans*, and *Once*. Here, a narrator outlined Bush's leading issues and campaign slogans about the American dream, reforming education, protecting Social Security, keeping America strong, and uniting, not dividing, but provided little detail of how these sere to be accomplished. These ads contained scenes of diverse adults and numerous children. Similar ads had Bush speaking directly to the audience about these issues while referring to the need to "do the hard things (*Hard Things*)".

Bush provided more specifics about his goals in ads related to education and Social Security, although many of his remarks relied upon the same conservative code words described above. *Education Agenda* included imagery of Bush addressing the Republican National Convention while a narrator described the components of his educational plan; local control, accountability, emphasis on reading, support for Head Start, and character related education. In other ads focusing on education, Bush described reading as a new civil right and said "without it, you can't have access to the American dream," and with the accompaniment of numerous children, said that we need to expect more from our public schools (*Phyllis Hunter*). His promises about Social Security were similar. In *No Changes, No Reductions*, Bush was shown, at both the Republican convention and in other settings, talking about the need for prescription drug benefits for seniors and the protection of Social Security. He provided yet another listing of general goals, this time about families and children, in *Tools*. Speaking directly to the audience once again, Bush named several tools that would help families with children. Included were internet filters, television family hours, character education, drug prevention, safety, discipline, and parental flex time.

In recent elections, some candidates have advertised in the Spanish language. Most ads are essentially the same as the ones employed in English with the narrator simply addressing the audience while using a different vocabulary. Sometimes the candidates may utter a few words in Spanish, particularly if they have some familiarity with it. Bush and Gore followed this pattern. The Bush campaign added a new feature this time, however, comments by a Latino family member. George P. Bush is the son of Governor Jeb Bush (Florida) and the nephew of George W. Bush. The P. stands for Prescott, the name of his great-grandfather, Senator Prescott Bush (Connecticut). His mother is of Latino background. The Bush campaign used the governor's nephew is several ads which emphasized the diversity in the Bush family. George P. Bush occasionally addressed his audience in Spanish and said that his uncle had the same name as himself (*Same as Mine*).

Bush also used a number of attack ads which compared the contrasting positions of the two candidates on major issues. Most of the ads restated Bush's general themes. In *58 Percent*, a narrator spoke of how 58 percent of the children in low income neighborhoods were having trouble reading. She then contrasted Bush's and Gore's educational plans on the various conservative themes that Bush had been advancing, accountability, local control, discipline, etc. Ads employing a similar contrasting approach focused on the candidates' policies related to prescription drugs and tax cuts (*Compare*).

The Bush campaign also made some attacks on Gore's character. In *Credibility*, a narrator mocked the vice president and raised questions about his trustworthiness because of his alleged inconsistent positions on debates with Bush. Another ad, *Nonsense*, used a similar approach in attacking Gore's positions on prescription drugs and for his statements relating to the fiscal weaknesses of Bush's goal of partial privatizing of Social Security. This ad was related to a theme that Bush had advocated throughout the campaign, the dichotomy between the "government" and the "people."

There were several minor party candidates in 2000, with Ralph Nader of the Green Party attracting the support of nearly three percent of the electorate. Two additional minor party aspirants were Pat Buchanan, who abandoned the Republican Party for the nomination of the Reform Party and Harry Browne, the standard bearer of the Libertarians. One Nader ad featured individual children speaking of what they wanted when they grew up. They said pollution, dishonesty, and disillusionment. The narrator asked parents if this is what they wanted for their children (*Grow Up*). A second Nader ad drew from a well known

MasterCard ad where prices were listed on campaign contributions, half truths, and promises to special interests compared to the truth, which was priceless (*Priceless Truth*). Buchanan focused his ads on the "culture war" by showing a tearing down of the Ten Commandments, children stopped from praying, and the Boy Scouts labeled as a hate group (*Culture Wars*). Browne relied more on humor. In one ad a woman confessed she had "battered voter syndrome" while in another, and using a reference to a movie from the 1960's, Browne said complaints that the Libertarians would "throw out the baby with the bathwater" included imagery of a baby with devil like eyes and a narrator telling viewers it was "Rosemary's baby" (*Battered, Baby*).

Bush maintained a lead over Gore in the polls during the nomination period but lost it during the Democratic convention in August. Gore led until the debates in late September and early October but saw that lead disappear with his questionable performances before the national television audiences. The two candidates ran even until mid October when Bush took the lead once again. Bush could not maintain that lead, however, and he lost it during the final days of the campaign. At this time, pollsters said the race was too close to call. Bush ultimately won the election because of an event over which he and Gore had little control; the vote counting difficulties and court cases related to Florida.

CHAPTER 5

THE 2004 ELECTION: NOMINATION CAMPAIGNS

GENERAL OVERVIEW AND REPUBLICANS

The presidential election of 2004 differed from other television age campaigns in the sense that the incumbent, George W. Bush, defied easy categorization as either a strong or a weak incumbent. Every successful incumbent since the 1950's attained high approval ratings from voters and led his general election challenger in public opinion surveys throughout the election year. In contrast, each unsuccessful incumbent had low approval ratings and trailed his challenger in the polls. Bush differed from the other incumbents in that voters were about evenly divided in both their approval of his performance in office and in their support for him and his challenger, Senator John Kerry (Massachusetts). Throughout the year, about fifty percent of the voters consistently approved of Bush and a nearly equal amount disapproved (Gallup Poll, 2006). This division of opinion was reflected in the general election popular vote where Bush attained 50.73 percent compared to Kerry's 48.27 and 1.00 for the nominees of several minor political parties (see Abramson, Aldrich, and Rohde, 2006; Ceaser and Busch, 2005; CQ Press, 2005; Cook, 2004; Crotty, 2005; Denton, 2005;

Jamieson, 2006; Nelson, 2005; Sabato, 2006, for a detailed discussion of the 2004 election).

This relatively even division of popular choices had unusual impacts on the perceptions and behavior of the two major political parties. The presidential Republicans viewed Bush as a strong incumbent and responded accordingly while the challenging Democrats clearly saw Bush as a weak incumbent and responded in vastly different ways from their partisan rivals. In previous elections marked by strong incumbents, the presidential party rapidly united behind the incumbent before the onset of the nomination campaign. This unity gave the incumbent an unusual opportunity to win renomination without opposition and to immediately begin his efforts for the general election. In contrast, weak incumbents tend to attract at least one major intra-party challenger for the nomination and must engage in a lengthy and frequently divisive battle for the nomination of their parties. Republicans were united in their perceptions that Bush had been effective during his first term in responding to terrorism, the economy, and important social values, and they believed he had earned the right to a second term as president. They were as united behind George W. Bush at the beginning of 2004 as they had been behind the three previous strong incumbents of their party who have won second terms during the television age; Dwight Eisenhower (1956), Richard Nixon (1972), and Ronald Reagan (1984). This unity allowed Bush to begin his reelection effort in early 2004 rather than delaying it until after defeating a formidable rival for the party nomination.

The opposition Democrats saw Bush in a very different light, however. They considered him to be an ineffective president who had misled the nation into a war which we could not win and that his taxing and spending policies were responsible for job losses, unaffordable health care, and a variety of other economic ills. Bush's Democratic detractors did not see him as a moral leader but instead thought of him as a polarizing ideologue. This set of beliefs encouraged Democrats to believe they could unseat Bush after one term. When a weak incumbent seeks another term, the challenging party tends to set aside many of its internal differences and unite behind the one candidate who holds out the promise of victory. The party unites because it believes it has a promising chance for attaining power. It is not so eager to unite when it believes the incumbent in unbeatable. The Democrats united relatively easily and early in the two previous television age elections that had weak incumbent Republicans and they went on to win those respective elections. These differences in perceptions by the two major parties about the incumbent's political strengths and policy successes are unusual. They resulted in a close and unchanging battle between Bush and Kerry that lasted for eight months and which left the nation as divided as before.

THE DEMOCRATIC CAMPAIGN

Ten individuals sought the Democratic nomination in 2004. The five with the broadest support were John Kerry, the eventual winner; Senator John Edwards

(North Carolina) Kerry's major rival and eventual vice presidential running mate; former Governor Howard Dean (Vermont), the front-runner throughout the latter part of 2003; Representative Richard Gephardt (Missouri), the Democratic minority leader in the House of Representatives, and retired General Wesley Clark (Arkansas), a former NATO commander who entered the race during the latter months of 2003. The five with the least amount of support were Senators Bob Graham (Florida) and Joseph Lieberman (Connecticut), former Senator Carol Moseley-Braun (Illinois), Representative Dennis Kucinich (Ohio), and Reverend Al Sharpton (New York). Graham and Moseley-Braun withdrew prior to the Iowa caucuses in mid-January, Lieberman ended his quest in early February after losing badly in the New Hampshire and Delaware primaries, Sharpton quit in March after disappointing results in South Carolina and New York, while Kucinich remained in the race until the last primaries took place in early June.

The public version of the nomination campaign, the part characterized by televised advertising and extensive media coverage of candidates' words and deeds, was very short. The candidates did not advertise nationally at this time but instead limited their efforts to those states with early votes, such as Iowa and New Hampshire which balloted in January, and a number of other states that voted during the weeks immediately afterwards. The audience for network news was far more extensive at this stage of the campaign since news coverage reached all parts of the nation rather than only selected states. Most voters were not exposed to any televised ads from the Democratic candidates during the nomination campaign.

The first electoral showdown, the caucuses in Iowa on January 19, developed in two stages. The first, which occurred during the late months of 2003, involved a battle between Dean and Gephardt, while the second, in December 2003 and January 2004, saw Kerry and Edwards expand their efforts and turn the caucuses into a four candidate battle. Dean started the campaign as the media proclaimed "front-runner" because of his lead in national public opinion polls. His lead was not overpowering, however, he rarely attained the support of even twenty percent of Democratic voters. Nonetheless, Dean had more support than any other candidate. Gephardt had won the Iowa caucuses during his previous presidential bid in 1988 and devoted most of his financial and organizational resources to Iowa this time. Kerry and Edwards had looked very promising as candidates during the early months of 2003 when they led their rivals in fundraising, but both saw their campaigns stall during the latter part of that year. Each recovered his momentum with an effective effort in Iowa and gained ground on Dean and Gephardt during the final days before the Iowa vote. Eventually, Kerry won the caucuses with 38 percent of the delegates elected to attend county conventions supporting him while 32 percent of the delegates backed Edwards. Dean and Gephardt trailed far behind as only 19 and 11 percent respectively of the convention delegates supported them. Gephardt withdrew from the race one day later.

Kerry, Edwards, and Dean moved their efforts to New Hampshire which held its primary election eight days after the Iowa vote. Clark and Lieberman joined them in what was to be their initial stands before voters. Kerry won again, also with 38 percent of the vote, while Dean came in second with 26 percent. The other candidates struggled to reach ten percent, although each of them did so. One week later, on February 3, Kerry became the decisive front-runner by winning primaries or caucuses in five states; Arizona, Delaware, Missouri, New Mexico, and North Dakota. He also finished second to Edwards in the South Carolina primary that day and third behind Clark and Edwards in Oklahoma. Kerry continued winning primaries, defeating both Clark and Edwards in Tennessee and Virginia one week later, Clark withdrew at this time, and Dean and Edwards in Wisconsin the following week. Dean ended his quest after this loss. Finally, Kerry won nine more primaries on March 2. This encouraged Edwards to withdraw and effectively clinched the nomination for Kerry. After a few weeks of planning for the next stage of the campaign, Kerry launched his general election efforts against Bush in early April.

Kerry

The Democratic candidates employed the same essential approaches in their televised advertising; reliance on the three themes of personal introductions, issue development, and attacks against rivals. They had few issue disputes among themselves since they belonged to the same political party, but differed in the ways in which they introduced themselves and in how they linked those introductions with issues. Kerry had been a nationally known political actor for a longer period of time than any of his rivals. He had emerged in 1971 as the most identifiable spokesman for a group of anti-war Vietnam veterans. During that time Kerry emphasized his opposition to the war at rallies and before congressional committees. Unlike many anti-war spokesmen of the time whose military experiences were either limited or non-existent, Kerry had served as an officer in the Navy, had commanded combat missions in Vietnam, and had won several awards for his heroic actions. He clearly had the ethos to attract national attention to himself and provide credibility to the anti-war cause that few other spokesmen could match. Kerry followed these efforts with a political career that eventually carried him to the Senate in 1984.

Kerry used his Vietnam experiences as a vital part of his personal introductions. One theme emphasized the relevance of his combat experiences to current matters of public policy. In *Believe*, a narrator initially described how Kerry had fought in the Vietnam War, had won several medals for heroism, and had then opposed the conflict after leaving the Navy. The narrator then linked these actions with Kerry's political life by saying that Kerry had the courage to do what was right, such as protecting a woman's right to choose and preventing oil drilling in the Alaska wildlife preserve. Several combat related photographs of Kerry serving in Vietnam complemented this audio component.

The Kerry campaign used a similar approach in the attack ad *Aircraft Carrier*. Once again the narrator spoke about Kerry's war background and then linked the past with the present. This time he emphasized how Kerry could take on Bush and change the direction of national policies relating to taxes, health care, and foreign relations. The video component contained imagery of Bush speaking of "mission accomplished" aboard the aircraft carrier Abraham Lincoln in May, 2003 when he was dressed in a combat flight suit. Finally, the ad *Change* followed a similar format but this time Kerry himself spoke about issues. The narrator began with references to Kerry's war experiences and once again linked them with his courage relating to abortion and oil drilling policies. Kerry then addressed the audience where he emphasized health care, Bush's tax cuts for the wealthy, and programs relating to children.

Kerry used two other military related themes in his introductory ads during the nomination campaign. One set of ads featured personal remarks about Kerry's character and leadership skills by individual veterans, including two who had served under his command in Vietnam and one who was a nationally prominent spokesman for disabled veterans. Del Sandusky told voters that Kerry knew what was right and pointed out that Kerry had made life and death decisions in Vietnam. Kerry then spoke about what he thought was right, telling viewers that it was right to guarantee health care, to roll back the Bush tax cuts, and to invest in children (*Del*). Another ad, similar to this in both content and style, featured David Alston speaking of Kerry's combat and leadership skills and by telling viewers that he believed Kerry would make a great president (*Alston*). These ads had a biracial appeal; Alston was black, Sandusky white. Max Cleland, a former U. S. Senator from Georgia, Veterans' Administrator director, and disabled Vietnam veteran emphasized that Kerry had been tested on the battlefield and tested in the Senate and was a fighter with character and courage. Cleland said these experiences had given Kerry the ability and personal capacity to lead the nation (*Cleland, AJC/Cleland*).

The final war related theme Kerry used emphasized the continuity between his military and political experiences. The ads *Fought for his Country* and *Trust* both used the phrase "for 35 years John Kerry has fought for his country" and then linked it with current conditions. The first of these ads featured Kerry talking about jobs, taxes, health care, and education while the second, used only in New Hampshire, mentioned the variety of newspapers that had endorsed Kerry and spoke of how he would "take the fight to Bush."

Kerry focused his issue related ads on themes related to economic difficulties while emphasizing the same topics mentioned in the above paragraph. The ads, although quite numerous, were similar in both style and content. They would show Kerry speaking at either a campaign rally or to a television audience about how the extensive job losses and other domestic problems of the past few years were a consequence of Bush's policies. Kerry often blamed Bush's tax cuts for a variety of troubles and promised to repeal them and then use the money for the creation of new jobs, affordable health care, improved educational funding, and the attainment of energy independence. He talked about job losses when he introduced himself to voters in some of the states with early caucuses and primaries. The ads *Iowa Announcement* and *Leadership*, included scenes of Kerry speaking at campaign rallies about job losses and tax cuts in Iowa and New

Hampshire respectively, while *Together* began in this manner but then focused on specific political endorsements that Kerry had received from leading South Carolina Democrats. Kerry emphasized how the middle class had not benefited from the tax cuts. In one ad, a woman, Elizabeth Hendrix, told of the financial difficulties she had encountered after her husband had died of cancer. She then spoke of how the tax cuts had not helped people such as herself but had been limited to the wealthy. She wanted these cuts rolled back in order to create more tax breaks for the middle class. Kerry then spoke about how he would try to achieve this goal (*Middle Class*). He used similar approaches with health care, saying he would promote family health care rather than higher profits for insurance and drug companies (*Families, Knowles*). He even said that all people should have the same high quality health care he had received during his recent battle with prostate cancer (*Cured Now*).

Kerry complemented his issue ads with attacks linking Bush with the problems he promised to address. Two ads he used during the Iowa caucuses emphasized Bush's close ties with energy companies and corporate lobbyists. In *Sided with Lobbyists* and *Corruption,* Kerry attacked Bush for his support for arctic oil drilling, for letting corporate lobbyists rewrite major environmental laws, and for trying to weaken the Clean Air Act. After questioning the Bush policies, Kerry, who spoke to the television audience in both ads, talked about how he would reduce the tax cuts, crack down on polluters, and promote energy independence. A similar ad, *Strength*, raised these same themes while relying on a narrator for the speaking. Kerry continued using this same approach, of questioning Bush's policies and then promising change, with his attack ads relating to other domestic issues. He placed a considerable amount of attention on health care. In an ad he used during the early part of the campaign, Kerry spoke directly to the television audience about Bush's support for the drug and insurance interests and of how this support worked against the achievement of affordable health care. He promised to fight these interests (*Health Care Coverage*). In an ad that was more confrontational in tone, Kerry relied upon a narrator to attack the Bush administration for creating a $130 billion tax break for drug and insurance interests. The narrator concluded his remarks by saying that Kerry would roll back this tax break and use the money to pay for health care and drug benefits (*Feeding Frenzy*). Kerry reiterated the same message in a number of other ads while varying his presentation styles. He had two ads, quite similar in both style and content, where he spoke to a campaign audience and attacked Bush for protecting "those at the top." Kerry says these policies had led to tax cuts for the rich, the loss of three million manufacturing jobs, and higher government deficits. He promised to repeal Bush's tax cut for the rich and to spend the money on education, health care, and the creation of new jobs. He used a slogan that linked his promises and attacks against Bush with the Vietnam related introduction he had used earlier in the campaign, "we need the courage to do what's right (*Deficit, Invest*)". In addition to ads where he spoke, Kerry also relied upon a narrator in ads with similar messages but which were harsher in their attacks on Bush. In *More than Anyone*, the narrator questioned Bush's past campaign contributions from the oil, insurance, and banking interests and the disgraced

Enron corporation while telling viewers about what Bush had done for them. The ad also accused Bush of attacking Kerry, an action that was now taking place with increasing frequency, because he could not defend his own record. Finally, Kerry combined the two styles in the ad *Jobs Lost*. Here, the ad began and ended with Kerry speaking from a podium to a campaign audience but with the narrator speaking during the middle portion of the ad. Kerry began by referring to the three million jobs that had been lost during the Bush term. The narrator followed Kerry and spoke about his position on job relocation and of how Kerry would seek tax incentives for new job creation and health care coverage. Kerry spoke for a second time and told his audience that Bush "will not do it but I will." A similar ad, but one that did not used any opening remarks by Kerry but included his concluding promise, had the narrator attacking Bush for his tax policies. The narrator denounced the incentives that existed in the tax code that encourage job relocation and then accused Bush of using misleading negative ads against Kerry (*Misleading America*).

While most of Kerry's attack ads against Bush focused on the damaging effects of the administration's policies and of Bush's financial ties to specific financial groups, they did not many raise questions about Bush's personal integrity. This pattern changed during the concluding phases of the nomination campaign, however. With most of his Democratic rivals already defeated or nearly finished, Kerry began raising questions about Bush's character. The ad *Keep Our Word* started with imagery of Bush speaking before Congress at one of his annual State of the Union Addresses. Here, Bush said "when we make a pledge, we keep our word." The ad included scenes of Bush making certain promises to Congress and the nation and then complemented his remarks with written statements showing he had actually done quite the opposite. There were several references about job creation, education funding, health care, the budget deficit, veterans' programs, and Social Security.

The war in Iraq proved to be one of the major issues of the 2004 campaign, but Kerry devoted very little of his televised advertising during the nomination campaign to it. He limited his remarks to attacking Bush's mismanagement while promising voters that he could lead more effectively. He did not question the wisdom or feasibility of American military involvement in Iraq, however. The ad *No, Mr. President* began with a scene of Bush appearing aboard the aircraft carrier Abraham Lincoln and involved a narrator accusing him of having no plan for winning the peace. The attacks also focused on the no bid reconstruction contracts the Bush administration had granted to the Halliburton Corporation. Kerry then told the television audience that we could not "go it alone in Iraq" while suggesting that he would seek allies to support our efforts. Finally, in an ad that was used at the end of the nomination campaign that brought many of Kerry's themes together, a narrator said that Kerry would stop Bush's radical agenda, including his "go it alone war," repeal his tax cuts, end corruption, and bring about energy independence (*100 Days*).

There were several features of the Kerry advertising campaign that defined and clearly enhanced, but in some instances hindered, his presidential bid in the general election. He directed his televised attacks toward Bush rather than his fellow Democrats. This strategy helped make party unity easier to attain and ultimately enabled the Democrats to offer a strong challenge against the incumbent. Kerry used his unique experiences as a combat veteran in an earlier and very controversial war to define himself as a fighter with the courage to do what was right. He complemented this introductory message by linking his personal experiences with an agenda for change that was predominately domestic rather than foreign in nature. He denounced the tax cuts Bush had brought about in 2001 as biased toward the wealthy. Kerry then promised to reduce them and use the new governmental revenues to address such pressing matters as job creation, affordable health care, education funding, and the creation of energy independence. These issues helped rally many Democrats, and particularly those with lower incomes, to his cause.

Unfortunately, Kerry failed to offer a significant change of policy related to Iraq other than to attack Bush over mismanagement of American military activities. This appears to have been a serious limitation because it left a major question unanswered about Kerry's candidacy. What message could one derive about Kerry's intentions for the Iraq war from his emphasis on his Vietnam experiences? Did his combat background mean he would lead the nation to the military victory that seemed to have eluded Bush? Instead, did Kerry's anti-war activities mean he would proclaim the war a mistake, as he had done with Vietnam in 1971, and then get the nation out of that mistake? He was not clear during the primaries about what meanings viewers should place on his biography and he still was not clear in July at the Democratic National Convention when he saluted the delegates and announced that he was John Kerry and was reporting for duty. His intentions for Iraq remained an unanswered question throughout the general election and may well have contributed to his eventual defeat. Kerry did not convince voters that he offered a real alternative to the incumbent on one of the most important issues of the year.

Edwards

John Edwards proved to be Kerry's strongest rival as the primaries unfolded. He did so by developing a far more populist oriented approach to domestic economic issues. He spent only a very limited amount of his advertising effort on the Iraq war, however, and when he did, sounded quite similar to Kerry in that he accused Bush of mismanagement without proposing any major changes of policy. In the ad *Strong*, Edwards blasted Bush for spending $87 billion in Iraq while having no end in sight and for fighting the war without allies. He attributed this lack of support to the administration's efforts as shutting out other nations from participating in the reconstruction effort because of large governmental giveaways to Halliburton. Edwards said that we should stop these inside deals, but then he changed the emphasis in this ad to domestic issues.

Edwards' leading theme was the great disparity in wealth and opportunity that continued to exist throughout the nation. One can clearly see this theme at work in his most important ad, *Two Americas*. Here, Edwards spoke to his television audience and contrasted various features of what he called the two Americas. In each instance he would refer to one America for the rich and another one for the rest. He said we had two health care systems, one for the privileged and another that was rationed by insurance companies. He added that we had two public school systems, one for the haves and one for everybody else; two tax systems, one for the wealthy where corporations paid less and another for working families which paid more; and two governments, one for the powerful interests and lobbyists and one for the rest of us. He promised that "together you and I can change America and make it work for all of us."

An appeal of this nature had credibility primarily because of the way in which Edwards had introduced himself. His political career had been relatively short in duration; he had first run for office only six years earlier with a self financed campaign for the U. S. Senate. His wealth derived from his practice of tort law where he had won some of the largest personal damage awards in North Carolina history. He frequently spoke of his humble origins, his father had worked in a textile mill, and he had been the first member of his family to attend college. Edwards spoke in nearly every one of his ads, regardless of whether it was introductory, issue related, or an attack against Bush. In fact, the only time he used a narrator was for telling voters how to reach his web site.

Edwards began his introductory ads by describing some aspect of his childhood background and then linked those personal features with economic themes similar to what he had spoken of in *Two Americas*. Initially, he focused the ads primarily on his background while offering only general policy related promises, but then expanded upon that theme later by talking more specifically about issues and goals. One can see the generality of the early appeals in his first two introductory ads. In *Right*, Edwards told his audience that he had been born fifty years before into a family with little material wealth. He then talked about how he had eventually gone both to law school and then to a successful career in law and politics. He linked himself with ordinary people by saying that he had never taken a dime from lobbyists while promising that he would be "your president, not theirs." In a similar ad, *Better Life*, Edwards once again used imagery of his childhood background while adding that his parents were not famous or rich but had worked hard every day. He used a new legal requirement of campaign advertising to emphasize the populist nature of his message. The Bipartisan Campaign Reform Act of 2002 requires candidates to announce their personal approval of every televised ad. Edwards told viewers "I approve this message because I believe that when you remember where you came from, you'll always know where you're going." He added that he wanted real change and would fight for an America that "works for all of us." In a similar ad, *Home*, Edward sat on the front porch of his childhood home and spoke about his intention to fight for opportunities for all, particularly with respect to jobs and health care. In *Hometown*, Edwards, dressed casually as he was in each of his introductory ads, walked along the main street of his childhood hometown and talked about the need for more jobs, better schools, affordable health care, and increased opportunities. He stressed that he was running in order to "keep the American dream alive in every hometown." He used a similar approach in *Chance* where he said he wanted to restore the promise of a better America. He concluded this ad by saying he would never forget where he came from, what he was fighting for, and "what Americans can accomplish if only given a chance."

The Edwards advertising campaign gradually transformed the personal background theme into a greater reliance on economic issues. There would be continued references to his experiences, but these were used primarily to enhance Edwards' credibility and distinguish him from his rivals. This approach is perhaps best illustrated in *American Jobs*. Here, Edwards told a campaign audience it was "easy for candidates to talk about manufacturing and jobs, but I've lived it, and I've not forgotten it. My dad worked in textile mills to put food on our table and clothes on our backs. Today, the mills are gone, and so are the jobs. That's why I opposed NAFTA and tax breaks to send jobs overseas." Edwards used a similar approach in other ads, including in *Jobs* where he stood in front of a closed textile mill and told the television audience about his opposition to tax laws that encouraged companies to relocate. He promised to change the law in ways that would encourage investment in this nation. In *College* he said he wanted to make college available to all were willing to work for it. He prefaced this by saying his grandmother had been a sharecropper.

He used the same approach in some of his attack ads. Like Kerry, Edwards also directed his attacks against Bush rather than at his Democratic rivals. In *Plan*, Edwards spoke directly to his television audience and began by referring to the usual features of his family background. He added that he had worked for ordinary people "whose voices are way too often ignored" during his years as a lawyer and Senator. He then attacked Bush for his interest in helping only those "at the top" and pointed out the economic failures of the Bush administration; millions of lost jobs, destroyed pensions, and higher health care and college costs.

Edwards used some attack ads where he spoke of the injustices that accompanied many of Bush's policies. In one instance, while speaking before a campaign audience as he did in all ads of this nature, he demanded to know why Bush's friends at Enron were not in jail. He then told his audience that when ordinary people steal milk, they go to jail. In another ad, he said Bush needed to explain why multimillionaires who were sitting beside their swimming pools paid lower taxes than teachers, secretaries, and police. He mocked Bush's claim that the nation was in an economic recovery while siding with individual people by saying "if you don't have a job, there is no recovery." He criticized the recent tax cuts by raising a question, "why don't we have the money for important needs." He answered his own question by saying that Bush had given the money away in tax breaks for the rich (*Milk, Pool, Create, Why Don't We?*). Finally, in an ad that addressed what some people believed was a major limitation of Kerry's and Edward's general election strategy, Edwards challenged Bush on values. He said he wanted to debate Bush about values and then defined them as a choice between children without health care or tax cuts for the rich (*Values*).

The Other Democrats

Howard Dean was more confrontational than either Kerry or Edwards and seemed more willing to attack his Democratic rivals. Moreover, he often posed his issues as contrasts to Bush and others. One can see an example of this style in Dean's leading introductory ad *Bio*. Here, a narrator told of how Dean had taken night classes in order to go to medical school, had worked in a Bronx emergency room, had become a family doctor, and had served as the governor of Vermont. In this latter capacity, the ad continued, Dean had turned a budget deficit into a surplus, had created jobs, raised wages, and, "while Washington talked," had provided health care coverage for nearly every child and prescription drug benefits for all seniors in his state. Now, he would repeal the Bush tax cuts, restore a foreign policy that reflected American values, break the special interest gridlock in Washington, and provide health care for every American. In an ad with a similar approach, *Leader*, a narrator spoke of how the test of a true leader was found in "standing up for what's right, even when it's not popular." The ad continued with the narrator saying that "when George Bush was riding high in the polls and other Democrats were silent, Howard Dean spoke out about the war and economy." Dean also attacked "some Democrats" in two other ads for supporting Bush on the war and taxes, although he did not use biographical information in these instances (*One Candidate, My Opponents*)." His only overt attack against a specific Democrat was in *Different View* when he used a female narrator to raise questions about how Gephardt, his major rival in the early stages of the Iowa caucuses, had supported both the congressional resolution authorizing the use of military force in Iraq, and an $87 billion supplemental request needed for funding the war.

Dean often linked his medical and political background in Vermont with health care. Three such ads contrasted Dean's accomplishments with Bush's alleged failures. In *Prescription Drug*, the narrator spoke of how Dean, as governor, had provided help for children and seniors and would, as president, repeal the Bush tax cut to pay for health insurance for every American. He added that we needed "to change the way Washington works," since this was the only to bring about health care for all. A similar ad, *Health Care* focused directly on the problems of children. The ad *Club for Truth* was similar in tone and style while focusing on government spending. After the narrator spoke of Dean's fiscal accomplishments in Vermont in balancing the budget, cutting taxes, raising wages, and providing more health care, he attacked Bush for bringing about a recession and the largest government deficit in history. Dean did not rely exclusively on a narrator; in the ad *Did It* he talked directly to a campaign audience about health care and the limitations of Bush's policies.

The two themes that Dean raised most frequently in his attacks against Bush were the Iraq war and the economy. On the war, Dean used a narrator in *Misled*, to accuse Bush of misleading the nation. This ad also contained Bush's controversial remarks from his 2003 State of the Union Address when he had said his administration had proof that Iraq had acquired materials for making weapons of mass destruction. Dean told the television audience that he had opposed the war from the beginning and added that we needed a foreign policy consistent with American values. Dean employed a similar approach; although this time he focused on the economy, in the ad *Enron Economics*. A narrator began by attacking Bush over his failures and then reviewed Dean's goals of creating two million new jobs, stopping tax breaks that encouraged industrial relocation, and investing more money in small businesses. Dean spoke next and said that Bush was doing to the economy what the executives at Enron had done to their company, "they get the benefits; we pay the bills." Dean complemented these two ads with two others where he was the only speaker. In *Every American*, he attacked Bush on both the war and economy while speaking before a campaign audience, and in *Join Us* he told the television audience he was running for president because he wanted to stop Bush's reckless policies (war and economic). He concluded by asking, "Don't you think it's time for someone to stand up to Bush and take our country back?"

While Dean's approach clearly differed from those of Kerry and Edwards, the reader should realize that the Dean campaign did not function on the same timeline as those of the two eventual nominees of the Democratic Party, and may well have made their work easier. Both Kerry and Edwards competed in major caucuses and primaries during January, February, and early March. They had emerged as the two leading candidates by mid-January and responded to this new designation by creating more ads as the voting progressed through a number of states. Dean was effectively finished as a candidate by the end of January. He had started his advertising in Iowa and New Hampshire earlier than either Kerry or Edwards. His relentless attacks against Bush in 2003, through advertising and public rallies, had excited Democratic voters and had elevated his candidacy to front-runner status. Dean's electoral failures in the early test states and his inability to raise enough money afterwards to compete effectively prevented his from adapting any of his advertising to the changing political conditions of the later primaries.

Dean needed to deal with an aggressive challenge from Gephardt in Iowa. Gephardt's introductions were similar to those of his previous effort in 1988, but he advanced different issues this time. This was evident in his attack ads. In one instance, in *Know*, Gephardt focused on Medicare and tried to link an unpopular proposal from the recent past with Dean. During the 1996 campaign, Bill Clinton attacked the Republicans, and Robert Dole and Newt Gingrich in particular, about their plans to reduce federal spending on Medicare by about $270 billion. Gephardt used quotes that Dean had made while serving as the governor of Vermont that appeared to support the Republican position. Gephardt concluded the ad by promising to protect Social Security. Gephardt also attacked Bush, and thereby forced Dean to response, in the ad *Jobs*. He said he wanted to stop Bush, who had lost more jobs than any president since Herbert Hoover, and promised that he would fight for the middle class. Gephardt claimed that the deficit was more than twice as high as it had been when Bush's father was president, that 41 million people were without health insurance, and ended his ad with the slogan "another Bush, another recession."

Another player in Iowa, although his electoral support turned out to be somewhat limited, was Kucinich. He used a number of short, 15 second, ads that focused mostly on the war in Iraq. His emphasis on the war kept the issue before voters and forced the other Democrats to respond. Kucinich used two slogans in his ads, "Fear Ends, Hope Begins" and "The eyes that see through the lies." The former usually appeared in written form at the end of the ad while the latter was advanced by the narrator (*Privacy, Listen, Inspire*).

Wesley Clark was the last major candidate to enter the race and compete in a primary; he made his first effort in New Hampshire. Clark used a military related theme in his introductions, focused many of his ads on character, and tried to link that theme to his personal ability to lead the nation in an uncertain and dangerous time. In the ad *Responsibility*, a narrator told viewers that Clark had led troops in combat and had been wounded in action. He said these experiences would make Clark an extraordinary president who would clean up the mess in Iraq. Another military related ad had a retired African-American officer, Major Patricia Williams, speaking about how well Clark had treated women while he was in the Army. Clark tried to link this background to economics in the ad *Secretary*. Here, a narrator said that Clark's father had died when the general was a child and that Clark's mother had supported the family while working as a secretary. These experiences meant that Clark would never forget what one job can mean to a family's life.

Clark used the character theme in several ads that had only vague references to specific issues. In one instance he used a narrator while in another he spoke directly to his television audience. In the former, the narrator, with supportive imagery of the White House, Bill Clinton, and Clark, told viewers that "everything has changed." After reminding viewers that Clark had dedicated his life to defending our security, the narrator added "At a time like this, don't we need a president like that?" In *Patriot*, Clark told television viewers that great leadership needed teamwork, spirit, sacrifice, and commitment. He concluded by adding that "to be strong on defense, you have to be strong on offense." He was much more specific in *Leader*, however. Here, once again speaking without the help of a narrator, Clark blasted the Bush administration for getting us into what he called the mess in Iraq. He said he had led troops into battle and would get us out of that mess.

While his background gave him a particular credibility and appeal on national security issues, Clark also directed some of his attention toward the same domestic issues as his rivals. He continued structuring his ads around the character theme. In *Hopes*, a narrator spoke of how Clark was raising our hopes, that he would put principle above politics and stand up to special interests, cut taxes for families, and bring about improvements in health care, education, and jobs. Clark also used a number of similar ads to focus individually on each of these issues; families (*Renewal*), taxes (*Future*), and education (*Respect*).

The various Democratic candidates were very similar to one another in their choices of issues. Each one focused his attention almost exclusively on Bush's recent tax cuts for the wealthy, job losses due to overseas relocation, and expensive health care while treating the Iraq war (Dean and Kucinich clearly excepted) as more of a management problem than a policy choice. They had no significant substantive disagreements on the direction the nation should take on the leading domestic concerns and essentially limited their differences to presentation style. They all tried to link their past backgrounds, either in combat, Congress, or in the practice of law or medicine, to domestic issues while emphasizing the theme that their unique personal background uniquely qualified them to lead a united Democratic Party. An opposition party tends to use this general strategy when it believes that a weak incumbent is vulnerable and that unification behind a candidate who holds out the promise of electoral victory is the preferred path to political power. There was only one important question that needed to be answered in the nomination campaign; which candidate held out the greatest promise of victory. The growing number of Kerry victories in the primaries and caucuses provided the answer and helped unify a party in the belief that it was on its way to defeating a weak incumbent.

CHAPTER 6

THE 2004 ELECTION: THE BUSH CAMPAIGN

General Overview

George W. Bush began his quest for a second term with his partisans united in their view that he was a strong and successful president deserving of reelection. This unity provided Bush with an opportunity similar to that enjoyed by the last two strong incumbents, Ronald Reagan and Bill Clinton, to begin his general election campaign at a time when the opposition party was still focused on resolving its nomination. Of course, John Kerry had emerged in mid-January as the likely Democratic nominee and few observers doubted that he would be denied the nomination. With this, the Bush campaign implemented an advertising strategy in early 2004 and perpetuated it throughout the year that had two distinctive themes; attacking the challenger Kerry and acclaiming the incumbent Bush (see Abramson, Aldrich, and Rohde, 2006; Ceaser and Busch, 2005; CQ Press, 2005; Cook, 2004; Crotty, 2005; Denton, 2005; Jamieson, 2006; Nelson, 2005; Sabato, 2006, for a detailed explanation of the 2004 election).

This chapter looks at how the Bush campaign emphasized these two themes, both independently of one another and by linking them together into a coherent message justifying his reelection. It also shows how the Bush advertising team altered the mix of themes across the five time periods of the election year. The chapter is subdivided into five sections for analysis with each corresponding to one of the year's major time periods. The first section, which covers the months of January, February, and March, focuses on the time when Kerry was competing against other Democrats in the primaries and could offer only a limited respond to any attacks from the Bush campaign. The second, encompassing April and May, looks at how the Bush campaign altered its approach after the conclusion of the primaries at a time when Kerry had difficulty reaching a national audience but while Bush was acting as president. The advertising during the summer months of June, July, and August comprises the third period. Kerry became more newsworthy because of the events related to the Democratic convention and the Bush campaign altered its strategy and its use of themes. The fourth, the pre-debate component of the general election campaign, consists of September. Bush was formally nominated by his party at the beginning of this month and started a new series of ads emphasizing the major goals of his second term while directing a limited number of attacks toward Kerry. The final, post-debate, period comprises October. The debates dominated the political news during this month. Moreover, a majority of voters, according to media generated polls, believed that Kerry had performed better than Bush in each of them. This was a problem for the Bush campaign. It responded by using more attack ads that were designed to strengthen the commitment of Republicans to the Bush reelection effort.

The Early Months: January to March

The Bush campaign used three different types of attack ads against Kerry during the nomination period with taxes and the Iraq war being the two most prominent. There was also a character related ad questioning Kerry's integrity. In *Unprincipled*, a female narrator talked about how Kerry had spoken against the influence of special interests in the Bush administration, but then she talked about the size of the campaign contributions Kerry had received from those same interests. With newspaper headlines and web sites as evidence, the narrator talked about Kerry's financial help from such interests as HMO's, telecommunication firms, and drug companies. As discussed in the last chapter, domestic issues had been the major focus of Kerry's ads during the nomination campaign. While the Bush campaign could not directly attack Kerry's goals of job creation, education, and health care since many people wanted expansions of these governmental actions, it could oppose them in a less obvious manner. Conservative candidates and organizations frequently oppose social welfare programs by emphasizing the increased taxes that may be needed to fund them. In the ad *Differences*, a narrator accused Kerry of planning to increase federal taxes by $900 Billion during his first one hundred days in office. In addition, he accused Kerry of voting to increase taxes on Social Security benefits and gasoline while opposing tax credits for health insurance. In another anti-tax ad, *Wacky*, the Bush campaign accused Kerry of voting to increase gasoline taxes eleven different times. With imagery of old cars driving in a circle and of several people riding a multi person bicycle, the narrator mocked Kerry's past statements by telling the audience that Kerry believed higher gasoline taxes would encourage people to drive less.

These accusations were only partially true. The $900 billion figure was an estimate of the amount of tax money that would be generated over several years if the tax cuts enacted at the beginning of the Bush presidency were not extended. Some of these cuts were due to expire at the end of 2004. Kerry had advocated the elimination of these cuts with the money generated used for funding his domestic programs. The remaining votes for which the ads attacked Kerry were for ones he had cast on comprehensive revenue bills that had numerous subsections and not on the specific issues mentioned. Congress is not inclined to hold votes on single issues where members must publicly record their support for unpopular positions on financial issues, such as increased taxes or reduced benefits. Instead, members cast votes for lengthy appropriations and revenue bills that often contain these controversial provisions.

While the Bush campaign attacked Kerry over his plans for increasing taxes in order to pay for more governmental spending, it also accused him of opposing more governmental spending. These attacks were related to funding of the war in Iraq. Federal law requires the president to submit a budget to Congress each year outlining expected revenues and proposed expenditures. The Bush budget for fiscal year 2004 contained no expenses for funding the war. Instead, Bush asked for an $87 Billion supplemental appropriation from Congress several weeks after submitting his budget. This proposal generated an intense debate over management of the war. In the ad *Troops*, the Bush campaign talked about Kerry's opposition to this supplemental funding and spoke of his votes against funding body armor and higher combat pay for soldiers and increased health care for military families. Once again, the members of Congress did not vote on each matter separately but instead cast votes on the entire appropriation as a comprehensive proposal. The ad also quoted Kerry as saying that he had voted for the bill before he had voted against it.

Finally, the Bush campaign combined the taxes and war themes in the ad *100 Days*. Here, the narrator attacked Kerry for his plans to increase taxes and for his lack of support for national defense and the war on terrorism. This ad referred to the $900 Billion in new taxes and to Kerry's lack of support for the Iraq war that had already been mentioned in other ads. The 100 days referred to the changes that Kerry would make in the first three months of his presidential term. Kerry, as mentioned above, had used ads that emphasized the goals he wished to accomplish in his first one hundred days as president.

There were two components of the acclaims portion of Bush's ads; relatively optimistic ones with Bush speaking, and more pessimistic ones with a narrator talking. In *Lead*, Bush remarked about the entrepreneurial spirit in private sector job creation. He told his audience that he knew what we needed to do for job growth and added that he was optimistic about America because he believed in people. He also identified himself as "President Bush" when he said he approved the message. He used a similar theme in the ad *21st Century*. Here, Bush also told the audience of his optimism and its relation to his belief in people. This ad focused more specifically on small business. In *Forward*, Bush told the audience that the nation had recently faced serious challenges but now faced a choice. He spoke of how "together we're moving America forward" while referring to such policy areas as fighting terrorism, creating new jobs, and improving education and health care. The ad included imagery of the each of these individual references as Bush spoke. The more pessimistic ads focused the attention on recent national troubles but then linked the solutions to those troubles with Bush. In *Tested*, a narrator told the audience that the past few years had tested America in many ways. He continued by adding that "America" had risen to the challenge and the values of "freedom, family, faith, and sacrifice" would see us through tough times. These remarks were complemented with imagery of Bush in a variety of settings. The ad concluded with a slogan that, as was often a recurring feature of similar ads employed by other incumbents, used the symbolic dimensions of the presidency and the presidential office to emphasize the competence of the current president. The slogan was "President Bush, Steady Leadership in Times of Change." Finally, the Bush campaign used an ad that relied exclusively on imagery to emphasize many of these same ideas. It included written references to January, 2001 by saying the economy was in recession, the stock market was declining, the computer, or dot com industry had crashed, and terrorists had attacked the nation. Bush, who was shown taking the oath of office as the new president, had met this challenge, as the ad depicted this chain of events. The ad, *Safer, Stronger*, also contained a scene at the end with Bush introducing himself to the television audience with the statement, "I am George W. Bush and I approve this ad."

The Post-Primary Months: April and May

The Bush campaign's advertising moved in a different direction after Kerry had secured the Democratic nomination and his rivals, including Edwards, had closed ranks behind him. The advertising was far more attack oriented with acclaims clearly limited to a secondary role. It contained only two new ads that were not attack oriented during this second time period. The attacks focused more on the Iraq war but included additional references to Kerry's personal integrity and to the usual Republican issue of high taxes. The personal attack ad, *Doublespeak*, began with a female narrator telling of how Kerry had been saying that he was not well known. She raised doubts about this contention and was then supported by a male narrator who mentioned statements from various newspapers about Kerry's positions. The doublespeak reference came from the Boston Globe. In addition, there were quotes from the Wall Street Journal, the Manchester New Hampshire Union Leader, and the National Journal on such issues as the Iraq war, taxes, and his liberal voting record. The female narrator concluded the ad by saying that Kerry's problem was not that "people don't know him, it is that they do." The new tax related ad, *Troubling*, made the same accusations as earlier ads about the so-called tax increase of $900 Billion that would take place during the first one hundred days of a Kerry presidency. This time, there were also references to some of the taxes that would increase. Included here were taxes on married couples, gasoline, Social Security benefits, and reduced deductions for children. These charges were also misleading. The higher taxes that had been mentioned in the ad were already required by law and would have to be paid unless Congress extended the temporary tax cuts that had been enacted in 2001. The tax changes that Kerry may have called for had he been elected were not brought out in this ad.

The Bush campaign used several new attack ads during this second time period that continued focusing attention on Kerry's votes related to funding military operation in Iraq. The actual relationship of the accusations to the conduct of the war was questionable, however, because some of the attacks were over issues that were not applicable to the war. Nonetheless, one cannot assume that the viewing public would necessarily know this; hence, a response by the Kerry campaign was necessary. There was a new version of the *Troops* ad during this time that was also critical of Kerry for voting against the $87 Billion supplemental appropriation, and there were several versions of the ad *Weapons*. In this particular set of ads, a narrator, a male this time in contrast to the female narrator of the *Troops* ads, attacked Kerry for voting against a number of military weapons systems. The ad began with a linkage to the Iraq war with the narrator stating "as our troops defend America in the war on terror, they must have what it takes to win." The narrator then told the audience that Kerry had repeatedly opposed the weapons systems that were vital to winning the war. He mentioned various weapons; Bradley fighting vehicles, Patriot missiles, the B-2 Stealth bomber, and F-18 fighter jets, and added that Kerry had "even voted against body armor for our troops on the front line in the war on terror." The ad concluded with the narrator saying that Kerry's votes on national security matters were troubling. Two additional versions of this ad were used exclusively in Arizona and New Hampshire. Here, the ad was changed slightly in order to point out that some of the components in the weapons systems were produced in the state in question. The misleading nature of these ads was similar to the tax related ones discussed previously; Congress rarely conducts votes on individual weapons but instead combines a number of procurement measures into one large annual appropriations bill.

A second anti-Kerry ad of this period focused on the Democratic candidate's recent opposition to the USA Patriot Act. This law had been enacted shortly after the bombings of September 11, 2001 in order to expand the powers of law enforcement agencies to fight terrorism. By 2004 a number of people had become quite critical of the law's potential threats to civil rights and liberties. The ad, entitled *Patriot Act*, began with a narrator saying that "President Bush signed the Patriot Act that has given law enforcement vital tools to fight terrorism." The narrator then spoke about the wiretapping, subpoena and surveillance powers that were already used against drug dealers. He added that Kerry had voted for the law but now wanted to remove those tools because of pressure from his fellow liberals. The ad concluded with the narrator accusing Kerry of "playing politics with national security."

The Bush campaign used only two new acclaims related ads during this time. Both were related to education and aimed at promoting the successes of Bush's major education program from his first term, the No Child Left Behind Act. One ad relied upon a female narrator to talk about Bush's accomplishments while the other used Laura Bush, his wife and a former teacher. The first of these, *Key to Success*, started out with the assertion that accountability and high standards were important to parents for measuring a child's progress. It continued by saying that, thanks to Bush, schools now had those standards, well qualified teachers, and accountability. Laura Bush, in *Take a Look*, said that children at risk needed help, pointed out how the new law had provided that help with greater funding, talked about how the president, as she referred to her husband on several occasions, looked at schools as a parent would, and concluded by also emphasizing the importance of standards and accountability. The focus of this ad then changed as a female narrator talked about how Bush had brought about the No Child Left Behind Act because of demands from parents, and then she attacked Kerry in a manner similar to what had been used in the *Patriot Act* ad. She told viewers that Kerry had initially supported the law but he had now turned against it because of pressure from education unions. The conclusion was similar as well; the narrator accused Kerry of "playing politics with education."

The National Convention Months: June to August

The themes in the Bush advertising during the summer months of 2004 differed from those of earlier times in the sense that they contained a greater balance of attacks and acclaims and focused more attention on a broader range of issues. There were five different topics in the attack ads; terrorism, intelligence, nuclear waste disposal, taxes and the economy, and a new one, Kerry's missed votes in the Senate. The acclaims ads featured Bush talking about the president's duty to lead the nation, his concept of an "ownership" society, and of his optimism about the economy in contrast to Kerry's pessimism. There were new ads that featured John McCain endorsing Bush and a controversial one that used imagery from the Olympics and which was quickly denounced by Olympic organizers and others as inappropriate politicizing of the quadrennial non-partisan games.

As mentioned earlier, new campaign finance laws now require presidential candidates to announce their personal approval of televised ads. The Bush campaign had been using this requirement to its advantage since the beginning of the campaign, but it made some changes in imagery during the summer months. Most ads, and particularly the attack one, began with a scene of Bush stating "I am George W. Bush and I approve this message." Each ad was accompanied with imagery linking Bush to the symbolic dimensions of the presidential office.

Most of them illustrated him walking or meeting with people at the White House. While the Bush advertising also contained such imagery during the summer months, it also had new imagery showing Bush campaigning and interacting with enthusiastic supporters. He was also dressed much more informally here. There was an additional change in the summertime ads, and particularly in the ones initially released in August. These included excerpts from Kerry's acceptance speech at the Democratic convention in July. After Bush's opening statement of approval, an ad would show Kerry's remarks about a specific issue. With this, a narrator would attack Kerry for his inconsistency on that issue, cite his congressional voting record, and conclude the ad with the statement "there's what Kerry says, and there's what Kerry does." For example, Kerry told the Democrats that he would reform the intelligence system. The narrator then said Kerry had missed about three-fourths of the meetings of the Senate Intelligence committee and had voted to reduce intelligence spending by about $6 Billion (*Intel*). A taxation related ad, *Taxing our Economy*, was similar in that it contained a scene of Kerry telling the Democrats he would not raise taxes on the middle class. The narrator then accused Kerry of voting to raise taxes on 98 different occasions while naming specific categories of taxes where those votes had taken place. The categories were gasoline, breaks for middle class parents, and Social Security benefits. Although released before the convention, the ad *Priorities* was similar in style in the sense that it attacked Kerry for missing congressional votes related to limitations on medical malpractice awards and defense spending and for voting against the so-called "Laci Peterson" law, a proposal that would criminalize fetal killing. This ad concluded with a statement and a question, "Kerry has his priorities, are they yours?" The other two issues that the Bush campaign used against Kerry during the summer months were terrorism, where they said that a pamphlet he had written about terrorism lacked any references to Osama Bin Laden but had spoken of a Japanese criminal gang, Yakuza, and nuclear wastes. This latter ad commented on Kerry's supportive votes for storing nuclear waste in Nevada (*Yakuza, Kerry's Yucca*).

The Bush campaign released a number of new acclaims ads during the summer that were similar in both style and substance to the ones it had used earlier in the first part of 2004. Bush would speak indirectly to the television audience, he would talk to an off camera person, about his optimistic beliefs relating to people and the nation. In *Ownership*, Bush said he wanted to encourage people to own their own homes, businesses, health care, and a piece of their retirements, and he understood "if you own something, you have a vital stake in the future of America." In another ad (*Pessimism*) Bush said he was optimistic about America because he believed in Americans. A narrator then spoke about how Bush's policies had improved the economy, reduced inflation and interest rates, cut taxes, and increased home ownership. He accused Kerry of focusing too much attention on the Great Depression while "reminding" viewers that "pessimism never created a job." Bush also emphasized foreign policy. In *Solemn Duty*, he said he had a solemn duty to protect the nation. Bush spoke about the 9-11 terrorist attack and proclaimed we could not hesitate and could not yield in bringing an enemy to justice. Two other ads with essentially the same foreign policy theme relied on narrators for the speaking roles. The ad *Changing World*, used a male narrator to tell the audience that the world was changing and we needed a vision and a sense of purpose and must depend on our values of freedom, faith, and family). A female narrator remarked that the last few years had tested America in many ways but we had become optimistic because of freedom, faith, family, and sacrifice. The ad ended with the statement of "President Bush, Moving us Forward" (*Together*).

One of the stronger Bush ads during the summer months featured John McCain who, while shown introducing Bush to a campaign audience, depicted the war on terrorism as a fight between right and wrong and good and evil. McCain called terrorists "depraved enemies" who hated our way of life and described the war on terrorism as "the great test of our generation." McCain told the audience that Bush had led the nation with "great moral clarity and firm resolve" and was determined to make the nation a safer and freer place and therefore deserved our support and admiration (*First Choice*). This ad was particularly important for Bush to make and use because extensive rumors had been circulating during this time that Kerry wanted to ask McCain to be his vice presidential running mate. A national ticket of two veterans of the Vietnam War talking about new efforts at fighting terrorism clearly posed a major threat to the Bush campaign since terrorism had been one of the president's strongest issues.

Finally, and in what turned into a major controversy and embarrassment for the Bush campaign, the ad *Victory* used imagery from the Olympics to advance the reelection effort. Here, a female narrator told viewers that only forty democracies had existed in 1972 but 120 existed now. With imagery of athletic competition, the narrator said there were two more new ones today (Afghanistan and Iraq were written on the screen), and added that "with strength and resolve, democracy will triumph over terror." There were many complaints that the ad was an inappropriate attempt to politicize the non-partisan games. The Olympics had taken place during the first three weeks of August, thus limiting news coverage of the presidential campaign. Republicans held their national convention within days of the Olympics' conclusion. This also provided the Bush campaign an opportunity to develop a new set of campaign ads.

The Post-Convention Campaign: September

The 2004 campaign reached an important turning point on September 2. The Republican National Convention ended this day with Bush's acceptance speech in the same city and very near the most famous site of the tragedy of 9-11. The speech was the most significant public event that occurred during this highly televised, but increasingly ignored, quadrennial institution of American politics. The last day of the convention marked the end of the middle period of the campaign that had taken place between the conclusion of the nominating primaries in early March and the beginning of the post-convention drive to the general election. The most intense part of the campaign was now underway. The candidates were devoting every day to personal campaigning; mass media were providing more intense, albeit of often questionable quality, daily coverage of political events; political parties were trying to mobilize their partisans in get-out-the vote drives; voters were waiting for the debates to help them reach decisions or reaffirm ones they had already made, and the airwaves were filled with even more advertising than before. The Bush campaign started a series of new ads in early September that placed far more emphasis on specific policy proposals than previous ads had done. This change of focus did not reduce the widespread use of attack ads by Bush campaign to convey the message that Kerry posed a threat to the goals of the Bush agenda, however.

Three new issue related ads that were similar in style and which drew attention to Bush's goals for a second term initially appeared in September. The second term theme was new as previous Bush acclaims ads had focused primarily on his past efforts at fighting terrorism or on his optimistic view of the nation and its people. These ads offered no great surprises, however, for numerous convention speakers had recently talked about these same issues or had attacked Kerry for his lack of support for many of them. Each of these three ads involved the use of two narrators, a male and a female, who alternated in talking about a variety of healthcare, economic, war on terror issues. The ads began with one of the narrators saying "President Bush and our leaders in Congress have a plan." The two narrators than took turns mentioning specific goals related to that broad issue, although neither offered any detained information about the content of Bush's plans. One ad, *Healthcare Agenda*, had one narrator promise "lower health care costs" while the next then added "allow small businesses to band together for insurance purchases." Similar statements followed; "tax free saving accounts families own," "stop junk lawsuits against doctors," "keep doctors in their communities," health centers in every poor county," and "every eligible child with health coverage." The economic ad (*Economic Agenda*) followed a similar format with short references made by the alternating narrators to "strengthen our economy," "lifelong learning," "invest in education," "new skills for better jobs," "fairer, simpler tax code," "reduce dependence on foreign oil," "incentives to create jobs," "strengthen Social Security," "legal reform," and "permanent tax relief." The *War on Terror Agenda*, had alternating promises calling for "enhance border and port security," "increase homeland security measures," "reform and strengthen intelligence services," "renew the Patriot Act," "create national terrorism center," "transform our military," "give the military all it needs," and "find terrorists where they live and hide." In addition to these three ads, the Bush campaign used another one, *Agenda*, where the president was shown speaking to an audience about many of the same economic goals mentioned above.

The Bush campaign also introduced some new attack ads that were designed to complement the goal related ones in the new *Agenda* series. The female narrator focused on Kerry's record on healthcare and economics while the male attacked Kerry on the war on terrorism. In *Healthcare: Practical versus Big Government*, the narrator reiterated some of the Bush goals from *Healthcare Agenda*, and then attacked "Kerry and the liberal Democrats in Congress" for wanting "big government" in charge of a new health care program she said would cost about $1.5 Trillion. The ad *Economy: Common Sense versus Higher Taxes* also began with the narrator reciting Bush's promises, and then attacking Kerry and the "liberal Democrats in Congress" for raising taxes on small businesses. The narrator in *Peace and Security* attacked Kerry for his congressional votes on national security issues such as reducing intelligence spending after the first bombing of the World Trade Center, elimination of forty weapons systems that he said were used in the war on terror, and for refusing to "support our troops with body armor." The ad ended with the narrator linking the Democratic presidential candidate with the "villains" that Republicans see as responsible for most national troubles, "John Kerry and congressional liberals, putting our protection at risk."

Three other attack ads that also appeared initially in September focused on Kerry's positions on issues and were designed both to raise, and reinforce, the claim by the Bush campaign that Kerry was inconsistent on some of the major issues he was advancing. The ad *Windsurfing* was by far the strongest personal attack during the month. It contained imagery of Kerry windsurfing in Boston Harbor during the July Democratic convention with a narrator accusing the Senator of inconsistencies in his positions relating to Iraq, education, and Medicare. The narrator followed his accusations, and with the accompaniment of the imagery of Kerry windsurfing, with the remark "John Kerry, whichever way the wind blows." A similar ad, this time focused on the Iraq war, had scenes of Kerry making what appeared to be contradictory statements relating to the war. The Bush campaign had used this imagery before. Here, Kerry was once again shown telling an audience he had voted for the $87 Billion supplemental appropriation that Bush had wanted for funding the war before he had voted against it. With this, the narrator asked the audience, "How can John Kerry protect us when he doesn't even know where he stands?" The third ad, which focused on Medicare spending, had a narrator accusing Kerry of voting to raise the premiums that Medicare recipients must pay for hospital coverage on 36 different occasions. In a remark designed to remind viewers of the Iraq related ad described above, the narrator concluded, "John Kerry, he actually voted for higher Medicare premiums before he came out against them (*Searching, Medicare Hypocrisy*)."

This combination of ads, some outlining the general goals for a second Bush term and others attacking Kerry for his alleged inconsistencies on many of the same issues, were initially used during the weeks between the end of the Republican convention and the first of the presidential debates, which was held in late September. The debates provided Kerry with an opportunity to address the charges of inconsistency. Kerry had a public relations problem that he needed to address; many people knew very little about him other than from what they might have learned from televised advertising. Kerry had directed his nomination campaign at only a limited part of the nation, those states with important primaries, while generally ignoring the remaining states. Moreover, television news media were preoccupied with their "horserace coverage," where they directed much of their attention to polls while trying to determine which candidates were leading or trailing, and were not providing voters with much information about the candidates or their promises. The Bush attack ads had raised questions about Kerry's integrity and ability to serve as president, questions he needed to address. The debates provided him with that opportunity. He performed well; polls indicated that voters saw him winning each debate. The debates ended about three weeks before the general election. With this, the two campaigns introduced their final sets of ads. Nearly all of Bush's were attack related.

The Final Round: October

The Bush advertising during the final campaign month, October, was almost completely comprised of attack ads. Twelve new ones were introduced this month compared to only two new acclaims related ads. The two acclaims ads dealt with economics and military families. One of them, *Nearly Two Million Reasons* featured a narrator who emphasized the number "two million" on a number of occasions while telling viewers about the economic accomplishments of the Bush presidency. The narrator began the ad by saying there were many reasons to be hopeful about America and then started his references to the number two million. He said there were "two million new jobs," and "two million more people working," "two million people with wages who were able to provide for their families," and concluded by telling the audience there were "two million reasons to be optimistic about our future." This ad was released several days prior to the final debate in mid-October. In what might have been a miscue, or a lost opportunity for reemphasizing a point, Bush did not use the phrase "two million" during the debate when he referred to the number of new jobs that had been created during his first term in office. He said that 1.9 million new jobs had been created. This number was far less memorable than the "two million" referred to in the ad and had less potential for reinforcing a phrase that debate viewers might have heard elsewhere.

The other acclaims ad, *Whatever it Takes*, included a scene of Bush speaking to an audience of military families. Bush told his audience about the difficulties he had faced in sending soldiers into battle and of how he had met with the families of the fallen. He added that he had seen the character of the nation and "will never relent in defending America, whatever it takes." The imagery, with began with a written reference to "President Bush," involved the power and symbolic dimensions of the presidential office. Bush was speaking to soldiers and their families at a military base, was accompanied by a number of high ranking uniformed officers, and was clearly acting in the presidential role of commander in chief. This role was unique in that Bush alone could perform it. Such a role was not available to his challenger.

The attack ads divided into three broad categories; taxes, health care, and war and terrorism. While the ads were new, the charges in the attacks were often similar or even identical with the ones the Bush campaign had used earlier in the year. The one new feature was to link Kerry with "liberals in Congress" as a major problem with which the nation had to contend. With respect to taxes, the ad *Clockwork* accused "Kerry and the liberals in Congress" of their "clockwork like" votes for increased taxes. There were specific references to Kerry's votes for increasing taxes on gasoline, Social Security benefits, and middle class parents. An ad with a similar theme, *Thinking Mom*, showed a woman listening to a radio ad while driving her car. The radio broadcast consisted of wording from the *Clockwork* ad. The woman clearly approved of the charges and indicated that she was not planning to vote for Kerry. In addition to reemphasizing the same charges that earlier ads had made against Kerry, this new group of tax related ads also suggested that he had cast votes on specific issues that, in reality, had not been brought to the floor of the Senate for consideration. Kerry had cast his votes on comprehensive revenue bills which contained these issues in some of their subsections.

The Bush campaign also introduced several new ads that attacked Kerry on health care. One set of ads dealt with medical malpractice lawsuits. In recent years, a number of Republicans, including Bush, have advocated that financial limits should be placed on the awards that juries can grant for punitive damages and for pain and suffering. They have placed the blame for the sharp recent increases in medical malpractice insurance on massive awards and claim they are forcing many doctors to abandon their practices in some fields of medicine. Democrats have denied that lawsuits are the primary force responsible for the increased costs. Instead, they attribute the problem to insurance companies that are gouging prices in hopes of generating even higher profits. The two Bush ads that focused on this controversy were aimed primarily at women. They included one with a female narrator (*Med Mal*) and another with a female doctor (*Tort Reform*), both of whom talked about access problems in women's health while clearly placing the blame on lawyers. The two narrators talked about the severity of the access problem and then blamed Kerry and liberals for voting against controlling awards and frivolous lawsuits from trial lawyers.

Other health care ads attacked Kerry for his alleged plans to increase the size of the federal bureaucracy. In three separate but related ads, the Bush campaign said that Kerry's health care proposals would result in the creation of a massive new federal bureaucracy that would make access to doctors particularly difficult. Of course, the ads did not raise questions about the massive size of the current private bureaucracy in the health insurance industry. The ad *Your Doctor* had images of a very large and complicated looking organizational chart of governmental agencies that a male narrator described as Kerry's plan. He told viewers that "Kerry and the liberals in Congress" were advocating a complicated health care plan that would cost about $1.5 Trillion and would include such governmental institutions as the Internal Revenue Service and the Department of the Treasury. There were references to how "your doctor is in here somewhere," and viewers were told that their doctor would not be able to make medical decisions. A similar ad, *Complicated Plan*, also featured the same chart and had a narrator tell viewers of how complicated the plan was and of the difficulties that people would likely encounter in getting care. He referred to such potential problems as rationing of care, less access, fewer choices, long lines, and the inability of doctors to make medical decisions. A nearly identical message appeared in *Don't take Chances*. Here, a female narrator talked about the organizational chart, accused "Kerry and the liberals in Congress" of wanting to create a $1.5 Trillion program which would have the same problems as mentioned in the *Complicated Plan* ad, and reminded viewers "you don't want to take chances with your health or health care."

The ads related to terrorism and Iraq also questioned Kerry's past voting record and some of his public comments on the issue. Kerry had once said that fighting terrorism was more of a problem of law enforcement than the military. The ad *World View* did not directly challenge this idea, but held Kerry up to ridicule for saying it. The narrator concluded the ad by asking the question of whether Kerry could fight terrorism if he did not understand the problem. One ad that seemed aimed more at scaring the audience then advancing a Bush position on terrorism was *Risk*. It began with a narrator telling viewers that "things have changed since 9-11." He said that if we did not fight the terrorists abroad we would have to fight them here. Bush had made some similar claims in justifying the military invasion of Iraq and he had encouraged the idea that the invasions of Afghanistan and Iraq were attempts to solve the same problem. There is a certain illogic to the argument that Iraqi fighters with limited mobility and inferior weapons would invade the United States if we were not fighting a war in their country. The ad reemphasized many of the same national security accusations of earlier; it attacked "Kerry and his liberal allies in Congress" for opposing certain weapons systems, some of which had been debated during the Reagan administration, that allegedly were needed for fighting terrorism. The ad concluded with a question asking if Kerry and his liberal allies were a risk we could afford today. In addition, there was yet another ad that questioned Kerry's vote against the $87 Billion supplemental appropriation for Iraq (*No Limit*).

In what was a fairly obvious attempt at copying the copy the famous *Bear* ad from the 1984 Reagan reelection effort, the Bush campaign attacked "Kerry and the Democrats in Congress" over their past votes at reducing the size of the intelligence budget. With an ominous sounding female narrator talking about an increasingly dangerous world where the spending cuts Kerry had supported would "attract those who seek to do American harm," the ad contained a scene of several grey wolves gathered in a forest. Viewers were apparently expected to assume the worst might result from such a group of vicious animals (*Wolves*).

While many candidates from campaigns in earlier years had used ads that contrasted the candidates on a number of issues, as discussed in previous chapters, Bush and Kerry tended to avoid using this style of advertising throughout much of 2004. Bush did use one such ad during the final days of the campaign, however. A narrator contrasted the goals of "Bush and his allies in Congress" with those of "Kerry and his liberal allies" in *The Choice*. Bush and his allies stood for strong leadership, tax relief, common sense health care, and protection of Social Security while Kerry and the liberals was for higher taxes, government run health care, and reckless cuts in intelligence and defense spending.

Summary and Analysis

The Bush campaign varied its combinations of attack and acclaims related ads throughout the five periods of the 2004 campaign. It used the two categories about equally during the early months of January to March when Kerry was competing for the Democratic nomination; during the summer months of June to August when the major political events were the national conventions, and in September during the time between the end of the conventions and the beginnings of the nationally televised debates. It relied mostly on attack ads during the other two periods; April and May after Kerry nearly disappeared from network news and was not visible to many voters, and in the final month of the campaign, October, when voters finally had to make their decisions. Throughout the campaign, the attack ads were directed toward three issues; taxes, health care, and terrorism and war, and were often aimed at questioning the consistency of Kerry's record and promises and at raising doubts about his personal character. The themes were not particularly original in that most of them had been used by Republican candidates in previous elections. Opposition to taxes and large governmental bureaucracies has been a major component of Republican promises at both the national and state levels for decades. The emphasis on greater spending on national security and war is a more recent phenomenon for Republican candidates, however. Republicans were often opposed to American internationalism prior to the Cold War but changed their views during the years following the Korean War.

The Bush campaign attacked Kerry for his votes against higher military spending, for supporting a number of tax increases, and for wanting to create a costly government controlled health care system. In some instances, the Bush ads misrepresented Kerry's actions by singling out specific components of comprehensive appropriations and revenue bills while accusing him of voting incorrectly on them as if the Senate actually conducted votes on each individual measure. In other instances, and particularly with respect to national security matters, the Bush campaign tried to use fear as a motivator. The nation faced ominous threats from abroad and Kerry did not seem sufficiently interested in confronting them with military means. Moreover, as seen in the health care ads, government was already too big and should not be increased in either size and funding. There was a certain illogic in the Bush ads and in the general Republican approach to modern American government, and it was one that Kerry needed to confront. The fiscal policies (taxing and spending) of the recent Republican presidents, Ronald Reagan and the two Bushes, had strong biases toward increasing national deficits. The policies had resulted in expanded military spending, reduced taxes, and little or no change in spending on popular entitlement programs such as Social Security or Medicare. Massive deficits marked the administrations of all three presidents. A successful war on terror would be costly and would require a bigger role for government. Foreign wars and tax cuts are not mutually compatible and wars cannot be carried out effectively while reducing the size of governmental programs. Wars require sacrifice on the part of citizens, and quite frequently, that sacrifice has to be economic. By 2004, a number of former military leaders, including Democratic candidate Wesley Clark, had accused Bush of failing to realize the manpower demands his Iraqi policy had placed on the armed forces. They believed that far more troops and equipment would be needed to win the war than Bush was willing to admit. There did not seem to be enough federal money to pay for an endeavor of the magnitude that Bush would need to accomplish his foreign policy goals. In response, Kerry needed to implement an advertising strategy that exposed these contradictions while developing an alternative vision of national leadership.

Bush's acclaims ads relied on the symbolic dimensions of the presidential office to call attention to his actions relating to the 9-11 attacks, to outline a vague collection of promises about health care, economics, and terrorism that he hoped to pursue in a second term, and on an upbeat attitude about America and American life that was linked to national myths of hope and economic progress. With respect to the first of these, the response to 9-11, the ads raised the theme that Bush, in his unique capacity as president, had responded effectively to the attacks and would continue doing so in future years. He used imagery were he acted in a manner that was available only to a president, to speak to soldiers and their families at a military installation in the statesmanlike role of commander in chief about the difficulties he had encountered in sending troops abroad. His second term promises, while general, were outlined in several ads that contained references to "President Bush." This title has dual meanings; the president in the unifying and statesmanlike leader of the nation and the divisive and partisan leader of a political party. The statesman was promising to implement a partisan agenda. Finally, the ads where he appeared upbeat when talking about economic growth contained imagery of the trappings of official power. They were made with scenes of the White House and the president speaking to an off camera person about what he saw as the primary sources of American greatness.

CHAPTER 7

THE 2004 ELECTION: THE KERRY CAMPAIGN

General Overview

The conclusion of the Democratic Party's nominating campaign in early March presented John Kerry with an altered set of conditions that forced an immediate change of tactics. Kerry had devoted months of his time, and a considerable part of his finances as well, to defeating his numerous intra-party rivals. With that task behind him, he now needed to respond to the strong attacks coming his way from the Bush campaign and its allies that questioned both his personal integrity and his commitment to the issues he had been using in defining himself. Kerry's advertising needs, which derived from his role as the challenger of an incumbent rather than as the incumbent himself, differed in a number of ways from those of Bush. In particular, Kerry needed to continue using introductory and biographical ads because he was not well known in far too many parts of the nation. Thus far, he had focused his campaigning only on those states with contested primaries or caucuses. Bush's attack ads had virtually served as Kerry's introduction in to many voters in several of the competitive states. This chapter looks at how Kerry presented himself, and attacked Bush, during the last seven months of the general election campaign. Since

Kerry's nomination campaign was discussed earlier, this chapter is structured around the final four time periods that were used in the previous chapter; the months of April and May that immediately followed the primaries and when the national news media showed little interest in the campaign; the summer months of June, July, and August when media interest increased because of the party conventions; September, the intense month of campaign activity between the conventions and debates; and October, the time of the debates and the concluding efforts of the two political parties to motivate their own partisans to actually cast ballots.

The Early Months: April and May

Kerry introduced two new biographical ads during this time, both of which directed attention to his background and then linked it with his political life. He filled the role of major speaker in one ad, *Heart*, while a narrator did so in the other one, *Lifetime*. Both ads began with references to how Kerry had been born in Fitzsimmons Army Hospital in Denver, that his father had served in the Army Air Corps, and that his mother had been a community leader. These remarks were followed by references to his education at Yale University and his combat experiences in Vietnam. There was imagery of Kerry in a combat uniform, statements by the narrator that he had volunteered for action and had won five medals for heroism, and statements by two veterans who had served under his command about his great leadership abilities. Kerry, or others, spoke of how his parents had taught him of the value of public service and of how this had guided him throughout his thirty year public career. This public career included service as a prosecutor when Kerry had fought for victims' rights; and as a Senator where he worked with John McCain to resolve long standing problems relating to prisoners of war and soldiers missing in action from Vietnam. Both ads concluded by claiming "a lifetime of service and strength."

The Kerry campaign also released two new issue related ads during April and May and Kerry spoke to the audience in each of them. In *Commitment*, Kerry said he would "set a few clear national priorities for America." He would start by keeping the country "safe and secure," and then put an end to the tax incentives that encouraged job relocation overseas and invest more money in education and health care. Kerry told his audience his priorities were jobs and health care and his commitment was to defend the country. He also talked about Iraq in *Risk*, but did not advocate a policy much different from that of the Bush administration. Kerry said we needed to reach out to other nations to share the burden and risk in that war. He was critical of the fact that we had already spent more than $200 Billion and were likely to spend even more.

These ads were complemented by a set of attacks aimed at Bush's record on an array of domestic issues including jobs, abortion, environment, taxes, and health care but not on foreign policy or war. This was a continuing feature of the Kerry advertising strategy through the remainder of the campaign. Kerry would be critical of Bush's management of the war in Iraq but did not question the major assumptions that justified it. Instead, Kerry emphasized his military credentials and then concentrated his promises on domestic issues. On jobs, Kerry used an ad where a narrator talked about job relocation overseas and quoted a Bush economic advisor saying that such practices were in the nation's interest. The narrator then told the audience that Kerry's plan would change tax laws in ways that would encourage rather than discourage domestic job creation and this would result in the creation of ten million new jobs (*10 Million New Jobs*). Other domestic related ads spoke of how the nation had lost three million jobs during Bush's tenure in office (*Join the Fight*), that Bush was allowing corporate polluters to rewrite environmental laws aimed at weakening the Clean Air Act (*Join the Fight for Our Environment*), that Bush had done nothing to fight the high cost of health care (*Time's Up*), but was trying to appoint anti-choice and privacy judges to the Supreme Court, something that Kerry clearly would not do (*Choice*). In one humorous ad, the Kerry campaign featured a child named George who had just prepared his first budget. The female narrator talked about how this child had failed to account for a number of important costs such as tax cuts and health care (*Very First Bush Budget*). These ads clearly addressed a broad range of domestic issues, but they did not challenge Bush on terrorism and war. Numerous polls continued to show that most voters saw Bush as more capable of dealing with these threats than Kerry.

The Summer Months: June to August

The Kerry campaign introduced several new ads during the summer months, but with the exception of two of them, all were either introductory or issue related rather than attack. The two attack ads were initially shown in August and were in response to the charges made by the Swift Boat Veterans for Truth about Kerry's Vietnam combat record. Both relied on statements and imagery of John McCain, although McCain had not agreed to participate in them. The Kerry campaign removed the ads after McCain objected. In *Old Tricks*, McCain was shown taking part in a televised debate in the South Carolina primary from the 2000 election where he denounced the smear tactics of a fringe veterans' group that had questioned his military experiences. He confronted Bush, who was seated next to him, for his part in the attacks and demanded that Bush condemn the group and its actions. McCain did most of the speaking in this ad. The other ad, *Issues*, relied on a narrator to talk about McCain's charges. The ad accused Bush of supporting the anti-Kerry attacks and then called on him to denounce them and return to the issues of Iraq, health care, and jobs. Kerry also used an ad that was more biographical than attack related in his responses to these attacks as well. James Rassmann spoke of how Kerry had saved his life during the battle in which the Swift Boat Veterans said that no combat action had taken place. This ad, *Rassmann*, also included remarks by a narrator who told the audience that the Navy had recognized Kerry's heroism in the battle.

The most important component of Kerry's summertime appeals was his new set of biographical and issue ads that were initially broadcast during the final weeks before the Democratic convention and shortly after its conclusion. Three different ads, but which were similar in style and content, introduced Kerry to a wider television audience than had seen him during the primary elections. One of them, *Pilot*, featured a narrator talking about Kerry's background and included references and imagery of him being a husband, father, airplane pilot, hunter, hockey player, prosecuting attorney, combat veteran, children's advocate, and member of the Senate intelligence committee. The two others differed only slightly from this ad. A second type of biographical ads involved the use of John Edwards, the newly acquired running mate, who appeared with Kerry in some instances or who spoke about him in others. The ad *New Team* featured a narrator describing both candidates with themes that each had used independently during earlier parts of the campaign. The narrator described Kerry as a combat veteran with thirty years of experience handling tough issues while Edwards was the son of a mill worker who had stood for ordinary people against powerful interests. Now, the narrator added, they were "a new team for a new America." In *Three Minutes*, Edwards said people would learn about his running mate's character if they could spend just three minutes talking with the veterans who had served under Kerry's command. Edwards told the audience that Kerry would leave no man behind. While this focused attention on character, the ad *Agenda* linked Kerry's personal background with his issues. Here, Edwards talked about Kerry's Vietnam record, his family life, character, and values and about of how Kerry would concentrate his presidency on issues such as taxes and health care.

Once again, the non-biographical issue ads focused almost entirely on domestic concerns while raising no major challenges to Bush's foreign policies other than criticism of bad management. Some of the issue ads were very general and focused attention on several different policy questions while others directed viewers to specific ideas. Kerry spoke in nearly every one of them, either directly to the television audience, or indirectly through portions of speeches he had delivered at campaign rallies. An example of the more general approach is the ad *Optimists*. Kerry told the television audience we were a nation of optimists. With this, a narrator then spoke about Kerry's issues that, when accomplished, would create a "stronger America." The leading issues were energy independence, health care, jobs, a strong military and better political alliances abroad. The ad concluded with a new slogan that was also used in several other summertime ads, "stronger at home, respected in the world." This slogan had appeared in *New Team*. A similar ad, and one that also looked at several domestic issues and concluded with the same slogan, was *Middle Class Help*. A narrator asked if anyone had a plan for the middle class and then reviewed Kerry's leading issues of job creation, taxes, education, health care, and investment in new technologies. Two of the issue specific ads looked at health care and two others at job creation. Kerry told television viewers we should reduce the $350 Billion we spend on health care paperwork annually (*Paperwork*) and, while proclaiming health care a right, state that since we are the richest country on earth; no one should be without health care (*Country*). Kerry denounced tax policies that encouraged manufactures to relocate their productions and jobs overseas and promised to end those (*Ohio Workers, Lifeline*). Both of these ads included imagery of Kerry making his promises before campaign audiences.

Kerry did not ignore foreign policy and war issues completely, however, although he still did not challenge the major assumptions behind them. He told a television audience that we needed to be tough and smart, rebuild our alliances, and strengthen homeland security in fighting terrorism (*War on Terror*), and reduce our dependence on oil from the Middle East (*Freedom and Independence*).

The summertime ads, while addressing many important domestic issues, lacked two necessary themes in addition to their foreign policy shortcomings. They did not include a strong and sustained response to the numerous attacks that the Bush campaign had aimed at Kerry since the primaries, and they did not convey a sense of outrage at the unsolved domestic problems that Kerry tried to address. Granted, Kerry had promised that he would enact programs related to jobs and health care, but he had not offered many details (of course, one cannot say much in thirty seconds). He did not convey very much passion about his commitment to the issues he raised. This lack of passion, when considered in light of the Bush character attack ads, helped make Kerry appear more as a governmental insider who was part of the problem than as an outsider determined to bring about major changes. Moreover, the attack ads had raised doubts about his voting record and consistency on crucial issues that he needed to address. The attacks were far from over; the Republican convention was approaching and it was to feature a number of speakers, including a Democratic U.S. Senator, who would question or distort Kerry's votes and remarks on a vast array of domestic and foreign policy related issues.

The September Strategy

The Kerry campaign altered its tactics in September and placed more reliance on attack ads, including a number related to the Iraq war. Nonetheless, Kerry continued to limit his criticism of the war to Bush's mismanagement. He started with an ad that accused Bush of using a juvenile attack related to Iraq and then questioned the developments of the war. The narrator talked about growing casualties in Iraq with Kerry promising to get more of our traditional allies involved (*Juvenile*). A similar ad, only with a female narrator speaking this time, hit Bush over his attacks while accusing him of playing politics with terror (*Despicable*). It concluded with the narrator telling viewers it was time for Bush to stop dividing the nation. Other ads featured male narrators telling viewers the war was not going well and that we needed some new leadership (*Different Story*), or attacked Bush for saying we were on the right track while over 1000 soldiers had been killed and many American civilian workers kidnapped and beheaded (*Right Track*), or accused him of lacking any plans for ending the war while using imagery of his appearance on an aircraft carrier under the banner of "Mission Accomplished" (*Doesn't Get It*), or talked about the variety of changing reasons Bush used to justify the war, such as non-existent weapons of mass destruction and links to the terrorists of Osama Bin Laden (*Reasons*). These ads offered little in way of alternatives, however. Only one of them, *Right Track*, had any proposals, and these were heavily related to the theme of Bush's mismanagement. The ad called for three changes; getting our allies involved, training more Iraqi soldiers to replace American fighters, and increased efforts aimed at enhancing the elections scheduled for late January, 2005. Each of these proposals essentially called for a continued war that would require an American presence but which would reduce our involvement by bringing someone else into the fray. These proposals were similar to the ones that Richard Nixon had offered in the early 1970's for ending the Vietnam War while Kerry was active in the anti-war movement.

Kerry introduced several attack ads during September that were both critical of Bush on leading domestic issues and complementary of his earlier policy related appeals. In a pattern similar to that of the summer months, some of these new ads focused attention on a variety of related issues while others were more directed at one particular concern. Three ads linked the high spending in the Iraq war with increased domestic troubles at home. All three emphasized the theme that the nation had lost numerous jobs and had health care costs rise while Bush had been spending over $200 Billion on the war. In the ad *Wrong Choices*, a narrator accused Bush of weakening the nation and used the slogan "stronger at home, respected in the world" in urging a vote for Kerry. Kerry delivered a similar message in *Defend America*, while promising viewers that he would fight terrorism and protect the middle class. The third ad attacked Richard Cheney for his past, and implied present, association with Halliburton. It began with imagery of a statement Cheney had made during the 2000 election where he said he had ended his ties with Halliburton, a corporation he had led for the previous five years, after becoming a candidate for vice president. A narrator then talked about how Cheney had received a financial payment of $2 Million after his resignation, mentioned the cost of the war, and linked it with the Bush policy failures on jobs and health (*Cheney-Halliburton*).

Several other ads focused on health care. One, partly aimed at countering Bush's attacks on Kerry's plans, talked about how recent tax giveaways to drug companies had caused five million more people to be without health insurance and then proclaimed that Kerry's plan would encourage choices for both patients and doctors (*Not True*). Additional ads emphasized that Bush's policies were harmful to businesses or would result in higher Medicare premiums for seniors while promising that Kerry's plans would reduce health care costs (*Uninsured, Immediate Help*).

The Kerry campaign used several new ads in September that did not directly attack Bush but focused attention on Kerry himself and on his goals in addressing the nation's economic needs. The style was similar; the ads contained imagery of Kerry speaking before campaign audiences and outlining general policy goals. The ad, *Economy-Ohio*, is one example of this approach. Here, Kerry spoke about the many industrial jobs Ohio had lost in recent years and then pro-claimed that a stronger America would begin at home. He referred to his major concerns of tax incentives for job creation and better health care. In other eco-nomic related ads, Kerry emphasized these same issues once again before cam-paign audiences and then spoke about the need for ending our dependence on Middle Eastern oil (*Time, Innovation*). Kerry summarized his economic goals in two additional ads that initially appeared during the last days of September and shortly before the beginning of the debates. He spoke directly to the television audience in one ad *Ingenuity*, where he outlined his three point plan, and at-tacked Bush, while relying upon a narrator, in another, *Powerful*, for the presi-dent's opposition to those goals. Kerry wanted to enact new programs that would help small businesses create jobs, reduce taxes for the middle class and lead to lower health care costs, and provide the nation with independence from Middle Eastern oil. He used these identical themes, and virtually the same words, while responding to economic related questions in the debates. Kerry employed the same approach with his war policy; he emphasized the three goals he thought would bring about an end to the Iraq war in the ad *Right Track* and then repeated them in nearly identical wording while answering war related de-bate questions. This may very well have improved his performance. A majority of viewers, according to public opinion polls, and many of the ubiquitous televi-sion pundits, saw Kerry defeating Bush in all three debates.

The Final Round: October

The Kerry campaign continued its strong reliance on attack ads during Octo-ber, but this time responded far more quickly to any and all new charges and distortions that came its way from the Bush media team. In addition, Kerry also developed several attack ads related to fast breaking stories that dominated news reporting during the month. These ads placed the blame for the problems first described in the reporting squarely on Bush's actions and policies. One can see examples of the quick responses in three ads that appeared after the first debate. Kerry had told the debate audience the nation needed to pass a "global test" be-fore deploying troops abroad. His definition of global was extensive and in-cluded the securing of public support for the military efforts through a dialogue where the merits of the idea were to be considered. Republicans, and even Bush, distorted the phrase and instead charged that Kerry planned to give for-eign nations the ability to veto American military intervention. In *He's Lost, He's Desperate*, a narrator began the ad by saying that Bush had lost the debate and then accused him of lying about Kerry's remarks and misleading the Ameri-can public by withholding vital information about why we had invaded Iraq. The ad concluded with the narrator remarking that we were paying the price the price for Bush's failures. The ad *You Saw* followed a similar script. With im-agery of various people watching the debate, the narrator told the audience they had seen Kerry say the president should always have the power to order a preemptive strike and that he would hunt down and kill the terrorists and that they had seen Cheney not tell the truth about his connections to Halliburton. The ad then focused on Bush's desperate attacks against Kerry and his failures on several vital issues. Included here, with the issues written on the screen, were problems related to Iraq, the economy, the deficit, gasoline prices, and health care. Finally, Kerry delivered essentially this same message to a campaign audience in the ad *Never*. He accused Bush of distorting his positions, emphasized that he would never cede national security to any organization, would never take his eye of Bin Laden, and would hunt down and kill the terrorists responsible for 9-11.

Three issues that developed suddenly, and which Kerry saw as failures or problems of the Bush presidency, were the sudden national shortage of flu vaccines, the discovery that about 380 tons of captured Iraqi explosives were missing and presumed to be in the hands of insurgents, and the publication of an article in the New York Times about how Bush planned to seek privatization of Social Security after the beginning of his second term. Kerry addressed the flu problem in an ad where a female narrator told the audience that medical experts had warned Bush three years earlier that "a dangerous shortage" loomed. Rather than fixing the problem, she said Bush had allowed vaccine production to be moved overseas and then added that such vaccines were now contaminated. The narrator followed by talking about an important contradiction in Bush's proposed solution; he wanted immediate help from Canada although his policies made the importing of Canadian drugs illegal. After saying that seniors and children had to wait and that not enough vaccines were available for pregnant women, the narrator concluded the ad by referring to "A George Bush mess, its time for a new direction (*Flu*)." In responding to the missing explosives, Kerry spoke to the television audience in the ad *Obligation*, where he said Bush had overextended our troops in Iraq and had failed to secure the explosives. He added that the commander in chief had the obligation to keep the country safe while proclaiming that Bush's misjudgments had put soldiers at risk and had made the country less secure. Kerry then accused Bush of promising to do more of the same and promised that he would make a "fresh start" in protecting the nation. With an opening remark that "the truth is coming out" a narrator in *January Surprise* talked about Bush's plans for changing Social Security. He said that Bush's budgetary deficits of more than $400 Billion annually were threatening the long term stability of the program and than added that Bush wanted to reduce benefits from somewhere between thirty and forty five percent. The ad concluded by referring to "The real Bush agenda, cutting Social Security."

In addition to implementing these new themes, Kerry also continued attacking Bush on the same issues as before, Iraq and terrorism, and jobs and the economy. Although his new Iraq related ads differed from earlier ones in style, Kerry's new ones did not raise fundamental questions about the ultimate wisdom of the war or seek to bring about a new direction in American foreign relations with Middle Eastern nations. The attacks were limited to criticism of Bush's alleged mismanagement of the war in Iraq and protecting the nation from terrorism. One of the more creative Iraq ads used imagery of a woman watching television with the camera increasingly focused on her eye. A female narrator told the audience that "we can see it ourselves," the mess in Iraq that Bush had created; over 1000 soldiers dead and many more people kidnapped and beheaded. Kerry, she added, had voted for the biggest increase in intelligence funding in history and was supported for president by two former chairmen of the Joint Chiefs of Staff. After this, Kerry told the audience that he would get the terrorists. The ad concluded with the camera imagery, which had moved closer to the woman's eye at the beginning, was now moving away from Bush's eye (*Looking*). In another war related ad, a group of West Virginia military veterans individually introduced themselves to the television audience and then criticized Bush over the conduct of the war. They said he had let Bin Laden escape, referred to the number of battle deaths, and concluded that a new commander in chief, John Kerry of course, was needed (*West Virginia Veterans*). The theme of Bush's failure to capture Bin Laden was also used in the ad *Bush's Mess* which accused the president of relying on Afghan warlords rather than American troops to capture the terrorist leader. This ad also drew attention to the continuing violence in Afghanistan and to the lack of anthrax vaccine for those troops.

These ads about Bush's failure to capture Bin Laden were the first attempt by Kerry to attack his rival over terrorism in a way that was distinct from the theme of war mismanagement. An accusation of mismanagement implied that Bush shared Kerry's, and presumably the voters,' goals, but was incapable of actually accomplishing them. A different approach would be to accuse Bush of not sharing the voters' values at all. Kerry attempted to accomplish this in two terrorism related ads. In *Ever Since*, a woman, Kristin Breitweiser, whose husband Ron had been killed at the World Trade Center attack, spoke to the television audience about how she had fought for the creation of the 9-11 commission, reminded viewers that Bush had opposed its existence from the beginning, and told them how disappointed she had been when the commission reported that the nation was no safer now than before. Breitweiser concluded the ad by saying she wanted to be able to look her infant daughter, who was shown with her, in the eyes and tell her she was safe. After mentioning that she and her husband had voted for Bush in the last election, Breitweiser told the viewers of her plans to vote for Kerry this time. The second ad was about Bush's unwillingness to prepare for possible future terrorist attacks while diverting money to Iraq instead. In *Can't Win* a female narrator said that 95 percent of the cargo containers that arrived in the nation's seaports from abroad were not inspected. She added that Bush had said we could not afford to pay for such inspections. The narrator followed this statement by directing attention to the $7 Billion in no bid contracts the Bush administration had given to Halliburton and to the $200 Billion it had spent paying for military actions in Iraq while leaving the nation unprotected from future terrorist attacks.

With respect to domestic issues, Kerry continued his attacks against Bush throughout October on both of his main themes of jobs and health care, particularly jobs. This time, Kerry introduced a new comparison; Bush's performance on economic matters was worse than that of any president since Herbert Hoover.

One can see an example of this style in the ad *Jobs*. A female narrator began by saying the election would give us a chance to set the country on a new direction. She then emphasized the extent of job losses under Bush, 2.7 million, attributed part of this to the existence of tax incentives that encouraged job relocation, mentioned the growing problems of low wages, a higher cost of living, and the financial difficulties of middle class families while linking this to the claim that only Hoover had a worse record on jobs than Bush. Similar ads placed the blame for the nation's economic troubles on Bush and the "right wing Republicans" in Congress. One ad referred to the 2.7 million lost jobs and used the Hoover reference while adding that new jobs paid $9,000 less than lost ones, (*Hoover*). A second referred to the windfall profits of the drug companies, *Middle Class Families*. In both ads, the narrator blamed Bush and his partisan allies for an array of problems such as higher priced health care and gasoline, tax breaks for job relocation, and the insider deals for Halliburton and Enron. There was even an ad directed to the battleground state of Ohio. Here, the narrator talked about the same problems as the other ads had done, but this time used numbers and references that were unique to Ohio. Included were statements of how Ohio had lost about 230,000 manufacturing jobs since Bush had become president. There were also quotes from Bush's Commerce Secretary who had once depicted reports of job losses as a myth. Viewers were then asked, during the ads' concluding seconds, if they thought job losses were a myth and "when is George Bush going to accept reality" (*Real Americans*).

Finally, Kerry responded to the Bush attacks against his health care plan. The female narrator in *Leading, Not True*, mentioned the charges that various Bush ads had said would occur under Kerry's plan, such as rationing, less access, fewer choices, and long waits, and then said these already existed while blaming them on Bush. She added that Kerry's plan would lower costs and allow people to choose doctors and make decisions.

The assertion made earlier that attack ads complement issue ads was clearly supported by the Kerry advertising strategy in October. The assertion is that an aspirant for office develops the rationale for his candidacy through the use of issue ads where he explains his goals and then links their accomplishment to his character and political skills. He then complements the issue ads with attack ads where he accuses, through the use of anonymous narrators, his rival or rivals of lacking any significant personal commitment to those same goals. Kerry used several acclaims ads during October that articulated essentially the same policy goals for his presidency that the attacks, discussed immediately above, questioned about Bush. There were two differences between the attack and acclaims ads; the acclaims did not mention Bush, and Kerry spoke in nearly every one of them. For example, two of Kerry's October ads focused attention on the issue of stem cell research. While Bush had made his opposition to the use of human stem cells in medical research well known, Kerry spoke of the scientific advances that could come from such research and of how this might lead to cures for a variety of diseases. He proclaimed to his television audience, in the ad *Stem Cell*, that "it's time to take America in a new direction." Actor Michael J. Fox, who has Parkinson's disease, said essentially the same thing in a similar ad while also mentioning the positions the presidential candidates had taken on stem cell research (*Michael J. Fox*).

Kerry used several issue related ads in October where he spoke directly to the television audience about his major issues. He emphasized taxes once again by telling his viewers that the middle class paid higher taxes while the "rich" received more breaks. He said this was wrong and promised to reduce, rather than increase, taxes on the middle class (*The Truth on Taxes*). With respect to the problem of high priced prescription drugs, Kerry promised to allow the importing of less expensive drugs from Canada and enact new laws permitting bulk purchases of drugs for the Medicare program. These actions would result in lower prices. Kerry proclaimed that "all we need for cheaper drugs is for a president to fight for it (*Rx Drugs*). He also addressed the major economic concern of his campaign, jobs, with new ads that complemented the accusations he was making against Bush. In *Economy Kick Start*, Kerry said we needed to change the tax laws in order to create more incentives for locating manufacturing jobs in this country that paid middle class wages and which provided secure and affordable health care. He also wanted to use this same approach to encourage more high technology industries that would reduce our dependence on Middle Eastern oil. Kerry had other economic oriented ads that were more general in their appeal. He said families needed someone to fight for them on tax incentives, job opportunities, and prescription drugs, (*Across America*), and talked about a variety of domestic concerns in an ad that appeared toward the end of the campaign where he urged people to vote (*Your Hands*). In this latter one, Kerry began by telling voters that the election was in "your hands" and then asked them if they believed in a particular issue which he then named. After mentioning a number of issues in this manner, Kerry ended the ad by proclaiming to the audience "then together we can change America." The issues he mentioned were the ones he had been talking about throughout the year long campaign; creating and keeping higher paying jobs, bringing health care costs under control, reducing the national deficit by repealing Bush's tax giveaways, and reducing our dependence on Middle Eastern oil. He also mentioned "making a fresh start in Iraq." This fresh start appeared to be more of a critique of Bush's poor management than a new direction in the stalemated war.

Kerry used two new war related ads in October that were uncritical of any aspect of the war other than Bush's leadership and which hinted at no fundamental changes of policy in the event of a Kerry election victory. One ad featured Kerry speaking directly to the television audience about his goals (*Protect*) while the other used a narrator and patriotic imagery of combat soldiers to emphasize a commitment to the status quo (*Heroes*). In the former, Kerry once again talked about our need for allies. He told his audience we could "no longer go it alone in the world" and that it was time to restore our respect. He promised to "stop at nothing to find and kill the terrorists" and committed himself to the goal that the nation would always have the strongest military. In the latter, the narrator attempted to co-opt an emotional appeal that Bush and his supporters had been using to implicitly generate support for the war. The appeal was for people to "support our troops." No definition of what constituted support was ever advanced by the war's advocates, however. The purpose of such an appeal was to silence critics whose questioning of the war would seem unsympathetic to the soldiers who were in harm's way in a foreign nation. Political leaders could then interpret this silence as proof of support for their policies. The ad began with imagery of soldiers in combat and of an eagle flying overhead with the narrator telling viewers that "our soldiers fighting in Iraq are heroes" who had "earned our thanks and support." Instead of then using this statement as an opportunity to question the policies that had led to the war and propose a change of direction, the ad simply reiterated the theme that Kerry would competently provide more of the same. The narrator put the election in perspective as he reminded voters, "as we see the deepening conflict and chaos and as we choose a new commander in chief and a fresh start, we will always support and honor those who served." The "fresh start" was then and continued to be as the election finally concluded, undefined.

Summary and Analysis

With the conclusion of the nomination battle in early March, the Kerry campaign needed to make a rapid transition from an advertising strategy where appeals had been aimed only at Democratic voters in selected primary states to a new strategy where it would focus attention on a far less partisan but much more national audience. Moreover, it needed to act quickly because of the heavy barrage of attack ads that were already coming its way from the Bush campaign. Initially, the new strategy relied extensively on attack ads that raised questions about Bush's policies and performance, and on biographical themes in which Kerry introduced himself to millions of voters who did not live in the states with early primaries. His biographical ads aired during two distinct time periods; shortly after the conclusion of the contested primaries; and after Edwards had become the running mate. The former set of ads used essentially the same theme of the primaries, Kerry was a man of courage and character who had been tested in combat and would now apply his character to solving the nation's problems. The second set added Edwards' populist appeal to this same theme. The attack ads were directed at Bush's domestic policies and emphasized such issues as the heavy losses of manufacturing jobs that had taken place during his first term, the new tax cuts that favored wealthier people, and increasingly unaffordable health care and the growing numbers of uninsured people that accompanied it. There were also some references to other issues, such as support for stem cell research, rights to abortion, more money for education, and far more vigorous enforcement of environmental laws, but Kerry did not place the same amount of attention on these as he did on jobs, taxes, and health care.

Kerry relied on a combination of attack ads related to Bush's record on his three domestic issues and biographical ads emphasizing character during the initial months of the general election campaign. He gradually introduced more issue oriented ads that focused attention on his promises rather than Bush's record as the campaign advanced into the summer and autumn months. This was an unusual appeal; a man with proven heroism in military combat relies on those experiences, while another war is underway, to demonstrate his competence for confronting domestic policies. He used this approach throughout the campaign. A strong majority of Kerry's televised advertising was related to emphasizing domestic issues. He would speak to his audience in his issue oriented ads, either directly or through a campaign appearance, and would promise to make important changes in existing policies. Meanwhile, an anonymous narrator would talk about Bush's failures on those same policies in the attack ads. Kerry's ads were often quite complementary of one another and taken together had a very straightforward theme; the proven fighter was qualified to lead the nation, he would address national failures on domestic issues, and those failures were direct results of the policies of the incumbent president, George W. Bush.

The one major limitation of this strategy was Kerry's response to the Iraq war and the continuing battle against Islamic terrorism. He was often critical of Bush's efforts in dealing with these matters, but he tended to limit his emphasis to the theme of mismanagement of a correct policy rather than one aimed at offering an alternative course of action. This may well have proven an unfortunate choice for Kerry in that voters constantly viewed Bush as the more qualified candidate to lead the nation on national security matters (Gallup Poll, 2006). This public perception did not change throughout the year, even at the time of the Democratic convention when Kerry directed considerable attention to his military experiences. An important event occurred during the last days of the campaign that Kerry claimed harmed his chances. This was a tape where Osama Bin Laden taunted the nation promised even more terrorist attacks. The fact that the architect of the 9-11 bombing was still at large should have hurt Bush by demonstrating to the nation that his policies in the Middle East had failed. Instead, it hurt the candidate who had not offered a strong alternative to the status quo.

CHAPTER 8

SUMMARY AND INTERPRETATIONS

Incumbent presidents and their challengers differ from one another with respect to their televised advertising in two important ways while being similar in another. As the various scholars quoted in Chapter One have demonstrated, incumbents as a group differ from challengers as a group in their choices of themes and styles of presentation. In addition, as the discussions in Chapters Two through Four have indicated, incumbents differ among themselves in ways that seem to be consistent with their political strength and status of strong, weak, or surrogate. There are four features of this status difference; strong incumbents tend to differ from other incumbents and from all challengers in their high usage of policy related themes; weak incumbents tend to differ from other incumbents and from challengers in their high usage of character related themes; surrogate incumbents do not appear to differ from all challengers in their usage of either policy and character related themes; and challengers do not appear to differ among themselves in their usages of either policy or character related themes in relation to the political strength of the incumbent. Finally, as described in Chapters Five through Seven, incumbents and challengers tend to remain consistent in their employment of themes over the course of a campaign year but also tend to alter the particular mix of themes at various times of the campaign year in ways that enable them to respond to short term changes in the electoral context.

Strong incumbents, as the discussions of Ronald Reagan (1984), Bill Clinton (1996), and George W. Bush (2004) have shown, enjoy a political opportunity that is quite simply not available to any other type of candidate. They are unopposed, or have only insignificant opposition, for the presidential nomination of their party. Other candidates, either weak or surrogate incumbents or any aspirants for the nomination of the challenging party, are opposed and must therefore devote a considerable part of the campaign year to competing with one or more formidable rivals for the party nomination. The strong incumbents have convinced the overwhelming majority of their own partisans that their first terms have been successful. These successes, they argue, qualify them for a second term. The partisans clearly agree and unite behind the incumbent prior to the beginning of the election year. The strong incumbent can begin his efforts aimed at winning the general election immediately without having to devote any time or money to securing the nomination.

Strong incumbents use this opportunity to generate imagery where they appear as successful national leaders. They do this in two ways; through their use of the "Rose Garden" strategy where they act as president and where television news media readily comply with their efforts by illustrating them performing in this role, and with their televised advertising where they emphasize their successes and question the ability of their rivals to continue with the same quality of political accomplishments. All three strong incumbents studied here structured their acclaims related advertising around the themes of their first term accomplishments in foreign, domestic, and economic policy, the plans they had for continuing these successes during second terms, and the political goals that guided their past and future actions. They frequently employed used the symbolic components and the legitimacy of the presidential office while doing so. In addition, they employed attack ads which questioned the commitments or abilities of their challengers to perpetuate those same deeds and goals.

A key tactical advantage that strong incumbents enjoy is their ability to attack their challengers during certain times of the campaign year when the challengers are unable to respond. Each of the three strong incumbents did so during two different time periods; the final weeks of the nomination campaign and the weeks preceding the onset of the national conventions. The challenger could not respond during the nomination campaign because he needed to orient his efforts at defeating his intra-party rivals. He could not respond effectively during the weeks preceding the national conventions because he needed to focus on uniting his partisans for the upcoming general election campaign and he had very little money remaining from the nomination battles. The strong incumbents dominated advertising for several weeks and used these opportunities to "introduce" the challengers to parts of the nation unfamiliar with them because of the limited number of states with competitive primary elections. In addition to this near monopoly, the strong incumbents were also aided by the growing practice of television news media interrupting their election year coverage during this time and not renewing it until the onset of the conventions. Many news broadcasts during this part of an election year are devoid of campaign related news. The challengers are harmed by this practice because they need news coverage in order to become better known in those parts of the nation where they have yet to campaign. The strong incumbents are helped because they continue to receive considerable news coverage simply by virtue of the fact that they hold the nation's highest political office.

Weak incumbents, as shown in the analysis of the ads used by Jimmy Carter (1980) and George Bush (1992), face very different political contexts. They have not enjoyed the same level of policy successes as the strong incumbents and have not convinced many of their own partisans they are deserving of re-election. They have not necessarily been rejected by their partisans, however, as was seen by the fact that both Carter and Bush, and Gerald Ford (1976) as well, ultimately won nominations after competitive battles. Instead, their political weaknesses appear to encourage intra-party rivals to openly oppose them and eventually deny them the same opportunities for presentation of self through videostyle that is available to strong incumbents. The weakness of these incumbents limits their abilities to use advertising that focuses on policy accomplishments with promises of extending them into a second term. An emphasis on policy questions might even have the opposite effect of encouraging even stronger opposition. The weak incumbents respond by using the one theme that allows them to address their difficulties; they possess personal characteristics, leadership skills, and values that distinguish them from their "flawed" intra-party rivals and general election challengers and which justify their ultimate reelection. Moreover, the weak incumbents lack a second feature enjoyed by their strong incumbent counterparts. The existence of opposition for their renomination requires them to devote the initial months of the campaign year to winning the support of their own partisans and eliminates opportunities to wage unanswered attacks against their general election challengers during the nomination and pre-convention time periods. Sometimes, their challengers even can start their general election efforts first, as occurred with Reagan in 1980.

In adapting their campaigns to the contexts of their respective years, the weak incumbents of 1980 and 1992 divided their efforts into two distinct parts. The first part aimed at defeating a rival for the party nomination while the second focused on winning the general election. Despite this division, the weak incumbents used essentially the same themes in both parts of their campaigns. They spoke of their skills and character, linked them with the symbolic imagery and legitimacy of the presidential office, and implied that their rivals, either for the nomination or in the general election, lacked those same qualities. Carter and Bush used ads which illustrated them working at the president's desk in the White House Oval Office, and ads where they spoke to groups of uniformed members of the armed forces in military settings where they appeared as the commander in chief. The underlying themes were that leadership was an attribute of only exceptional persons of character and they were such persons. Their corresponding attack ads complemented these themes by arguing that their rivals in the nomination campaigns, Kennedy and Buchanan, and the ones from the general election, Reagan and Clinton, were flawed in ways that would certainly prevent them from leading the nation. The rivals were not trustworthy, were reckless, often failed to tell the truth, and lacked the integrity to protect the nation's interests in a crisis.

The challengers focused their attention on issues they believed were responsible for the incumbents' failures and attempted to link them to an alternative view of national leadership. This is not easy, as the challengers of weak incumbents often encounter some troubles of their own in constructing electoral majorities. Reagan gained slightly less than 51 percent of the popular vote while Clinton won a three candidate battle with only 43 percent of the vote. Carter won his first term by defeating a weak incumbent, Ford, with about 51 percent of the vote.

Surrogate incumbents face an unusual set of conditions that all too frequently prove difficult and are sometimes nearly impossible to overcome. They do not have the luxury of running unopposed for their nominations and therefore must devote substantial time and resources to winning them. This need often prevents them from freely attacking their general election challengers during the nomination and pre-convention time periods. Moreover, they are not the actual incumbents and consequently cannot employ the symbolic and legitimating dimensions of the presidency and the trappings of office to articulate their past deeds and future plans. Their role as presidential surrogate has provided them with an important advantage over intra-party rivals, and this usually results in their nominations, but the surrogate role is not always so advantageous in the general election. A surrogate is often less well known to the voting public than popular wisdom might suggest. Vice presidents must devote some of their advertising to the challenger task of introducing themselves to the voters. This need can become an obstacle if they wish to pursue a character oriented advertising strategy. They are not known well enough to make convincing arguments that their leadership skills and personal characteristics are better than those of their challengers. Unlike strong or weak incumbents who appear to have some distinct opportunities or constraints that derive from their unique vantage points and which differ from those of all other candidates, surrogate incumbents appear to be far more like challengers. They cannot take much credit for the accomplishments of an administration of which they were not the most important actor, nor can they demonstrate that their leadership skills and character are necessarily superior to those of their rivals.

Surrogate incumbents have differed among themselves in the approaches they have employed, however. The greatest difference appears to rest with the manner in which they link their candidacy with the policies and actions of the retiring incumbent. Each surrogate must convince voters that he has been a significant player in a successful administration and that such an administration is deserving of another term of office. However, he must also convince those same voters that he is his "own man" and not merely an understudy who is trying to substitute for a much more impressive actor. Bush appears to have accomplished this task while Gore did not. Bush directed a major part of his advertising themes to the record of Reagan presidency and to his presence when its major accomplishments had taken place. In contrast, Gore attempted to place some distance between himself and Clinton, perhaps because of Clinton's personal scandals. This does not appear to have worked. He ran for president as if he were a member of Congress seeking higher office rather than the second most important member of a successful administration who was trying to extend its tenure in office to a third term. He said he was a fighter who would come through on the economic issues of the day, but he did not appear to convince a majority of voters that he was the necessary man for continuing the peace and prosperity they had been enjoying for the past few years. The vice presidency did not seem to be any more significant as a qualification for the presidency than the governorship of a major state. In 1988, George Bush had made this case against Governor Dukakis of Massachusetts but in 2000 Albert Gore failed to make it against Governor Bush of Texas.

All challengers, regardless of the political strength of the incumbent, must direct their televised advertising to accomplishing certain essential tasks. They must start their quests for their party's nomination by employing image and issue ads in order to introduce themselves to their fellow partisans. They often do so in ways that suggest they possess specific character qualities that will prove helpful in implementing their policy goals. They also use attack ads to raise doubts about the commitment of their rivals to attaining those same goals. Challengers tend to rely less upon attack ads during the nomination campaigns than they do during general elections. This is because the rivals for party nominations are more similar than distinct in their policy views, and because the large number of aspirants for a nomination makes focused attacks more difficult. A general election candidate has only one major rival to attack and that rival speaks for a different ideology.

Despite these common needs, challengers differ among themselves in the issues and images they advance. These differences seem to result from the personal preferences of the candidates. For example, in 2004 Howard Dean directly attacked Bush's policies and rationale for the Iraq war. In contrast, John Edwards rarely spoke about the war while John Kerry talked about mismanagement and then emphasized his skills as a military leader from his own experiences in a previous conflict. On domestic issues, Edwards linked his working class background with redistributive economic policies while Dean emphasized his background as a medical doctor and small state governor while talking about health care financing. In addition, Kerry's ads often relied on a narrator while Edwards spoke tended to directly address his television audience.

Despite their advertising efforts, challengers rarely can influence the outcome of an election. Instead, they seem more likely to be the unlucky victims or fortunate beneficiaries of the incumbents' political strength and communicative competence. If the challenger has the misfortune to face a strong incumbent who has united his partisans, he may fall so far behind the incumbent in public support during the nomination and pre-convention periods that a general election victory becomes impossible. If he is fortunate in getting to oppose a weak incumbent who must use these same campaign periods to secure his own partisan base, the challenger can emerge as a credible alternative to a beleaguered president and win an election. The challenger of a surrogate incumbent may have the greatest opportunity to influence an election outcome than other challengers because his rival is, in many ways, also a challenger. Presidential elections are increasingly serving as referendums on the performance of the incumbent with the challengers being of secondary importance. The status of the incumbent, strong, weak, or surrogate, seems to be a better determinant of election outcomes than challenger effort.

The descriptions of advertising strategies employed in the 2004 election demonstrate that candidates, incumbents and challengers, vary the mix of their image, issue, and attack related themes throughout the year in response to changing political contexts. The incumbent and challenger, Bush and Kerry, were consistent in their uses of specific themes during the year, but both varied the particular mix of acclaims (images-issues) oriented and attack related ads as their campaign efforts advanced through different time periods. Kerry used the nomination period to define himself in contrast to his intra-party rivals while Bush used this time to speak about the policy successes of his first term. Bush then attacked Kerry during the weeks that followed the nomination campaign as Kerry tried to make himself better known to the voters in those parts of the nation where he had not yet made any effort. The two combatants continued varying their particular mixes of acclaims and attacks by giving more emphasis to the former during and immediately after the national conventions and to the latter during the final weeks of the election year when the mobilization of their partisans to actually vote became the overriding emphasis of their political efforts.

In 2004, for the sixth time over the past fifty years, an incumbent president entered the election year with a majority of voters approving of his performance in office. This approval translated into the important political fact that the incumbent would encounter no major opposition from within his own party as he sought a second term. With his partisans unified and highly supportive, the incumbent was free to attempt to use televised advertising to convince other voters that he deserved another term. And for the sixth consecutive time during these decades, the incumbent won the election.

REFERENCES

Books, Journals, and News Sources

ABC World News Tonight.

Abramson, Paul R., Aldrich, John H., and David W. Rohde. *Change and Continuity in the 1980 Elections.* Washington, D.C.: Congressional Quarterly Press, 1982.

Abramson, Paul R., Aldrich, John H., and David W. Rohde. *Change and Continuity in the 1984 Elections.* Washington, D.C.: Congressional Quarterly Press, 1986.

Abramson, Paul R., Aldrich, John H., and David W. Rohde. *Change and Continuity in the 1988 Elections.* Washington, D.C: Congressional Quarterly Press, 1990.

Abramson, Paul R., Aldrich, John H., and David W. Rohde. *Change and Continuity in the 1992 Elections.* Washington, D.C.: Congressional Quarterly Press, 1994.

Abramson, Paul R., Aldrich, John H., and David W. Rohde. *Change and Continuity in the 1996 Elections.* Washington, D.C.: Congressional Quarterly Press, 1998.

Abramson, Paul R., Aldrich, John H., and David W. Rohde. *Change and Continuity in the 2000 Elections.* Washington, D.C.: Congressional Quarterly Press, 2002.

Abramson, Paul R., Aldrich, John H., and David W. Rohde. *Change and Continuity in the 2004 Elections.* Washington, D.C.: Congressional Quarterly Press, 2006.

Ansolabehere, Stephen, Behr, Roy L., and Shanto Iyengar. *The Media Game: American Politics in the Television Age.* Boston: Allyn & Bacon, 1993.

Ansolabehere, Stephen, and Shanto Iyengar. *Going Negative: How Political Advertisements Shrink and Polarize the Electorate.* New York: Free Press, 1995.

Atkin, C. and G. Heald, Effects of Political Advertising. *Public Opinion Quarterly, 40,* 216-228.

Ballotti, R. John, Jr. Verbal Style in Presidential Advertising: Computer Analysis of the 1996 Campaign Spots. In Lynda Lee Kaid and Dianne G. Bystrom, *The Electronic Election: Perspectives on the 1996 Campaign Communication,* pp. 223-232. Mahwah, NJ: Lawrence Erlbaum Associates, Publisher, 1999.

Barilleaux, Ryan J. *The Post-Modern Presidency.* New York: Praeger Press, 1988.

Bartels, Larry M. *Presidential Primaries and the Dynamics of Public Choice.* Princeton, NJ: Princeton University Press, 1988.

Benoit, William L. *Seeing Spots: A Functional Analysis of Presidential Advertisements, 1952-1996.* Westport, CN: Praeger, 1999.

Benoit, William L. *Campaign 2000: A Functional Analysis of Presidential Campaign Discourse.* Lanham, MD: Rowman & Littlefield, 2003.

Benoit, William L., Joseph R. Blaney, and P. M. Pier. *Campaign 96: A Functional Analysis of Acclaims, Attacks, And Defending.* Westport, CN: Praeger, 1998.

Benoit, William L., P. M. Pier, and Joseph R. Blaney. A Functional Approach to Televised Political Spots: Acclaiming, Attacking, Defending. *Communication Quarterly.* Vol. 45, No. 1. Winter 1997, pp. 1-20.

Bennett, W. Lance. *The Governing Crisis: Media, Money, and Marketing in American Elections.* New York: St. Martin's Press, 1992.

Brians, Craig L. and Martin P. Wattenberg. Campaign Issue Knowledge and Salience: Comparing Reception from TV Commercials, TV News, and Newspapers. *American Journal of Political Science, 40* (February): 172-193.

Busch, Andrew E. *Outsiders and Openness in the Presidential Nominating System.* Pittsburg: University of Pittsburg Press, 1997.

Bush, George W., Presidential Campaign. *Georgewbush.com.*

CBS Evening News.

Ceaser, James W. et al. The Rise of the Rhetorical Presidency. *Presidential Studies Quarterly 11* (Spring 1981), pp. 158-171.

Ceaser, James W. and Andrew Busch. *Upside Down and Inside Out: The 1992 Elections and American Politics.* Lanham, MD: Rowman & Littlefield, 1993.

Ceaser, James W. and Andrew Busch. *Losing to Win: The 1996 Elections and American Politics.* Lanham, MD: Rowman & Littlefield, 1997.

Ceaser, James W. and Andrew Busch. *The Perfect Tie: The True Story of the 2000 Presidential Election.* Lanham, MD: Rowman & Littlefield, 2001.

Ceaser, James W. and Andrew Busch. *Red over Blue: the 2004 Elections and American Politics.* Lanham, MD: Rowman & Littlefield, 2005.

Cook, Rhodes. *Race for the Presidency: Winning the 2004 Nomination.* Washington, D.C.: Congressional Quarterly Press, 2004.

CQ Press. *Presidential Elections: 1789-2004.* Washington D.C.: Congressional Quarterly Press, 2005.

Cronin, Thomas. *The State of the Presidency, 2nd. Ed.* Boston: Little, Brown, 1980.

Cronin, Thomas E. and Michael A. Genovese. *The Paradoxes of the American Presidency.* New York: Oxford University Press, 1998.

Crotty, William J. *A Defining Moment: The Presidential Election of 2004.* Armonk, NY: M. E. Sharpe, 2005.

Denton, Robert E. Jr., Ed. *The 1992 Presidential Campaign: A Communication Perspective.* Westport, CT: Praeger, 1994.

Denton, Robert E. Jr., Ed. *The 1996 Presidential Campaign: A Communication Perspective.* Westport, CT: Praeger, 1998.

Denton, Robert E. Jr., Ed. *The 2000 Presidential Campaign: A Communication Perspective.* Westport, CT: Praeger, 2002.

Denton, Robert E. Jr., Ed. *The 2004 Presidential Campaign: A Communicative Perspective.* Lanham, MD: Rowman and Littlefield, 2005.

Devlin, L. Patrick. An Analysis of Presidential Television Commercials: 1952-1984. In Lynda Lee Kaid, Dan Nimmo, and Keith R. Sanders, *New Perspectives on Political Advertising,* pp. 21-54. Carbondale, IL: Southern Illinois University Press, 1986.

Devlin, L. Patrick, ed. *Political Persuasion in Presidential Campaigns.* New Brunswick: NJ: Transaction Books, 1987.

Devlin, L. Patrick. Contrasts in Presidential Campaign Commercials of 1988. *American Behavioral Scientist.* Vol. 32, No. 4, March/April 1989, pp. 389-414.

Devlin, L. Patrick. Contrasts in Presidential Campaign Commercials of 1992. *American Behavioral Scientist.* Vol. 37, No. 2, November 1993, pp. 272-290.

Devlin, L. Patrick. Contrasts in Presidential Campaign Commercials of 1996. *American Behavioral Scientist.* Vol. 40, No. 8, August 1997, pp. 1058-1084.

Devlin, L. Patrick. Contrasts in Presidential Campaign Commercials of 2000. *American Behavioral Scientist.* Vol. 44, No. 12, August 2001, pp. 2338-2369.

Diamond, Edwin and Stephen Bates. *The Spot: The Rise of Political Advertising on Television*. Cambridge, MA: The MIT Press, 1984.

Dolan, Christopher. Three Cheers for Negative Ads. In David Schultz, *Lights, Camera, Campaign! Media, Politics, and Political Advertising*, pp. 45-72. New York: Peter Lang, 2004.

Dover, E. D. *Presidential Elections in the Television Age: 1960-1992*. Westport, CT: Praeger, 1994.

Dover E. D. *The Presidential Election of 1996: Clinton's Incumbency and Television*. Westport, CT: Praeger, 1998.

Dover, E. D. *Missed Opportunity: Gore, Incumbency, and Television in Election 2000*. Westport, CT: Praeger, 2002.

Edwards, Janis L, and Stacey M. Smith. Myth and Anti-Myth In Presidential Campaign Films 2000. In Lynda Lee Kaid, John C. Tedesco, Dianne G. Bystrom, and Mitchell S. McKinney, *The Millennium Election: Communication in the 2000 Campaign*, pp. 17-26. Lanham, MD: Rowman and Littlefield Publishers Inc., 2003.

Farnsworth, Stephen J. and S. Robert Lichter. *The Nightly News Nightmare: Network Television's Coverage of U.S. Presidential Elections, 1988-2000*. Lanham, MD: Rowman and Littlefield, 2003.

Fiorina, Morris. *Retrospective Voting in American National Elections*. New Haven, CT: Yale University Press, 1981.

Fisher, Louis. *The Politics of Shared Power: Congress and the Executive, 4th ed.* College Station: Texas A&M University Press, 1993.

Gallup-CNN-USA Today Polls.

Garramone, G. M., C. K. Atkin, B. E. Pinkleton, and R. T. Cole. Effects of Negative Political Advertising on the Political Process. *Journal of Electronic Media, 34*, 299-311.

Germond, Jack W., and Jules Witcover. *Blue Smoke and Mirrors: How Reagan Won and Why Carter Lost the Election of 1980*. New York: Viking Press, 1981.

Germond, Jack W. and Jules Witcover. *Wake Us When It's Over: Presidential Politics of 1984*. New York: Macmillan, 1985.

Germond, Jack W. and Jules Witcover. *Whose Broad Stripes and Bright Stars: The Trivial Pursuit of the Presidency 1988*. New York: Warner Books, 1989.

Germond, Jack W. and Jules Witcover. *Mad as Hell: Revolt at the Ballot Box, 1992*. New York: Warner Books, 1993.

Goldstein, Joel. *The Modern American Vice Presidency: The Transformation of a Political Institution*. Princeton, NJ: Princeton University Press, 1982.

Goldstein, Kenneth M. and Patricia Strach. *The Medium and the Message: Television Advertising and American Elections.* Upper Saddle River, NJ: Pearson/Prentice Hall, 2004.

Graber, Doris. *Media Power in American Politics.* Washington D.C.: Congressional Quarterly Pres, 2002.

Hacker, Kenneth L., ed. *Presidential Candidate Images.* Lanham, MD: Rowman & Littlefield, 2004.

Hale, Katherine. The Spinning of the Tale: Candidate and Media Orchestrating in the French and U.S. Presidential Elections. In Lynda Lee Kaid, Jacques Gerstle, and Keith R. Sanders, eds., *Mediated Politics in Two Cultures: Presidential Campaigning in the United States and France, pp. 195-210.* New York: Praeger, 1991.

Hart, John. *The Presidential Branch: From Washington to Clinton, 2nd. ed.* Chatham, NJ: Chatham Hall, 1995.

Hatfield, Mark. *Vice Presidents of the United States: 1788-1993.* Washington, D.C.: U.S. Government Printing Office, 1997.

Hess, Stephen. *Organizing the Presidency, 3rd ed.* Washington, D.C.: Brookings, 2002.

Hinckley, Barbara. *The Symbolic Presidency: How Presidents Portray Themselves.* London: Routledge, 1990.

Iyengar, Shanto and John R. Petrocik. "Basic Rule" Voting: Impact of Campaigns on Party- and Approval-Based Voting. In James A. Thurber, Candice J. Nelson, David A. Dulio, eds. *Crowded Airwaves: Campaign Advertising in Elections*, pp. 113-148. Washington, D.C.: Brookings Institution Press, 2000.

Jacobson, Gary C., and Samuel Kernell. *The 2000 Elections and Beyond.* Washington, D.C: Congressional Quarterly Press, 2000.

Jamieson, Kathleen Hall. The Evolution of Political Advertising in America. In Lynda Lee Kaid, Dan Nimmo, and Keith R. Sanders, *New Perspectives on Political Advertising,* pp. 1-20. Carbondale, IL: Southern Illinois University Press, 1986.

Jamieson, Kathleen Hall. Context and the Creation of Meaning in the Advertising of the 1988 Presidential Campaign. *American Behavioral Scientist.* Vol. 32, No. 4, March/April, 1989, pp. 415-424.

Jamieson, Kathleen Hall. *Dirty Politics: Deception, Distraction, and Democracy.* New York: Oxford University Press, 1992.

Jamieson, Kathleen Hall. *Packaging the Presidency: A History and Criticism of Presidential Campaign Advertising.* Oxford: Oxford University Press, 1996.

Jamieson, Kathleen Hall. *Everything You Think You Know about Politics. . ..: And Why You're Wrong.* New York: Basic Books, 2000.

Jamieson, Kathleen Hall. *Electing the President 2004: An Insider's View.* Philadelphia, PA: University of Pennsylvania Press, 2006.

Jamieson, Kathleen Hall, Ken Auletta, and Thomas Patterson. *1-800 President: The Report of the Twentieth Century Fund Task Force on Television and the Campaign of 1992.* New York: The Twentieth Century Fund Press, 1993.

Jamieson, Kathleen Hall and Paul Waldman, eds. *Electing the President 2000: The Insiders View.* Philadelphia: University of Pennsylvania Press, 2001.

Jamieson, Kathleen Hall, Paul Waldman, and Susan Sherr. Eliminate the Negative? Categories of Analysis for Political Advertisements. In James A. Thurber, Candice J. Nelson, David A. Dulio, eds. *Crowded Airwaves: Campaign Advertising in Elections*, pp. 44-64. Washington, D.C.: Brookings Institution Press, 2000.

Johnson-Cartee, Karen S. and Gary A. Copeland. *Manipulation of the American Voter: Political Campaign Commercials.* Westport, CT: Praeger, 1997.

Johnston, Anne. Political Broadcasts: An Analysis of Form, Content, and Style in Presidential Communication. In Lynda Lee Kaid, Jacques Gerstle, and Keith R. Sanders, eds., *Mediated Politics in Two Cultures: Presidential Campaigning in the United States and France*, pp. 59-72. New York: Praeger, 1991.

Johnston, Anne, and Lynda Lee Kaid. Image Ads and Issue Ads in Presidential Advertising: Using Videostyle to Explore Stylistic Differences in Televised Political Ads From 1952 to 2000. *Journal of Communication*, 52, 281-300.

Just, M. A., A. N. Crigler, and L. Wallach. Thirty Seconds Or Thirty Minutes: What Viewers Learn From Spot Advertisements and Candidate Debates. *Journal of Communication 40*, 120-133.

Kaid, Lynda Lee. Political Advertising in the 1992 Campaign. In Robert E. Denton Jr., ed., *The 1992 Presidential Campaign: A Communication Perspective*, pp. 111-127. Westport, CT: Praeger, 1994, pp. 111-127.

Kaid, Lynda Lee. Videostyle and the Effects of the 1996 Presidential Campaign Advertising. In Robert E. Denton Jr., ed., *The 1996 Presidential Campaign: A Communication Perspective*, pp. 143-159. Westport, CT: Praeger, 1998.

Kaid, Lynda Lee. Political Advertising: A Summary of Research Findings. In Bruce Newman, ed. *The Handbook of Political Marketing* (pp. 423-438). Thousand Oaks, CA: Sage Publishers, 1999.

Kaid, Lynda Lee. Videostyle and Political Advertising Effects in the 2000 Presidential Campaign. In Robert E. Denton Jr., ed., *The 2000 Presidential Campaign: A Communication Perspective*, pp. 183-197. Westport, CT: Praeger, 2002.

Kaid, Lynda Lee, ed. *Handbook of Political Communication Research.* Mahwah, NJ: Lawrence Erlbaum Associates, 2004.

Kaid, Lynda Lee and Dianne G. Bystrom, eds. *The Electronic Election: Perspectives on the 1996 Campaign Communication*. Mahwah, NJ: Lawrence Erlbaum Associates, Publishers, 1999.

Kaid, Lynda Lee, and Dorothy K. Davidson. Elements of Videostyle: Candidate Presentations through Television Advertising. In Lynda Lee Kaid, Dan Nimmo, and Keith R. Sanders, *New Perspectives on Political Advertising,* pp. 184-209. Carbondale, IL: Southern Illinois University Press, 1986.

Kaid, Lynda Lee, Jacques Gerstle, and Keith R. Sanders, eds. *Mediated Politics in Two Cultures: Presidential Campaigning in the United States and France.* New York: Praeger, 1991.

Kaid, Lynda Lee, and Anne Johnston. *Videostyle in Presidential Campaigns: Style and Content of Televised Political Advertising.* Westport, CT: Praeger, 2001.

Kaid, Lynda Lee, Dan Nimmo, and Keith R. Sanders, eds. *New Perspectives on Political Advertising.* Carbondale, IL: Southern Illinois University Press, 1986.

Kaid, Lynda Lee and John C. Tedesco. Presidential Candidate Presentation: Videostyle in the 1996 Presidential Spots. In Lynda Lee Kaid and Dianne G. Bystrom, *The Electronic Election: Perspectives on the 1996 Campaign Communication,* pp. 209-221. Mahwah, NJ: Lawrence Erlbaum Associates, Publishers, 1999.

Kaid, Lynda Lee, Tedesco, John C., Bystrom, Dianne G., and Mitchell S. McKinney, eds. *The Millennium Election: Communication in the 2000 Election.* Lanham, MD: Rowman and Littlefield Publishers Inc., 2003.

Kamber, Stephen. *Poison Politics: Are Negative Campaigns Destroying Democracy?* New York: Insight Books, 1997.

Kern, Montague. *30 Second Politics: Political Advertising in the Eighties.* New York: Praeger, 1989.

Kernell, Samuel. *Going Public: New Strategies of Presidential Leadership, 3rd ed.* Washington, D.C.: Congressional Quarterly Press, 1997.

Kerry, John, Presidential Campaign. *Johnkerry.com.*

Lau, Richard R. and Lee Sigelman. Effectiveness of Political Advertising. In James A. Thurber, Candice J. Nelson, David A. Dulio, eds. *Crowded Airwaves: Campaign Advertising in Elections,* pp. 10-43. Washington, D.C.: Brookings Institution Press, 2000.

Lazarsfeld, Paul, Bernard Berelson, and Hazel Gaudet. *The People's Choice: How the Voter Makes Up His Mind in a Presidential Campaign.* New York: Columbia University Press, 1948.

Light, Paul C. *Vice Presidential Power: Advice and Influence in the White House.* Baltimore: Johns Hopkins University Press, 1984.

Light, Paul C. *The President's Agenda: Domestic Policy Choice from Kennedy to Reagan*. Baltimore: Johns Hopkins University Press, 1991.

Light, Paul C. *Thickening Government: Federal Hierarchy and the Diffusion of Accountability*. Washington, D.C.: Brookings, 1995.

Lowi, Theodore J. *The Personal President: Power Invested, Promise Unfilled*. Ithaca, NY: Cornell University Press, 1985.

Maarek, Philippe J. *Political Marketing and Communication*. London: John Libbey and Co., 1995.

Maltese, John Anthony. *Spin Control: The White House Office of Communications and the Management of Presidential News, 2nd. ed. rev*. Chapel Hill, NC: University of North Carolina Press, 1994.

Mayer, Kenneth R. *With the Stroke of a Pen: Executive Orders and Presidential Power*. Princeton, NJ: Princeton University Press, 2001.

Mayer, William, ed. *In Pursuit of the White House: How We Choose Our Presidential Nominees*. Chatham House, NJ: Chatham House, 1999.

Mayer, William G., ed. *The Making of the Presidential Candidates 2004*. Lanham, MD: Rowman & Littlefield, 2004.

Mickelson, Sig. *From Whistle Stop to Sound Bite: Four Decades of Politics and Television*. New York: Praeger, 1989.

Milkis, Sidney M. and Michael Nelson. *The American Presidency: Origins and Development: 1776-1993*. Washington, D.C: Congressional Quarterly Press, 1994.

Morreale, Jeanne. *The Presidential Campaign Film: A Critical History*. Westport, CT: Praeger, 1997.

NBC Nightly News.

Nathan, Richard P. *The Administrative Presidency*. New York: Wiley, 1983.

Nelson, John S. and G. R. Boynton. *Video Rhetorics: Televised Advertising in American Politics*. Urbana: University of Illinois Press, 1997.

Nelson, Michael. *The Elections of 1984*. Washington, D.C.: Congressional Quarterly Press, 1985.

Nelson, Michael. *A Heartbeat Away: Report of the Twentieth Century Fund Task Force on the Vice Presidency*. New York: Priority Press Publications, 1988.

Nelson, Michael. *The Elections of 1988*. Washington, D.C: Congressional Quarterly Press, 1989.

Nelson, Michael. *The Elections of 1992*. Washington, D.C.: Congressional Quarterly Press, 1993.

Nelson, Michael. *The Elections of 1996.* Washington, D.C.: Congressional Quarterly Press, 1997.

Nelson, Michael. *The Elections of 2000.* Washington, D.C.: Congressional Quarterly Press, 2001.

Nelson, Michael. *The Elections of 2004.* Washington, D.C.: Congressional Quarterly Press, 2005.

Neustadt, Richard. *Presidential Power and the Modern Presidents: The Politics of Leadership from Roosevelt to Reagan.* New York: Free Press, 1990.

Newman, Bruce I. *Handbook of Political Marketing.* Thousand Oaks, CA: Sage Publications, 1999.

Nie, Norman H., Sidney Verba, and John R. Petrocik. *The Changing American Voter.* Cambridge, MA: Harvard University Press, 1979.

O'Reilly, Richard. Television Advertising in the Reagan Campaign. In L. Patrick Devlin, ed. *Political Persuasion in Presidential Campaigns,* pp. 53-61. New Brunswick, NJ: Transaction Books, 1987.

Ornstein, Norman J. and Thomas E. Mann, eds. *The Permanent Campaign and its Future.* Washington, D.C.: American Enterprise Institute, 2000.

Patterson, Thomas, and Robert McClure. *The Unseeing Eye: The Myth of Television Power in National Politics.* New York: Putnam, 1976.

Pfau, Michael and Henry C. Kenski. *Attack Politics: Strategy and Defense.* Westport, CT: Praeger, 1990.

Pfiffner, James P. *The Managerial Presidency, 2nd. Ed.* College Station: Texas A&M University Press, 1999.

Polsby, Nelson W. *Consequences of Party Reform.* New York: Oxford University Press, 1983.

Polsby, Nelson W. and Aaron Wildavsky. *Strategies and Structures of American Politics.* Lanham, MD: Rowman and Littlefield, 2004.

Pomper, Gerald M. *The Election of 1980: Reports and Interpretations.* Chatham, NJ: Chatham House Publishers, 1981.

Pomper, Gerald M. *The Election of 1984: Reports and Interpretations.* Chatham, NJ: Chatham House Publishers, 1985.

Pomper, Gerald M. *The Election of 1988: Reports and Interpretations.* Chatham, NJ: Chatham House Publishers, 1989.

Pomper, Gerald M. *The Election of 1992: Reports and Interpretations.* Chatham, NJ: Chatham House Publishers, 1993.

Pomper, Gerald M. *The Election of 1996: Reports and Interpretations.* Chatham, NJ: Chatham House Publishers, 1997.

Pomper, Gerald M. *The Election of 2000: Reports and Interpretations.* Chatham, NJ: Chatham House Publishers, 2001.

Popkin, Samuel L. *The Reasoning Voter: Communication and Persuasion in Presidential Campaigns.* Chicago: University of Chicago Press, 1991.

Richardson, Glenn W. Jr. *Pulp Politics: How Political Advertising Tells the Stories of American Politics.* Lanham, MD: Rowman and Littlefield, 2003.

Ridout, Travis. Campaign Advertising Strategies in the 2000 Presidential Nominations: The Case of Al, George, Bill and John. In Kenneth M. Goldstein and Patricia Strach, *The Medium and the Message: Television Advertising in American Elections,* pp. 5-26. Upper Saddle River, NJ: Pearson/Prentice Hall, 2004.

Sabato, Larry. *Divided States of America: The Slash and Burn Politics of the 2004 Presidential Election.* New York, NY: Pearson/Longman, 2006.

Schramm, Martin. *The Great American Video Game: Presidential Politics in the Television Age.* New York: Morrow, 1987.

Schultz, David A. ed. *Lights, Camera, Campaign! Media, Politics and Political Advertising.* New York: Peter Lang, 2004.

Somit, Albert, Wildenmann, Rudolf, Boll, Bernard, and Andrea Rommele, eds. *The Victorious Incumbent.* Aldershot, England: Dartmouth Publishing, 1994.

Spero, Robert. *The Duping of the American Voter: Dishonesty and Deception in Presidential Television Advertising.* New York: Lippincott & Crowell, 1980.

Swanson, David L., and Paolo Mancini. *Politics, Media, and Modern Democracy: An International Study of Innovations in Electoral Campaigning and Their Consequences.* Westport, CN: Praeger, 1996.

Tally, Steve. *Bland Ambition: From Adams to Quayle-the Cranks, Crooks, Tax Cheats, and Golfers Who Made It to Vice President.* San Diego: Harcourt Brace Jovanovich, 1992.

Tulis, Jeffrey. *The Rhetorical Presidency.* Princeton, NJ: Princeton University Press, 1987.

Tedesco, John C., and Lynda Lee Kaid. Style and Effects of the Bush and Gore Spots. In Lynda Lee Kaid, John C. Tedesco, Dianne G. Bystrom, and Mitchell S. McKinney, *The Millennium Election: Communication in the 2000 Campaign,* pp. 5-16. Lanham, MD: Rowman and Littlefield Publishers Inc., 2003.

Tenpas, Kathryn Dunn. *Presidents as Candidates: Inside the White House for the Presidential Campaign.* New York: Garland Publishing, 1997.

Trent, Judith S., and Robert V. Friedenberg. *Political Campaign Communication: Principles and Practices, Fifth Edition.* Lanham, MD: Rowman & Littlefield, 2004.

Thurber, James A., Candice J. Nelson, and David A. Dulio, eds. *Crowded Airwaves: Campaign Advertising in Elections.* Washington, D.C.: Brookings Institution Press, 2000.

Vanderbilt Television News Archive.

Walch, Timothy. *At the President's Side: The Vice Presidency in the Twentieth Century.* Columbia: University of Missouri Press, 1997.

Wayne, Stephen J. *The Road to the White House: The Politics of Presidential Elections.* New York: Wadsworth Publishing, 2003.

West, Darrell M. *Air Wars: Television Advertising in Election Campaigns: 1952-2004., Fourth ed.* Washington, D.C.: Congressional Quarterly, 2005.

White, Theodore H. *The Making of the President: 1960.* New York: Atheneum Publishers, 1965.

White, Theodore H. *The Making of the President: 1964.* New York: Atheneum Publishers, 1965.

White, Theodore H. *The Making of the President: 1968.* New York: Atheneum Publishers, 1969.

White, Theodore H. *The Making of the President: 1972.* New York: Atheneum Publishers, 1973.

White, Theodore H. *America In Search of Herself: The Making of the President 1956-1980.* New York: Harper & Row, 1982.

Wildavsky, Aaron and Naomi Caiden. *The New Politics of the Budgetary Process, 5th ed.* New York: Pearson/Longman, 2004.

Winebrenner, Hugh. *The Iowa Precinct Caucuses: The Making of a Media Event, Second edition.* Ames: Iowa State University Press, 1998.

Witcover, Jules: Marathon: *The Pursuit of the Presidency: 1972-1976.* New York: Viking Press, 1977.

Witcover, Jules: *Crapshoot: Rolling the Dice on the Vice Presidency from Adams and Jefferson to Truman and Quayle.* New York: Crown Publishers, 1992.

Television Ads

Candidates

Alexander, Lamar. Presidential Campaign of 1996. *Comparison Wave, Facts, Freedom New Hampshire, Future, Hello New Hampshire, Honey, Jobs, Mud Balls, New Hampshire Aim, New Hampshire Switch, New Leadership, New South, Only, Party-Iowa, Sleeves, Smokey, Snow,* 1996.

Alexander, Lamar. Presidential Campaign of 2000. *Auction,* 2000.

Anderson, John. Presidential Campaign of 1980. *Buy Votes, Fact, Independent, Secret Solo,* 1980.

Babbitt, Bruce. Presidential Campaign of 1988. *Bio, Guts, Turned Off,* 1988.

Baker, Howard. Presidential Campaign of 1980. *Iranian Student, New Hampshire Pictures, New Hampshire Platform,* 1980.

Bauer, Gary. Presidential Campaign of 2000. *Advisor, China Threat, Newport,* 2000.

Bradley, Bill. Presidential Campaign of 2000. *Agenda, Always, Chicago, Crystal City, Intro, Listen, Mom, Objective, Positive Values, Real Risk,* 2000.

Brown, Jerry. Presidential Campaign of 1992. *Care, Documercial, Fast Track, Promo,* 1992.

Browne, Harry. Presidential Campaign of 2000. *Baby, Battered,* 2000.

Buchanan, Patrick. Presidential Campaign of 1992. *Behind the Mask, Broken Promises, Check Your Socks, Foreign Agents, Freedom to Abuse, I Won't Sign, Pay to Pray, Protect, They Don't Care,* 1992.

Buchanan, Patrick. Presidential Campaign of 1996. *Advisor, Advisor, Alternative, Affirmative Action, Alaska, Bob, Deal With Mexico, Generation, Immigration, Jobs Go Overseas, Louisiana Trade, No New Taxes, That Ain't Conservative, Women,* 1996.

Buchanan, Patrick. Presidential Campaign of 2000. *Auction, Culture Wars, Meatball,* 2000.

Bush, George. Presidential Campaign of 1980. *Exterior, Interior,* 1980.

Bush, George. Presidential Campaign of 1988. *Accomplishments, Bush America, Bush Positive Economy, Crime Quiz, Effective, Eliminating Nuclear Weapons, Family, Free World Leadership, Gorbachev, Harbor, His Mistakes, I Am That Man, Inaugural, Period/Straddle, Quiz, Revolving Door, 16 of 34, Strong Defense, Tank, Tax Blizzard, Texas Opportunities, The Mission, Unbelievable,* 1988.

Bush, George. Presidential Campaign of 1992. *Agenda, Arkansas Record, Cincinnati-Barney, Cincinnati-Fred, Crisis, Debate, Determined, False, Federal, Federal Taxes, Gray Dot, Guess, Health Care, Joined, Mayor, Nation, Opposed, Peter, Presidency, Reunited, Send a Message, The Leader, Trust, What am I Fighting For, Wolverine,* 1992.

Bush, George W. Presidential Campaign of 2000. *America in Education, America's Spirit, Challenging Status Quo, Compare, Credibility, Debate, Fifty Eight Percent, Education, Education Agenda, Education Miami, Every Child, Expect More, Hard Times, Hard Things, How About You, Integrity, New Americans, No Changes-No Reductions, Nonsense, Once, Phyllis Hunter, Promised, Solid Values, Successful Leader, Tools, Trust,* 2000.

Bush, George W. Presidential Campaign of 2004. *Agenda, Changing World, Clockwork, Complicated Plan, Differences, Don't Take Chances, Doublespeak, Economy: Common Sense v. Higher Taxes, Economic Agenda, First Choice, Forward, Health Care Agenda, Health Care: Practical v. Big Government, Intel, Kerry's Yucca, Key to Success, Lead, Med Mal, Medicare Hypocrisy, Nearly Two Million Reasons, No Limit, One Hundred Days, Ownership, Patriot Act, Peace and Security, Pessimism, Priorities, Risk, Safer-Stronger, Searching, Solemn Duty, Take a Look, Taxing our Economy, Tested, The Choice, Thinking Mom, Tort Reform, Troops, Troops-Fog, Troops, Fog Revision, Troubling, Twentieth Century, Unprincipled, Victory, Weapons, Weapons-Arizona, Weapons-New Hampshire, Wacky, War on Terror Agenda, Whatever it Takes, Windsurfing, Wolves, World View, Yakuza, Your Doctor,* 2004.

Carter, Jimmy. Presidential Campaign of 1980. *Akron, Cities, Commander, EMK Choice, Family, Farmer, Hope, Kennedy, Light, Light Roll, Lorraine, Mary, Mideast, Oval Interior, Reagan Record, Security, Street Concern, Street Hip, Things,* 1980.

Clark, Wesley. Presidential Campaign of 2004. *Future, Hopes, Independence, Leader, Major, Patriot, Prepared, Renewal, Respect, Responsibility, Secretary, What If,* 2004.

Clinton, Bill. Presidential Campaign of 1992. *Best, Billion, Boot, Casualties, Change, Curtains, Eleven Years, Energy, Even, Fact, Family, Fighting, Hip Parade Jobs, Hope, Idea, Industry, Journey, Leaders, Looking, Maine, Morning, New Covenant, People Plan, Politics, Promise, Rebuild America, Remember, Restore, Scary, Steady, Time, We Can Do It, Which, You're Not Alone,* 1992.

Clinton, Bill. Presidential Campaign of 1996. *Cherish, Closely, Dayton, Desperate, Drums, Empty, First Time, Front, Gamble, Growth, Guide, Hold, King, Look, Missing, Next Century, Nobody, Parents, Preserve, Real Ticket, Real Record, Running, Sad, Safe, Seconds, Spirit, Wrong in Past,* 1996.

Cranston, Alan. Presidential Campaign of 1984. *First Day, Still Bald, Trivial Pursuits,* 1984.

Dean, Howard. Presidential Campaign of 2004. *Across Iowa, Bio, Caucus, Club For Truth, Did It, Different View, Enron Economics, Every American, Health Care, Iraq, Join Us, Leader, Misled, My Opponents, One Candidate, Prescription Drugs, Record,* 2004.

Dole, Elizabeth. Presidential Campaign of 2000. *Announcement Ad*, 2000.

Dole, Robert. Presidential Campaign of 1988. *Difference/Dole/Bush, Difference-Iowa, Freeze, Gorbachev, Interesting/Footprints, Lessons*, 1988.

Dole, Robert. Presidential Campaign of 1996. *A Better America, America, At Stake, Agenda, An American Hero, Balanced Budget, Classroom, Conservative Agenda, Courage and Commitment, Crossfire, Defeat, Deficits versus Cuts, Defining Moment, Do Better, Elizabeth, Fool, From the Heartland, Gravy Train, How to Speak Liberal, Keep More, Lamar's Income Tax, Leadership, Midwest Values, Nicole, Plan, Riady, School, Security, Serious Business, Sorry Taxes, Stop the Presses, Tested, The Great Pretender, The Threat, The Stakes, Too Late, Truth on Spending*, 1996.

Dukakis, Michael. Presidential Campaign of 1988. *Anthem, Bio, Budget, Bush False Advertising, Central America, Counterpunch, Crunch, Debate, Education, Effort, Furlough from Truth, Homeless, Leadership/Responsibility, List, Little Miracles, McIntyre, New Era, Oval Office, Packaging/Crazy, Plant Closing, Record Hop, Seabrooke, Tip, Two Paychecks*, 1988.

DuPont, Pierre. Presidential Campaign of 1988. *Farm Subsidies, Scarecrow*, 1988.

Edwards, John. Presidential Campaign of 2004. *American Jobs, Answer, Believe, Better Life, Chance, College, Create, Home, Hometown, Jobs, Milk, Now, Plan, Pool, Right, Strong, Two Americas, Values, Why Don't We, Yours*, 2004.

Forbes, Steve. Presidential Campaign of 1996. *Army, Bio Vision, Blue, Concord, Conservative, Education, Future, Generic Flat Tax, Graft, Health Care, Humphrey, Interest, Lamar, Less-Not More, Little Mo, Man, Married, My Powerbrokers, Orlando, Pensions, Power, Reagan, Sea, Ski/Bicycle, Stop, Stretch, Strike, Time, Treasury, Words*, 1996.

Forbes, Steve. Presidential Campaign of 2000. *Abortion, Bio/Dream, Catherine, Face, Family, Lunch Counter, Mary, Other People, Social Security*, 2000.

Ford, Gerald. Presidential Campaign of 1976. *Accomplishments*, 1976.

Gephardt, Richard. Presidential Campaign of 1988. *Belgian Endive, Change, Soul, Trade, Voice*, 1988.

Gephardt, Richard. Presidential Campaign of 2004. *Jobs, Know*, 2004.

Glenn, John. Presidential Campaign of 1984. *Better Man, Leader, Pursuit of Peace*, 1984.

Gore, Albert Jr. Presidential Campaign of 1988. *Bio, Debate, South, Triple*, 1988.

Gore, Albert Jr. Presidential Campaign of 2000. *Accountability, Baby, Bean Counter, Best, Care, Champion, Check, Child, Coast, Confused, Cover, Doesn't, Down, Experience, Frush, Help, Honor, Ian, Interview, Jackpot, Momentum, Morph, 1969, Only, Super, Reporter, Teachers, Two Promises, Veteran*, 2000.

Gramm, Phil. Presidential Campaign of 1996. *Allowance, Common Sense, Courage, I Know Who I Am, Look Inside, Remember Senator Straddle, Something New, Three Candidates, Working Families,* 1996.

Haig, Alexander. Presidential Campaign of 1988. *In Charge, Peace, Pizza,* 1988.

Harkin, Thomas. Presidential Campaign of 1992. *Builder, Danette, Echoes, Frank, Sister, Trickle Down, Work,* 1992.

Hart, Gary. Presidential Campaign of 1984. *Breaking Chains, Cake, Central America, Chicago, Leadership, New York, PAC, Past/Future, Proud Democrat,* 1984.

Hart, Gary. Presidential Campaign of 1988. *Character, Different,* 1988.

Hatch, Orrin. Presidential Campaign of 2000. *Announcement Ad,* 2000.

Humphrey, Hubert. Presidential Campaign of 1968. *Ahead of His Time,* 1968.

Jackson, Jesse. Presidential Campaign of 1988. *Cosby, Iowa Farmer, Only One, Stood,* 1988.

Johnson, Lyndon. Presidential Campaign of 1964. *Daisy Girl,* 1964.

Kemp, Jack. Presidential Campaign of 1988. *Bio, Difference, Deficit,* 1988.

Kennedy, John F. Presidential Campaign of 1960. *Kennedy-Kennedy,* 1960.

Kennedy, Edward. Presidential Campaign of 1980. *Apollo, Fingers Crossed, Four More Years, Senate Effectiveness, Spokesman,* 1980.

Kerrey, Robert. Presidential Campaign of 1992. *Cause, Counterfeit, Firefight, Growing Up, Net, Shattered, Valor,* 1992.

Kerry, John. Presidential Campaign of 2004. *Across America, Agenda, Aircraft Carrier, AJC/Cleland, Alston, Alston-Extra, Believe, Best Prepared, Born in Colorado, Bush's Mess, Can't Win, Change, Cheney-Halliburton, Choice, Cleland, Commitment, Corruption, Country, Cured Now, Defend America, Deficit, Del, Despicable, Different Story, Doesn't Get It, Economy Kick Start, Economy-Ohio, Endorsements, Ever Since, Experience, Families, Feeding Frenzy, Flu, Freedom and Independence, Fought For His Country, Health Care Coverage, Heart, Heroes, He's Lost--He's Desperate, Hoover, Husband and Father, Immediate Help, Ingenuity, Invest, Innovation, Iowa Announcement, Issues, January Surprise, Join the Fight, Join the Fight for Our Environment, Jobs, Jobs Lost, Juvenile, Keep Our Word, Kids, Knowles, Leading Not True, Leadership, Lifeline, Lifetime, Looking, Michael J. Fox, Middle Class, Middle Class Families, Middle Class Help, Misleading America, More than Anyone, Never, New Team, No Mr. President, Not True, Obligation, Ohio Workers, Old Trick, One Hundred Days, Optimists, Paperwork, Pilot, Powerful, Promise, Protect, Rassmann, Real Americans, Reasons, Right Track, Risk, Rx Drugs, Shaheen, Sided With Lobbyists-Iowa, Stem Cell, Strength, Strength-New Hampshire, Team for America, Ten Million New Jobs, The Truth on Taxes, Three Minutes, Time, Time's Up, Together, Trust, Uninsured, Very*

First Bush Budget, War on Terror, West Virginia Veterans, Who is this Man, Wrong Choices, You Saw, Your Hands, 2004.

Keyes, Alan. Presidential Campaign of 2000. *Kids, Rush, Second Amendment*, 2000.

Kucinich, Dennis. Presidential Campaign of 2004. *Inspire, Listen, Privacy, Re-Awake, U.N.*, 2004.

Lugar, Richard. Presidential Campaign of 1996. *Common Sense, Dignity, Genuine Courage, Straight Up, Trust with Your Life*, 1996.

McCain, John. Presidential Campaign of 2000. *Can Win, Commander, Duty-Honor-Country, Every Dime, Leader, Message to America, Ready to Lead, Reagan Conservative, Trust, Wrong*, 2000.

McGovern, George. Presidential Campaign of 1984. *Conscience, McGovern*, 1984.

Mondale, Walter. Presidential Campaign of 1984. *America for Mondale, American Jobs, Biography, Cincinnati, Computer, Debate, Deficits, Domestic, Elderly, Hole, Hotline Illinois, Limo, New Ideas, Roller Coaster, Plan, Safety Net, Teach, Ticket, Trade, Truth, Victory, You've Made us Proud*, 1984.

Nader, Ralph. Presidential Campaign of 2000. *Grow Up, Priceless Truth*, 2000.

Nixon, Richard. Presidential Campaign of 1968. *Law and Order*, 1968.

Nixon, Richard. Presidential Campaign of 1972. *McGovern Defense, Russia*, 1972.

Perot, Ross. Presidential Campaign of 1992. *Chicken Feathers, Children, Cities, Don't Waste Your Vote, Health Care, No More Voodoo, Oops, People versus Pollsters, Purple Heart, Storm, Time, Trickle Down, Who's Best*, 1992.

Perot, Ross. Presidential Campaign of 1996. *Afraid Conscience, Commission, Don't Waste Your Vote, Don't Waste Your Vote II, Faces-Non Voters, Generation X, Listen to Me, NAFTA Debate, 76 percent for Ross, What Are They Afraid Of, Where's Ross, Why Campaign Reform, Why Campaign Finance, Why Referendum*, 1996.

Reagan, Ronald. Presidential Campaign of 1980. *American Newspapers, Carter, Defense, Documentary, Everything Up, Flip Flop Economy, Ford/Inflation, Foreign Affairs, Government Regulations, Kennedy Foreign Policy, Kennedy Inflation, Nancy, No More Jimmy Carter, Peace, Podium, Record*, 1980.

Reagan, Ronald. Presidential Campaign of 1984. *America's Back, Bear, Convention Movie-Economic Choice, Normandy Excerpt, Democratic Switch, Hart on Mondale, Inflation, Man on the Street: Mondale, Man on the Street 2, Peace, Prouder-Stronger-Better, Reaganomics versus Mondalenomics, Roosevelt Room, Side By Side, Spring 84, Tax Vignettes, Train, Unity, Unity-Five Minute Version, Youth Future*, 1984.

Robertson, Pat. Presidential Campaign of 1988. *Communists, Iowa Post, Families*, 1988.

Simon, Paul. Presidential Campaign of 1988. *Bio, Bowtie, Trust,* 1988.

Tsongas, Paul. Presidential Campaign of 1992. *Alone, Change, Difference, Leadership, Old Politics, Straight Answers, Swim, The Latest, This is Paul Tsongas,* 1992.

Wilson, Pete. Presidential Campaign of 1996. *Courage, First,* 1996.

Videotape Collections

Devlin Archive, University of Rhode Island . *Types of Presidential Ads, 1952-2000 Collection of Longer Ads, 1952-2000 Collection of Negative Ads, 1952-2000 Historic Short Presidential Ads, 1980 Presidential Campaign Ads, 1984 Presidential Campaign Ads, 1988 Presidential Campaign Ads, 1992 Presidential Campaign Ads, 1996 Presidential Campaign Ads,1996 Presidential Primary Campaign Ads,2000 Presidential Campaign Ads,2000 Presidential Primary Campaign Ads.*

London International Advertising Awards. *Political Advertising of the '60's, Political Advertising of the '80's, The Best Campaign Commercials of 1984, The Best Campaign Commercials of 1988, The Best Campaign Commercials of 1992.*

Candidate Web Sites, 2004. *Bush, George W; Clark, Wesley; Dean, Howard; Edwards, John; Kerry, John; Kucinich, Dennis; Gephardt, Richard.*

INDEX

Alexander, Lamar, 27, 43, 45–47, 102, 105
Anderson, John, 24, 53, 55, 56, 68–71

Babbitt, Bruce, 96, 98
Baker, Howard, 24, 56, 69, 70
Bauer, Gary, 102, 105
Bradley, Bill, 85, 91–93
Brown, Jerry, 24, 53, 57, 74, 76, 84
Browne, Harry, 106, 107
Buchanan, Patrick: advertising 1992, 51, 54, 56, 62–65, 73, 155; advertising 1996, 27, 43–47; advertising 2000, 102, 106, 107
Bush, George H. W., 3, 18, 19, 23, 24, 28, 51–57, 79, 83, 84; advertising strategy 1980, 70, 71; advertising strategy 1988, 86–91, 156, 157; advertising strategy 1992, 62–67, 155; attacked by opponents 1988, 99–101; attacked by opponents 1992, 74–78
Bush, George W., 3, 6, 17–19, 25, 85, 86, 109, 110; advertising strategy 2000, 101–107, 156, 157; advertising strategy 2004, 123–137, 154, 157, 158; attacked by opponents 2000, 92–95; attacked by opponents 2004, 139–151

Carter, Jimmy, 3, 14, 18, 19, 23, 24, 38, 51, 53–57; advertising strategy 1980, 57–62, 155, 156; attacked by opponents 1980, 67–69, 71, 72
Cheney, Richard, 144, 146
Clark, Wesley, 111, 112, 121, 137
Clinton, Bill, 3, 4, 14, 18, 19, 24, 25, 54–57, 68; advertising strategy 1992, 72–77, 155; advertising strategy 1996, 33–37, 154; attacked by opponents 1992, 63, 65–67, 77, 78; attacked by opponents 1996, 43, 45, 47, 48; election of 2000, 91–94, 96, 101, 102, 104, 120, 121, 123, 156
Congress, general references, 4, 5, 22–24, 34, 35, 37, 44, 45, 52, 54, 59, 63, 64, 68, 71, 75, 87, 91–93, 95, 102, 112, 115, 119, 122, 125, 127, 131, 132, 134, 135, 148, 157
Cranston, Alan, 26, 41

Dean, Howard, 111, 112, 119–121, 157
Democratic Party, general references, 22, 23, 26, 38, 40, 43, 48, 52, 82, 84, 100, 102, 107, 116, 120, 122, 124, 129, 132, 139, 142, 151
Dole, Elizabeth, 43, 48, 102
Dole, Robert, 18, 24, 25, 27, 38, 56, 83, 84, 120; advertising 1980, 70; ad-

vertising 1988, 87, 88; advertising strategy 1996, 43–48; attacked by opponents 1996, 33–37, 45

Dukakis, Michael, 18, 24, 84; advertising strategy 1988, 95–101, 157; attacked by opponents 1988, 88–91

DuPont, Pierre, 84, 88

Edwards, John, 19, 110–112, 116–120, 126, 142, 150, 157

Eisenhower, Dwight, 2, 14, 22, 24, 81, 82, 89, 110

Election of 1952, 1, 13, 19, 22

Election of 1956, 2, 15, 21, 22, 110

Election of 1960, 3, 8, 14, 19, 22, 23, 79–82, 89, 95, 99

Election of 1964, 2, 11, 15, 21, 22, 68, 76, 83

Election of 1968, 3, 5, 9, 14, 18, 23, 51, 52, 54, 56, 68, 79–83, 89, 95, 100

Election of 1972, 2, 7, 11, 14, 15, 18, 21–23, 69, 110

Election of 1976, 3, 7, 9, 15, 20, 23, 51–53, 56, 58, 69, 72, 99, 155

Election of 1980, 3, 4, 15, 18–20, 23, 24, 51, 52, 55–57, 74, 101, 155; challengers' campaigns, 68–72; incumbents' campaigns, 57–62

Election of 1984, 2, 4, 15, 18, 21, 22, 24, 99, 101, 110, 112, 135, 154; challengers' campaigns, 38–43; incumbents' campaigns, 28–32

Election of 1988, 3–5, 18, 22, 24, 52, 54, 64, 76, 77, 79–81, 83, 85, 102, 157; challengers' campaigns, 95–101; incumbents' campaigns, 86–91

Election of 1992, 3, 8, 9, 15, 18, 24, 28, 48, 51–57, 101, 155; challengers' campaigns, 72–78; incumbents' campaigns, 62–67

Election of 1996, 1, 2, 4, 7, 13, 15, 18, 19, 21, 22, 25, 27, 87, 120, 154; challengers' campaigns, 43–49; incumbents' campaigns, 33–37

Election of 2000, 1, 3, 6, 10, 18–20, 25, 33, 79–81, 83, 85, 89, 100, 141, 144, 157; challengers' campaigns, 101–107; incumbents' campaigns, 91–95

Election of 2004, 3–5, 7, 9, 10, 12, 13, 16–20, 25, 33, 154, 157, 158; Bush general election campaign, 123–137; Kerry general election campaign, 139–151; nomination campaigns, 109–122

Elections with strong incumbents, 2, 18, 21–49, 95, 110, 153–155; challengers, 37–49; incumbents, 27–37

Elections with surrogate incumbents, 2, 18, 79–107, 153, 154, 156; challengers, 95–107; incumbents, 86–95

Elections with weak incumbents, 2, 18, 51–78, 95, 110, 122, 153, 155, 156; challengers, 67–78; incumbents, 57–67

Forbes, Steve, 27, 43, 45–47, 102, 105

Ford, Gerald, 3, 9, 18, 19, 23, 24, 51–54, 56, 69–72, 101, 155, 156

Gingrich, Newt, 34–37, 120

Glenn, John, 26, 41

Gore, Albert Jr., 3, 18, 19, 79, 80, 83–85, 96, 99; advertising strategy 2000, 91–95; attacked by opponents 2000 86, 88, 89, 104, 106, 107

Gephardt, Richard, 84, 96–99, 111, 119, 120

Goldwater, Barry, 11, 22, 68

Gramm, Phil, 27, 45, 47

Haig, Alexander, 84, 88

Harkin, Tom, 24, 57, 73–75

Hart, Gary, 26, 28, 40, 41

Health care as an issue, 10, 24, 34, 35, 42, 45, 48, 65–67, 73–76, 78, 91–94, 99, 104; election of 2004, 110, 113–121, 124–126, 129, 131–137, 140–150, 157

Humphrey, Hubert, 3, 9, 14, 18, 22, 23, 79, 82, 83, 88, 89

Iowa precinct caucuses; election of 1980, 23, 56, 70, 91; election of 1984, 26, 40; election of 1988, 83, 84, 88, 96–98; election of 1992, 57; election of 1996, 27, 44, 45, 47, 73; election of 2000, 85, 102;

election of 2004, 111, 113, 114, 119–121
Iraq war as an issue, 115–116, 119, 121, 124–127, 130, 132, 135, 137, 140, 141, 143–147, 149–151, 157

Jackson, Jesse, 26, 84, 96, 99
Jobs as an issue, 10, 29, 35, 41, 46, 47, 59, 64, 65, 74–78, 97, 98, 100; election of 2004, 113–115, 117–121, 126, 131, 133, 140–150
Johnson, Lyndon, 2, 3, 8, 9, 11, 22–24, 51, 52, 54–56, 79, 82, 83, 101

Kemp, Jack, 84, 88
Kennedy, Edward, 53, 56–60, 62, 71, 72, 155
Kennedy, John F., 8, 9, 22–24, 73, 82, 89, 97, 99, 100
Kennedy, Robert F., 23, 55, 82
Kerrey, Robert, 24
Kerry, John, 17, 19; advertising strategy 2004 nomination campaign, 112–116; advertising strategy in 2004 general election, 139–151, 157, 158; attacked by opponents 2004, 116–120, 122–137
Kucinich, Dennis, 111, 121

Lieberman, Joseph, 111
Lugar, Richard, 24, 27

McCain, John, 85, 102–105, 128, 130
McGovern, George, 11, 14, 23, 26, 41
Mondale, Walter, 18, 24–26, 71; advertising strategy 1984, 38–43; attacked by opponents 1984, 28–32, 40–41

Nader, Ralph, 85, 106–107
New Hampshire Primary, 33, 82, 83; election of 1968, 54, 55; election of 1980, 23, 56, 70; election of 1984, 26, 27, 40; election of 1988, 84, 85, 96, 97; election of 1992, 63, 64; election of 1996, 44, 45, 47, 73, 74; election of 2000, 102; election of 2004, 111, 113, 120,

121, 126, 127
Nixon, Richard, 2, 3, 9, 11, 14, 18, 22–24, 52, 55, 56, 68–70, 110

Perot, Ross, 24, 25, 54, 55, 63–66, 68, 73; advertising strategy 1992, 77, 78; advertising strategy 1996, 48, 49
Presidential office, description, 4–6; general references, 9, 12, 13, 15, 29, 34, 37, 66, 126, 128, 133, 137

Quayle, Dan, 100–102

Reagan, Ronald, 2, 9, 14, 18, 19, 23, 25, 37, 39, 44, 45, 52, 53, 55, 56, 110, 123, 135, 136; advertising strategy 1980, 68–72, 155, 156; advertising strategy 1984, 28–34, 36, 154, 155; attacked by opponents 1980, 58, 60–62; attacked by opponents 1984, 38–43; election of 1988, 83, 84, 86, 87, 89, 90, 97, 100, 101, 104
Republican Party, general references, 22–25, 27, 28, 33, 44, 48, 53, 55, 68, 69, 71, 81, 83, 85, 87, 89, 101–103, 105, 106, 130, 132, 143, 145, 148
Robertson, Pat, 84, 88
Rockefeller, Nelson, 23, 69, 83

Simon, Paul, 84, 96–98
Stevenson, Adlai, 22, 82

Taxes as an issue, 10, 29–32, 35, 39, 45–48, 54, 62, 64–66, 69, 71, 72, 74–77, 87, 88, 91, 94, 97, 98; election of 2004, 103–105, 124–129, 132–136
Tsongas, Paul, 24, 56, 57, 74, 75

Vice Presidential office, 4, 39, 81, 156, 157

Wallace, George, 23, 83
Wilson, Pete, 47

ABOUT THE AUTHOR

E. D. Dover is Professor of Political Science, Public Policy and Administration at Western Oregon University. He has taught a wide variety of courses in American government and public administration at Western Oregon for the past nineteen years, including ones about elections, political parties and interest groups, political communication, congress, the presidency, constitutional law, community politics, federalism, governmental budgeting, and public personnel administration and labor relations. He has also taught at the University of Wyoming, University of Colorado, and University of Tennessee at Martin. He is the author of five books about various aspects of American presidential elections. Previous works include *Presidential Elections in the Television Age: 1960-1992; The Presidential Election of 1996: Clinton's Incumbency and Television; Missed Opportunity: Gore, Incumbency, and Television in Election 2000;* and *The Disputed Presidential Election of 2000.* Dover is a long time labor union activist and has served as the president of local 2278 of the American Federation of Teachers which represents the Western Oregon faculty. He also has chaired several collective bargaining teams in contract negotiations. Dover was born and raised in Wyoming, is a veteran of the U.S. Army, and served as a delegate to the 1976 Democratic National Convention. He has a Bachelor's degree in Political Science, a Master's in Public Administration, and a Master's in Communication, all from the University of Wyoming, and a Doctor of Philosophy degree in Political Science from the University of Colorado. He lives on a small tree farm several miles west of Monmouth, Oregon with his wife Molly Mayhead, Professor of Speech Communication at Western Oregon University and co-author *of Women's Political Discourse: A Twenty First Century Perspective* (Rowman and Littlefield, 2005).